ROMAN BRITAIN: THE FRONTIER PROVINCE

ROMAN BRITAIN: THE FRONTIER PROVINCE

COLLECTED PAPERS

by

Mark Hassall

**Studies in the history of Roman Britain
based on the documentary sources**

THE HOBNOB PRESS

First published in the United Kingdom in 2017

by The Hobnob Press,
30c Deverill Road Trading Estate, Sutton Veny, Warminster BA12 7BZ
www.hobnobpress.co.uk

British Library Cataloguing in Publication Data
A catalogue record for this book is available from the British Library

ISBN 978-1-906978-42-6

Typeset in Scala 11/14 pt. Typesetting and origination by John Chandler

Printed by Lightning Source

CONTENTS

PREFACE

THE ARTICLES REPUBLISHED here are all concerned with the history of Roman Britain, and they are all based on contemporary documentary sources, whether the writings of Roman and Greek authors or Roman inscriptions found both within and outside the province.

Inscriptions have been a particular subject of study of mine, as for well over 30 years, from 1971 to 2007, I helped to compile the annual reports of new finds of Roman inscriptions from Britain in the journal *Britannia*, originally in collaboration with Richard Wright, and then from 1975 with Roger Tomlin. Roger also helped to compile two of the *corpora* of inscriptions from the province. The first of these was R.G. Collingwood and R.P. Wright, *The Roman Inscriptions of Britain, Volume II: Instrumentum Domesticum* (*RIB* II), encompassing personal belongings and similar, bearing inscriptions, found before 31 December 1986, edited by S.S. Frere and R.S.O. Tomlin (1990–5). The second was *The Roman Inscriptions of Britain, Volume III: Inscriptions on Stone* (*RIB* III), found or notified between 1 January 1955 and 31 December 2006, compiled by R.S.O. Tomlin, R.P. Wright and myself (2009).

Besides inscriptions and contemporary literary sources, a key document of study and in a class of its own is the unique *Notitia Dignitatum*, a handbook devoted to the civil and military administration of the later Roman Empire. This emanated originally from the offices of two high-ranking Roman 'civil servants': the *Primicerius Notariorum in partibus Occidentis* and his equivalent in the eastern parts of the empire, the *Primicerius Notariorum in partibus Orientis* (see especially Articles 17–19 below).

In so far as the present reprint of articles has a model, it is the inspirational collection of papers by Eric Birley, *Roman Britain and the Roman Army* (1953). The number of papers was less than those included in the present collection – some sixteen rather than twenty – and of those only eleven were specifically devoted to Roman Britain, the remaining five relating to the officers and personnel of the Roman army, their origins, and career structure. As with the items included in that book, the present articles are reprinted according to their subject matter rather than their date of publication, and are grouped according to four broad categories: (I) Early Military History: Articles 1–2; (II) Frontier: Articles 3–6; (III) The Province: Articles 7–16; and (IV) Later Military History: Articles 17–20 (see the table of contents above).

It is realised, firstly, that not all possible topics in these categories have been covered – for example, there is nothing on villas or native British settlement in the countryside. This is in part a reflection of the 'historical' source material on which the collection is based. Thus, monumental inscriptions are very seldom found on villas – a rare example is *RIB* III, 3045, a tombstone with, unusually, a consular date found at Tarrant Hinton in Dorset, from which it is learnt that in the middle of the third century the owner was one Cupitus, the son of Verus, who died on 26 August 258. Secondly, it is realised that there is a degree of overlap between some of the articles. This is especially true of the four articles in Part IV, Later Military History. However, even where this is so, there is always a somewhat different emphasis on the way the topics are treated, so that hopefully their contents can be regarded as complementary rather than duplicating what has already been said. Indeed, in some cases new evidence has come to light. A note at the end of the relevant article draws attention to such cases, but the original wording or views in the body of the text has not been altered.

ACKNOWLEDGEMENTS

O F THE TWENTY articles republished here, six were originally published as contributions to volumes produced in honour of half a dozen scholars, whether teachers or colleagues. The six in question are Jocelyn Toynbee (Article 5), A.R. Birley (Article 9), W.F. Grimes (Article 10), Hugh Chapman (Article 11), John Wacher (Article 13), and Harvey Sheldon (Article 15). There are further individuals to whose honorary volumes I have contributed but where the scope of the contribution has not in most cases been limited to Roman Britain. Their names can be found in the titles in the chronological bibliography of articles by the author, included at the end of this volume, and they are S.S. Frere (1983), B.R. Hartley (1998), and George Boon (2000).

It goes without saying that I owe a great amount to each of these nine individuals whose names are mentioned above, but if two names only were to be selected for the influence they have had on my career in archaeology, they would be Jocelyn Toynbee and Sheppard Frere. To Jocelyn Toynbee I owe an immense debt of gratitude, as it was she who really set me on the road to becoming a student of Roman Britain at the tender age of thirteen – see the first item in the chronological bibliography (1954), which was largely 'ghosted' by her. She also arranged for me to address the January 1954 meeting of the Council for British Archaeology in the rooms of the Society of Antiquaries of London in Burlington House (*Daily Telegraph*, 16 January 1954). This she achieved by liaising with the then Secretary of the CBA, Beatrice de Cardi – who celebrated her 102nd birthday in 2016, sadly her last. Turning to Sheppard Frere, it was under his guidance that I first learnt the techniques of excavation at the site of Verulamium (St Albans) in the 1950s. After completing my BA in Classics at Magdalen College, Oxford, I subsequently became Frere's pupil at the Institute of Archaeology, University of London, where I took the Postgraduate Diploma in Iron Age Europe and the Archaeology of the Western Roman Provinces. Finally, after Sheppard moved to Oxford, I became attached to the staff of the Institute as Assistant Lecturer in the Archaeology of the Western Roman Provinces, then Lecturer, and eventually Reader in Roman Archaeology.

Besides thanking these two eminent and generous scholars, I should also name two others without whom this collection would never have been published: Giles Standing and John Chandler. Giles was one of my last pupils at the Institute and also one of my best. His first published article, in *Britannia* 34 (2003), is very much along the lines of the items of my own which have been selected for the present work, but in one respect Giles far surpasses me – technical expertise in information technology – and it is for these two reasons, the academic and the technical, that I am deeply grateful to him for agreeing to edit the various items presented here and for producing the copy for this print-on-demand edition. Where Giles left off, John Chandler of the Hobnob Press took over. I offer them both my sincerest thanks. Finally, I am most grateful to Ann Hudson for compiling the indexes.

Mark Hassall
London, May 2017

NOTE ON THE TEXT

THE TWENTY ARTICLES in this collection span four decades of archaeological publication, from 1970 to 2010. The range of publications across this period necessarily means that the texts, as originally published, were produced in a variety of different formats, styles, and dimensions.

A central goal of the present work has been to bring these varied papers together into a single volume, and accordingly to take this opportunity to correct any original typographical errors which may have occurred. In this way, whilst the present collection serves as a historiography, as well as an account of archaeology, it is not intended to be a facsimile. As such, some light editing has been undertaken, and minor changes of formatting and spelling made, to standardise, as appropriate, the various texts reproduced in the present collection.

Whereas different referencing styles were originally applied, each article has now been reformatted with Harvard references, as endnotes, and a corresponding complete bibliography of cited works compiled. A separate bibliography of all works published by the author, arranged chronologically, has also been included.

G.S.

ABBREVIATIONS

Series and catalogues

The following are cited by item number and not page number

AE	*L'Année épigraphique*, 1888– , Paris (cited by year and item number)
BMC	*Coins of the Roman Empire in the British Museum*, 1923– , London
CIL	*Corpus Inscriptionum Latinarum*, 1863– , Berlin (cited by volume and item number)
CSIR	*Corpus Signorum Imperii Romani*, 1967– , Oxford
IDR	*Inscriptiones Daciae Romanae*, 1975– , Bucharest
ILS	*Inscriptiones Latinae Selectae*, H. Dessau (ed.), 1892–1916, Berlin
Pap. Lips.	*Griechische Urkunden der Papyrussammlung zu Leipzig*, L. Mitteis, 1906– , Leipzig
PIR²	*Prosopographia Imperii Romani* (2nd edn), 1933–2015, Berlin
RIB	*The Roman Inscriptions of Britain. Volume I: Inscriptions on Stone*, R.G. Collingwood and R.P. Wright, 1965, Oxford (revised edn (R.S.O. Tomlin (ed.)), 1995)
RIB II	*The Roman Inscriptions of Britain. Volume II: Instrumentum Domesticum*, R.G. Collingwood and R.P. Wright (S.S. Frere and R.S.O. Tomlin (eds)), 1990–5, Stroud (cited by fascicule and item number)
RIB III	*The Roman Inscriptions of Britain. Volume III: Inscriptions on Stone, Found or Notified between 1 January 1955 and 31 December 2006*, R.S.O. Tomlin, R.P. Wright and M.W.C. Hassall, 2009, Oxford
RIC	*The Roman Imperial Coinage*, 1923– , London
RMD	*Roman Military Diplomas 1954–1977*, University of London, Institute of Archaeology Occasional

	Publication 2, M.M. Roxan, 1978, London
RMD III	*Roman Military Diplomas 1985–1993*, University of London, Institute of Archaeology Occasional Publication 14, M.M. Roxan, 1994, London
RMD IV	*Roman Military Diplomas IV*, Bulletin of the Institute of Classical Studies Supplement 82, M.M. Roxan and P.A. Holder, 2003, London
RPC	*Roman Provincial Coinage*, 1992– , London/Paris
SEG	*Supplementum Epigraphicum Graecum*, 1923–, Amsterdam/Leiden

Classical sources

Amm. Marc.	*Roman History*, Ammianus Marcellinus
ARS	*Ancient Roman Statutes*, A.C. Johnson, P.R. Coleman-Norton and F.C. Bourne, 1961, Austin, Texas
Caes.	*Commentaries on the Gallic War*, Julius Caesar
CTh.	*Codex Theodosianus*
Dig.	*Digest*
Dio	*Roman History*, Dio Cassius
Not. Dig. Occ.	*Notitia Dignitatum... in partibus Occidentis*, O. Seeck (ed.), 1876/1962, Berlin (repr. 1962, Frankfurt)
Pan. Lat.	*Panegyrici Latini Veteres*
Pliny *NH*	*Natural History*, Pliny
SHA	*Scriptores Historiae Augustae*
Suet.	*Lives of the Caesars*, Suetonius
Tac. *Agr.*	*Agricola*, Tacitus
Tac. *Ann.*	*Annals*, Tacitus
Tac. *Germ.*	*Germania*, Tacitus
Tac. *Hist.*	*Histories*, Tacitus

Modern sources

BRGK	*Bericht der Römisch-Germanischen Kommission*, 1904– , Frankfurt/Berlin
CA	*Current Archaeology*, 1967– , London
JRS	*Journal of Roman Studies*, 1911– , London
L&S	*A Latin Dictionary*, C.T. Lewis and C. Short, 1879, Oxford

OCD[2]	*Oxford Classical Dictionary* (2nd edn), N.G.L. Hammond and H.H. Scullard (eds), 1970, Oxford
OLD	*Oxford Latin Dictionary*, P.G.W. Glare (ed.), 1982, Oxford
PSAN[4]	*Proceedings of the Society of Antiquaries of Newcastle-upon-Tyne* (4th series), 1855–1956, Gateshead
RCHM	*An Inventory of the Historical Monuments in London. Volume III: Roman London*, Royal Commission on Historical Monuments (England), 1928, London
RE	*Realencyclopädie der classischen Altertumswissenschaft*, Pauly–Wissowa, 1894–1980, Stuttgart

FIGURES

All figures are reproduced from the original publications, with permission. Line drawings are by the author

TABLES

Part I

Early Military History: AD 43–122

I

THE LOCATION OF LEGIONARY FORTRESSES AS A RESPONSE TO CHANGES IN MILITARY STRATEGY: THE CASE OF ROMAN BRITAIN AD 43–84

Originally published:
'The location of legionary fortresses as a response to changes in military strategy: the case of Roman Britain AD 43–84', in Y. Le Bohec and C. Wolff (eds), *Les légions de Rome sous le Haut-Empire: Actes du Congrès de Lyon (17–19 septembre 1998)*, Collection du Centre d'Études Romaines et Gallo-Romaines nouvelle série 20, 2000, Lyon, 441–57

I N THE OPENING papers of this conference, colleagues presented a series of papers on individual legions, with particular emphasis on the changing locations of the legionary bases. In the case of a 'one-legion' province such as Africa, such an exercise is relatively easy. In the case of a multi-legion province such as Britain, with four legions for the first half-century of its existence, it is not, and this is especially so during the fluid conditions of conquest and early military occupation. The reason for this is the paucity of the evidence. The primary evidence might be expected to come from notices in contemporary or near-contemporary authors, but historians such as Tacitus, writing for a readership that knew little of the geography of a far-off province such as Britain and cared less, are often less than helpful. This type of evidence is, of course, finite, but is supplemented by epigraphic and, in the cases of some fortunate provinces, papyrological and other documentary discoveries. A third type of evidence comes from archaeology, which can provide the actual remains of the legionary bases themselves. But reconstructing legionary movements in a multi-legion province is like a jigsaw where not all of the pieces may be present. From archaeology we know where the bases – or some of them – may be. From the historical, epigraphic or other documentary evidence we know the identity of the legions – or some of them – which occupied the bases. Where the evidence is lacking, we have to rely on guesswork and reconstructions that make 'the best fit' of such evidence as does survive. The best and most economical way of presenting such reconstructions is the one adopted by Ernst Stein,[1] that is in tabular grid form with one axis devoted to legions and the other to the bases. Not only do such tabular grids make immediate visual sense in a way that narrative text does not, but the weaknesses and anomalies in such reconstructions are at once apparent. Such an approach also emphasises the truth that if one piece of the jigsaw is misplaced – one legion attributed to the wrong base during a specific period – it will affect the rest of the picture.

In a recent article,[2] the present writer reviewed the changing opinions as to the locations of the legions in Britain from the Claudian invasion in AD 43 to the reign of Hadrian. These attempts at reconstructing the changing legionary dispositions were presented in a series of tabular grids on the model of those produced by Stein for the German provinces. That review began with Emil Hübner's survey of 1881,[3] naturally included that of Emil Ritterling in 1924/5,[4] and concluded with the reconstructions of Sheppard Frere, Graham Webster, and the writer's own.[5] Looking at all ten tabular grids in that article, it at once becomes apparent how the increase in knowledge – particularly archaeological knowledge – leads to increasingly complex reconstructions. When Hübner wrote, he knew that the normal standing garrison of the province in the first 60 or 70 years of existence was four legions – actually represented by six, since Legion IX was replaced by Legion VI Victrix, and Legion XIV by Legion II Adiutrix – but he only knew of four certain legionary bases, at Caerleon, York, Chester and Lincoln, where plentiful epigraphy indicated the presence there of Legions IX and II Adiutrix. He guessed at the existence of four others: on the sites later occupied by the *coloniae* at Colchester, Gloucester – both since confirmed by archaeology – and Silchester, and either Bath or Cirencester. In the present writer's opinion, he may have been correct about Silchester, but was probably wrong about Bath or Cirencester, though both had auxiliary units stationed there in the conquest period.[6]

Ritterling of course accepted the existence of the certain legionary fortresses of Caerleon, Chester, Lincoln and York, and Hübner's tentative suggestions of Gloucester and Cirencester. He rejected Hübner's suggested legionary bases at Colchester and Silchester, certainly wrongly in the first case and perhaps wrongly in the second, but correctly added a new base at Wroxeter.

Since the appearance of Ritterling's 'Legio', archaeology has confirmed the base at Wroxeter, (probably) disproved the existence of a legionary base at Cirencester, and added three certain new ones at Exeter, Colchester and Inchtuthil, and three probable ones at Lake Farm near Dorchester, Usk and Kingsholm on the outskirts of Gloucester. Others can be postulated at such sites as Silchester, Dorchester (?) and Leicester, the later capitals of the *civitates* of the Atrebates, Durotriges and Corieltauvi, and in the vicinity of Carlisle. Archaeology has also shown the existence of sixteen or seventeen so-called 'vexillation' fortresses. These Frere believes accommodated legionary troops – sometimes half a legion, sometimes less. The 'tabular grid' of pre-Hadrianic legionary dispositions according to Frere is thus complex. In the present writer's opinion, the proposed existence of bases (*hibernae*) for vexillations of half a legion or less is an unnecessary complication: it is anyway *a priori* unlikely at a time when many legions in other provinces of the empire so far from being split up were actually paired together in double fortresses like Vetera I. The 'vexillation fortresses' could, it has been argued, have been the winter quarters for concentrations of auxiliary units, possibly attached to specific legions, which with the start of the next year's campaigning season operated in conjunction with them.

If the proposed reconstruction of legionary dispositions (Table 1), or something like it, is accepted, one interesting conclusion is reached. If one ignores Caerleon from *c.* AD 75 (when it was occupied by Legion II Augusta), Chester from *c.* 87 (when it was certainly occupied by Legion XX) and York from 122 (when it was occupied by Legion VI), the average period that a legion spent in one particular fortress was only a dozen years. Sometimes, of course, the period of occupation might be much longer: Legion IX spent 45 years at York. But it could also be much shorter; the all-time record is held by the legion at Inchtuthil, Legion II Adiutrix (or, as is usually assumed, Legion XX), which was there for only four years, but Legion XX comes close with only five years at Colchester. The movements of Legion II Augusta before it arrived at Caerleon in *c.* 75 are controversial. On the reconstruction proposed here it spent only

	Leg. II Aug.	Leg. IX	Leg. XIV	Leg. II Ad.	Leg. XX	Leg. VI
Silchester	43–9					
Dorchester or Lake Farm	49–55					
Exeter	55–75					
Caerleon	75–>					
Leicester (double)		43?–55?	43–55			
Lincoln		55–71 or 43–71		71–8		
York		71–122				122–>
nr Carlisle		122–5				
Colchester					43–8	
Kingsholm					48–57	
Usk					57–67	
Gloucester (*colonia* site)					67–75	
Wroxeter			55–67 & 69		75–83/4	
Chester				78–83/4	83/4–>	
Inchtuthil				83/4–7		

Table 1 The location of the legions in Britain (after Hassall 2000a, table 10)

half a dozen years at Silchester, and the same period at either Dorchester or Lake Farm before going on to Exeter, while Legion II Adiutrix spent comparable periods at Lincoln and Chester. Put another way, if one removes the period of 45 years spent by Legion IX at York from the equation, the average length of time spent by the legions in Britain at any particular base comes down to less than ten years. If one considers the periods of office of the first eleven governors of the province, whose names and achievements are known from the testimony of Dio and Tacitus, only under three of them was there no change in the legionary dispositions: Suetonius Paulinus (58–61), whose conquests in North Wales and Anglesey were abandoned on the outbreak of the Boudiccan revolt, his successor, Petronius Turpilianus (61–3), who maintained the status quo, and Vettius Bolanus (69–71), whose capability for action was limited by a reduced garrison of three, rather than four, legions. What now follows is a brief survey, governor by governor,[7] of the military history of the province, with reference to the changing strategic situation and the way in which this was reflected in the relocation of legions.

PERIOD I: 43–61, ADVANCE[8]

This period of eighteen years, from the initial invasion of Britain under Claudius in 43 to the Boudiccan revolt of 60/1, saw the incorporation of the whole of the south and south-east of Britain into a Roman province with the exception of the client *regnum* of king Cogidubnus, which remained *extra formulam provinciae*. The northern boundary of the province was secured by the alliance of the powerful tribe of the Brigantes beyond its borders. Attempts to find a military (or political) solution to the problems posed by hostile tribes in Wales ultimately ended in failure. There were five governors of the province during these years.

A. Plautius, 43–7
The avowed objective[9] of the campaign undertaken by Claudius' first governor, Aulus Plautius, with the four legions under his command was to reinstate Verica as client king of the Atrebates. To do this he had to crush the power of the Catuvellauni, who had taken over the Atrebatic state and driven Verica into exile. In this he was successful. Camulodunum (Colchester), once the capital of the Trinovantes and subsequently of the combined power of Trinovantes and Catuvellauni, was captured and became the permanent base of Legion XX, while the whole of the south-eastern part of the island was overrun. This comprised the territory of nine tribal states. Of these, the Iceni retained nominal independence as a client kingdom, and part of the territory of the Atrebates was handed back to Verica (or his successor, Cogidubnus or perhaps Togidubnus[10]), his subjects henceforth known as the Regnenses, 'People of the Kingdom' – *regnum*. It is likely that Legion II Augusta had permanent winter quarters at Calleva Atrebatum (Silchester, near Reading) in that part of the territory of the Atrebates that was not included in the *regnum*, and what would appear to be part of the timber *principia* has been found beneath the later civil forum and basilica. The whereabouts of the other legions are not certain. Legion XIV may have been stationed in Catuvellaunian territory. But it is possible that the presence of Legion XX in Trinovantian lands may have been thought sufficient to overawe the tribe, since by this date the Trinovantes and Catuvellauni may have been at least politically indistinguishable. Ratae (Leicester), later the capital of the canton of the Corieltauvi and linked to Colchester by a new strategic road (the so-called Gartree Road), would be an obvious site for a legionary fortress, perhaps Legion XIV. Indeed, it could have been a

double legionary base and accommodated Legion IX as well, unless this was already based at Lincoln. A number of auxiliary (?) 'campaign bases' are also known in this area. The area under Roman occupation was criss-crossed by strategic roads, and auxiliary *castella* were established at road junctions, river crossings, and at or near native centres of population to enforce security. Finally, beyond the frontier, the Brigantes certainly, and the Cornovii probably, were allied either formally or informally to Rome.

P. Ostorius Scapula, 47–52

Scapula was faced with trouble on the western front with attacks by the tribes in Wales on 'Rome's allies',[11] presumably the Dobunni within the frontier and the Cornovii beyond it. He probably incorporated the territory of the Cornovii within the province and continued the network of roads with forts at strategic points in the area thus occupied. Auxiliary 'campaign bases' were moved forward into the tribal territory but Legion XIV may at first have remained at Leicester. Further south, however, Scapula transferred Legion XX from its base at Colchester to a new one in the western part of the tribal territory of the Dobunni, which was threatened by the Silures tribe of South Wales. This was at Kingsholm, a suburb of the city of Gloucester. To fill the military vacuum thus created, he established a military colony at Colchester.[12] Using Legion XX as the core of the army, Scapula was able to defeat the Silures and ultimately capture their leader, the renegade Catuvellaunian prince Caratacus, even if he was not able to claim total victory in the 'Silurian War'.[13] Southwards again, Scapula extended the territory of Verica's old kingdom, the *regnum* of his successor Cogidubnus, by adding to it several *civitates*. These will have been the northern part of the Atrebates, up to now under direct Roman rule, and the tribe of the Belgae based around Winchester (Venta Belgarum), possibly even the Cantiaci. The reason for this action will have been the same as the reason for creating the colony at Colchester: to 'free up' a legion for transfer to the west. The Durotriges, like the Belgae, had resisted the Roman advance under Vespasian, legate of Legion II Augusta,[14] and Scapula now decided to station the legion in their territory, either at Lake Farm or at Dorchester (Durnovaria Durotrigum). If one of these sites became a legionary base, the other may have become an auxiliary 'campaign base'. The fate of the *regnum* of Cogidubnus need not concern us but it may have lasted into the Flavian period when, with the death of its ruler, it was incorporated into the province, perhaps as the responsibility of *legati iuridici* who are first attested for Britain at this time.[15] This brief survey ignores the suppression of the first Icenian revolt, the campaign against the Deceangli, and the subsequent intervention in Brigantia, all recorded in the *Annals*, since none of these events appear to have led to changes in legionary dispositions.

A. Didius Gallus, 52–7

Written off by Tacitus as inactive and ineffective, the historian grudgingly admits that this elderly officer did 'push forward a few forts'.[16] In fact it may be that during the double *triennium* in which Gallus remained in office, no less than three of the four legions in the province moved to new forward bases, and if so the work of construction alone would represent a considerable expenditure of manpower and resources. Internal trouble had broken out in the kingdom of the Brigantes, where Gallus had to intervene in support of the client queen Cartimandua.[17] Perhaps it was now that Legion IX was stationed at Lincoln in the northern territory of the Corieltauvi in order to facilitate such intervention in Brigantia as might be necessary in the future, though the transfer may have taken place earlier; indeed it is possible that the legion was stationed in Lincoln or its immediate vicinity even since 43. Again, it was probably during the relatively long governorship of Gallus that Legion XIV took up quarters at Wroxeter (Viroconium), later to become the tribal capital of the Cornovii, while it is almost certain that Legion II Augusta moved westwards from Durotrigan territory to the territory of their neighbours, the Dumnonii. It was based at Exeter,[18] and, as with so many of the sites of first-century legionary fortresses, once the legion moved on, Exeter became the tribal capital – Isca Dumnoniorum. Only Legion XX may have remained in its old base at Kingsholm. This was already in the frontier zone and would remain so until a serious attempt was made to eliminate the threat posed by the Silures, a task that was to be left to Gallus' successor.

Q. Veranius, 57

Quintus Veranius' successful campaigns in Wales were cut short by his premature death after only a year in office.[19] Nevertheless, it may be due to him that Legion XX was moved forward to Usk in the newly-conquered territory. And even if the actual work of construction fell on the shoulders of his successor, that surely will have been his intention.

C. Suetonius Paulinus, 58–61

Suetonius Paulinus continued the work of Quintus Veranius in Wales but operated in the north rather than the south, where he was responsible for the initial occupation of Anglesey (Mona).[20] It is likely that he would have moved the XIV westwards from Wroxeter to a base in the newly-conquered territory of the Deceangli if the outbreak of the Boudiccan revolt had not occurred. As it was, he was fully occupied with the suppression of the revolt and the repressive measures that followed.

PERIOD 2: 61–71, RETRENCHMENT[21]

The appointment of Petronius Turpilianus marks a change in overall strategy on the part of Rome. The period 43–61 had seen a general forward movement in the island. Under the first governor, Aulus Plautius, this had been rapid. The pace had slowed under his successor, Ostorius Scapula, and almost come to a full stop under his successor, Didius Gallus, though even under Gallus conquered territory had been consolidated and legionary bases had been pushed forward to the edges of the frontier zone. The next phase, under Quintus Veranius and Suetonius Paulinus, had promised more rapid results and the final subjugation of Wales. However, with the outbreak of the Boudiccan revolt, the realisation of this objective had had to be postponed, and the years 61–71 were basically ones of retrenchment. There were changes in legionary dispositions in Britain during this period, but they were not carried out in order to implement a pro-active military policy but as a reaction to events which were taking place elsewhere in the empire.

P. Petronius Turpilianus, 61–3

No active military campaigning and no change in the location of legionary fortresses (unless Legion XX was removed from Usk to Gloucester (*colonia* site), but the archaeological evidence from the latter site favours a slightly later date).

M. Trebellius Maximus, 63–9

Nero's withdrawal of Legion XIV from Wroxeter for a projected campaign in the Caucasus may have resulted in a partial redeployment of the remaining legions, with Legion XX transferring from Usk to Gloucester (Glevum), on the site later to be occupied by the *colonia*.

M. Vettius Bolanus, 69–71
Despite the dislocation caused by the civil wars of 69, Vettius Bolanus was involved in a short, sharp campaign in Brigantia where the pro-Roman Cartimandua was defeated by the anti-Roman faction led by her husband, Venutius.[22] There were no changes in legionary dispositions, although Legion XIV did return briefly during the course of 69, to leave the province for good the following year to serve on the Rhine frontier with a base at Mainz.

<h2 style="text-align:center">PERIOD 3: 71–84, ADVANCE[23]</h2>

The arrival of Q. Petillius Cerealis in 71 with Legion II Adiutrix brought the military establishment in the province back from three to four legions and gave scope for the further advances that followed. Tacitus characterises this period as one which saw great generals as governors, Roman victories, and the dwindling hopes of the native opposition.[24]

Q. Petillius Cerealis, 71–4
Logic demanded that Cerealis turn his attention to the subjugation of Wales, begun by Ostorius Scapula and almost completed by Veranius and Suetonius Paulinus, but interrupted by the Boudiccan revolt, the civil wars of 69, and expulsion of Cartimandua. The immediate priority, however, was to stabilise the situation in the north after the collapse of the Brigantian client kingdom, and this Cerealis appears to have done.[25] Legion II Adiutrix took up quarters at Lincoln, while Legion IX moved northwards to York (Eboracum). Legions XX and II Augusta remained at Gloucester and Exeter respectively.

Sex. Julius Frontinus, 74–8
Frontinus finally carried out the long-awaited subjugation of the Silures of South Wales. The Dumnonii of south-western Britain were now pacified, and it was possible to transfer Legion II Augusta from Exeter (Isca Dumnoniorum) to Caerleon (also Isca) in the territory of the Silures. The presence of Legion XX at Gloucester was now unnecessary and it was transferred to Wroxeter,[26] finally vacated by Legion XIV in 70. Gloucester itself was to become a colony, the *deductio* perhaps occurring under Domitian, rather than Nerva as usually assumed.[27] It is possible that at the very end of his governorship, Frontinus began operations against the Ordovices in North Wales,[28] in which case work may also have started on the legionary fortress of Chester.

Cn. Julius Agricola, 78–83/4

It is not certain whether at the outset of his governorship Agricola had
his eyes set on the total conquest of the island of Britain, but it is certain
that this had been his aim by the time he left the island – indeed those
partial to him, and presumably he himself, believed that he had done
it[29] and that his conquests had then been abandoned. His first priority
was to round off the conquest of North Wales, which he achieved by
decimating the tribe of the Ordovices.[30] Now, if not before, the legionary
fortress at Chester will have been established. In the present writer's
opinion, this was for Legion II Adiutrix – not initially for Legion XX
– which had previously been based at Lincoln. Whatever the legion in
garrison, its function will have been to support operations should they
become necessary in two areas – North Wales and northern Britain west
of the Pennines. It was thus the equivalent both of Caerleon in South
Wales and of York in northern Britain east of the Pennines.

After operations in North Wales came the final pacification of
Brigantia, the conquest of southern Scotland, and finally north-eastern
Scotland north of the Forth–Clyde line and east of the Highland massif.
At the very end of Agricola's governorship, or in the early years of that
of his successor, the legionary fortress of Inchtuthil will have been
established, perhaps for Legion II Adiutrix, rather than Legion XX as is
usually assumed. What was the intended function of the new legionary
fortress? Not, surely, as I.A. Richmond long ago suggested, to 'block' the
Dunkeld Gorge and prevent Highland tribes from issuing out to attack
Roman forts in eastern Scotland – such a strategy would have been
useless – but as the key site from which the penetration and pacification
of the Highlands would have taken place. There can be little doubt that
if Agricola's victory at Mons Graupius had been followed up, Roman
engineers would have pushed a road, the equivalent of the modern A9,
up Glen Tay to the Great Glen, one of the main arteries of a system that
would eventually have encompassed the Highlands, as the Roman road
network did the mountains of Wales or the Pennines. Inchtuthil, at the
point where the Tay issues out from the Grampians, bears the same
relationship to that river as the Rhineland legionary bases of Vetera and
Mainz do to the Rivers Lippe or Main. All three were established when
Roman strategic thinking was based on the concept of further advance
rather than defence, and the river valleys provided natural avenues for
advance.

POSTSCRIPT – PERIOD 4: FROM AGRICOLA TO THE DEPARTURE OF
LEGION IX, 84–C. 125?[31]

In some ways, the period following the departure of Agricola is a 'dark age'. The books of Tacitus' *Histories*, which would have covered the latter part of the reign of Domitian, are lost, and while all Agricola's predecessors are known, we do not even know the name of his successor. We do know, however, that in *c.* 87, Legion II Adiutrix was withdrawn for service on the Danube. Whether, as suggested above, it had been in garrison at Inchtuthil, or had occupied Chester, the result was the same: the reduction in the legionary establishment from four to three legions meant that the legionary base at Inchtuthil could not be maintained and a staged withdrawal from Scotland followed. As Tacitus recognised, the chance to round off the complete occupation of the island was lost, and, as it turned out, lost forever. Henceforth there was always to be a frontier within the island itself. The result was that Britain remained a frontier province with a permanent military establishment of three legions, unlike Spain where the whole peninsula had been conquered under Augustus and the garrison could be progressively reduced until it stood at a single legion. Nevertheless, it is in this period that we can say without question where the legions in Britain were actually stationed: Legion XX was based at Chester, Legion IX at York and Legion II Augusta at Caerleon.

Then, at some time in the first quarter of the second century, Legion IX was withdrawn. It appears briefly in Lower Germany at Nijmegen but its subsequent history is uncertain. When did this withdrawal take place? Many think that it was removed from Britain under Trajan or early in Hadrian's reign, and that it was replaced at York in 122 by Legion VI Victrix, which arrived from Lower Germany with the new governor, Aulus Platorius Nepos, in that year. The replacement of Legion IX by Legion VI Victrix at York is not in question, but did it really take place before 122? On balance it seems unlikely, for if it had been, it would have meant that the military establishment had been reduced to two legions only. Of course, such a reduction is possible, but at no other time from the middle of the first century to the beginning of the fourth was the legionary establishment so low. It seems more likely that when Hadrian ordered Legion VI to be sent to the province, his intention was to bring the military establishment back to its pre-87 strength of four legions. The reason for this will have been his decision to construct the great frontier barrier that bears his name. It is true that Legion IX does not figure among the numerous epigraphic building records from the Wall, but here absence of evidence does not necessarily imply evidence of absence since the legion could have been employed in the western sector, which was constructed in turf and where building records do not survive – or it could have been employed in purely military duties while the other legions were entrusted to the actual work of construction. If Legion IX did remain in the province after 122, the question arises as to where it was based. One suggestion is that it was stationed in the vicinity of Carlisle, from near which tile-stamps have been found.[32] It is known that work on the Wall, or rather its attendant forts, continued into the late 130s,[33] but it may be that Legion IX itself was removed earlier than that and an approximate date of 125 is adopted here. With the arrival of Legion VI and the withdrawal of Legion IX – whenever these events occurred – the legionary establishment and indeed the legionary bases became permanent, and both were to remain so for perhaps the next two centuries.

CONCLUSION

There is much in the above reconstruction of legionary movements presented here that may appear controversial, and the hope is that new evidence from sites like Leicester or Dorchester will prove or disprove some of the ideas here presented. However, the main conclusions of this article should stand: that the Roman high command was very flexible in the location of legions during the initial stages of the incorporation of new territory into the empire. To the cost-effective modern mind, the abandonment of whole legionary fortresses or major engineering undertakings such as Hadrian's Wall (by Pius) or Trajan's Bridge over the Danube (by Hadrian) shortly after completion – or even before completion, as in the case of the legionary fortress at Inchtuthil (abandoned by Domitian) – seems both extraordinary and yet horrifyingly familiar. However, in the case of the changing locations of the legionary fortresses in Britain, flexibility in response to changing military strategies was surely a strength rather than a weakness, and can be accounted as one of the reasons for the success of the Roman imperial army in the island.

ACKNOWLEDGEMENTS

I am most grateful to May Hesslefors for permission to include the maps of legionary dispositions, in the original article, from her Mémoire de Maîtresse, *Organisation militaire et défense de territoire conquis en*

Bretagne Romaine, 1995, Paris. These maps were themselves based on an article by the present writer.[34]

Illustration note: This article was originally published with illustrations of fifteen maps, not included in the present collection, but referred to in the notes below.

Addendum: Since this article was written, an important discovery has been made at Alchester in Oxfordshire, where the later Roman town is now known to have been preceded by an early fortress. A tombstone from the site records the death of Lucius Valerius Geminus, a veteran of Legion II Augusta.[35] As Eberhard Sauer, the excavator of the site, argues, this strongly suggests that Alchester, at the junction of Akeman Street and the North–South Road linking Silchester with Towcester and beyond, was the base of Legion II in the early conquest period, rather than Silchester.[36] See also Article 9 in the present collection, under Aulus Plautius, the first governor, and again in the 'Postscript' for Aulus Plautius at the end of that article, where it is proposed that the initial legionary fortresses were: Colchester (Legion XX), Chichester (Legion IX), Alchester (Legion II Augusta) and, possibly, Irchester (Legion XIV) or a site further north (Table 2).

	Leg. II Aug.	Leg. IX	Leg. XIV	Leg. II Ad.	Leg. XX	Leg. VI
Alchester	43–9					
Dorchester or Lake Farm	49–55					
Exeter	55–75					
Caerleon	75–>					
Chichester		43–55				
Irchester (?)			43–55			
Lincoln		55–71		71–8		
York		71–122				122–>
nr Carlisle		122–5				
Colchester					43–8	
Kingsholm					48–57	
Usk					57–67	
Gloucester (*colonia* site)					67–75	
Wroxeter			55–67 & 69		75–83/4	
Chester				78–83/4	83/4–>	
Inchtuthil				83/4–7		

Table 2 The revised location of the legions in Britain (after Table 1; Sauer 2005; Article 9 'Postscript' for Aulus Plautius)

[1]   Stein 1932.
[2]   Hassall 2000a.

3   Hübner 1881.
4   Ritterling 1924; 1925.
5   Frere 1967; 1978; 1987; Webster 1993; Hassall 2000a.
6   The *Ala Indiana* and *Ala Thracum* at Cirencester, *RIB* 108–9, and the *Ala Vettonum* at Bath, *RIB* 159.
7   Reference should be made to the useful survey by Birley (1981, 37–81), with its full citation of the literary sources.
8   Hassall 2000b, maps 1–5.
9   Dio 60.19.
10   *RIB* 91 + add.
11   Tac. *Ann.* 12.31.
12   Tac. *Ann.* 12.32.
13   Tac. *Ann.* 12.39.
14   Suet. *Vesp.* 4.1.
15   Birley 1981, 208–18.
16   Tac. *Agr.* 14.
17   Tac. *Ann.* 12.40.
18   The identity of the legion is indicated indirectly by the presence of antefixes from the same mould as are found at the later legionary base of Legion II Augusta at Caerleon: Bidwell and Boon 1976.
19   Tac. *Agr.* 14; *Ann.* 14.29.
20   Tac. *Agr.* 14; *Ann.* 14.29.
21   Hassall 2000b, maps 6–8.
22   Tac. *Hist.* 3.45. Bolanus is not actually mentioned by name in this passage.
23   Hassall 2000b, maps 9–12.
24   Tac. *Agr.* 17.
25   Tac. *Agr.* 17. At Carlisle, a dendrochronological date of AD 72 shows that military occupation began here at this time: *Britannia* 21 (1990), 320, no. 2.
26   *RIB* 293; cf. Tomlin 1992, 141–5.
27   Hassall 1999.
28   cf. Tac. *Agr.* 18 for an *ala* which had been stationed in the territory of the Ordovices before Agricola's arrival.
29   Tac. *Hist.* 1.2: *perdomita Britannia et statim missa.*
30   Tac. *Agr.* 18: *caesaque prope universa gente.*
31   Hassall 2000b, maps 13–15.
32   *RIB* II.4, 2462.2–4.
33   e.g. Carvoran, *RIB* 1816, 1818, 1820, n. on *RIB* 1820.
34   Hassall 2000a.
35   *Britannia* 36 (2005), 478, no. 4.
36   Sauer 2005.

2
BATAVIANS AND THE ROMAN CONQUEST OF BRITAIN

Originally published:
'Batavians and the Roman Conquest of Britain', *Britannia* 1, 1970,
131–6

TACITUS' ACCOUNT OF the Claudian invasion of Britain and the campaigns that followed it down to the year AD 47 is unfortunately lost,[1] and historians have to be content with Dio, who gives the only consecutive account,[2] supplemented by scattered references in other sources. This short article is an attempt to extract a few more fragments of information from these literary sources, and in particular it concerns the part played by Rome's Batavian auxiliaries.[3]

The first definite evidence we have that Batavians were stationed in Britain comes from Tacitus, who, in describing the preparations made by Nero for an expedition against the Albani of the Caucasus, says that units were withdrawn from several provinces including Britain, and from his later narrative it is clear that these included Legion XIV and eight cohorts of Batavians who were attached to it.[4] The date is 67. However, there is strong reason to suppose that there were Batavians serving in Britain before this date, indeed from the invasion of 43 onwards. This is an inference derived from the known methods of fighting employed by the Batavians, and the descriptions of auxiliaries in action in Britain given by Tacitus and Dio. It was the proud boast and peculiar skill of the Batavians that they could swim rivers fully armed, the cavalry still retaining control over their horses. This skill they had exhibited in the campaign of Germanicus against Arminius in attempting to cross the Ems,[5] and were later to show in crossing the Po during the civil wars of 69.[6] Batavian cavalry could cross great rivers like the Rhine[7] and Danube[8] under arms and without breaking ranks. Accordingly, the Κελτόι, who during the invasion of 43 crossed the Medway and later the Thames in the face of strong enemy opposition to form a bridge-head for the army of Aulus Plautius,[9] are usually identified with Batavians. The term Κελτόι is not a difficulty since Dio regularly calls Germans, among whom the Batavians were generally classed,[10] by this name, while he calls Gauls Γαλάται.[11] Again, it is very likely that Suetonius Paulinus used Batavian cavalry for his attack on Anglesey in 60, for on this occasion too Tacitus says that the troopers forded the straits and, where the water was too deep, swam by the side of their horses.[12]

Are these Batavians, whose presence in Britain from the time of the conquest until AD 60 has been argued, identical with those Batavian cohorts withdrawn by Nero in 67? These early references mention cavalry, but this does not invalidate an identification with the eight cohorts of 67 since these latter were part-mounted, as we know from their demand at the outset of their mutiny in 69 that the cavalry element be increased.[13] The real difficulty in assuming that these cohorts had been in Britain since 43 lies in the fact that Nero sent auxiliary as well as legionary reinforcements to Britain after the Boudiccan revolt of 60 and that this involved precisely eight cohorts.[14] The number is suspiciously reminiscent of the eight Batavian cohorts to be recalled by Nero half a dozen years later. Cichorius[15] held the view that they were the same and was therefore of the opinion that there was no evidence for Batavians in Britain before 61. The circumstantial evidence for Batavians here during the conquest period is, however, strong and, even if one accepts Cichorius' point, the case for *other* Batavian units taking part in the opening phases of the conquest is not affected. Is there, in fact, additional evidence to suggest that they did serve before the year 61?

In a much-quoted passage, *Histories* 4.12, Tacitus says as a general comment on the Batavians that they increased the renown won in long wars with the Germans by service in Britain, to which some cohorts had been sent under the command of their own nobles. As Professor Frere has pointed out,[16] the period 61–7 is not one in which they would have acquired a great reputation in Britain. They will have taken no part in the defeat of Boudicca when Legion XIV won the title Martia Victrix, and indeed the whole period will have fallen in the governorships of P. Petronius Turpilianus, who, after the suppression of the revolt dared 'nihil ultra', and of M. Trebellius Maximus, under whom the army, accustomed to campaigns, '*otio lasciviret*'.[17] Even if we discount the desire of Tacitus to belittle the achievements of these two 'unmilitary governors', and thus draw a contrast with '*viri militares*' of the succeeding Flavian period, it is likely enough that this was a time of consolidation and it is difficult to see how reputations can have been won. If Tacitus in *Histories* 4.12 cannot be referring to the period immediately after 61, because of the absence of serious fighting, he cannot refer to the subsequent Flavian period when the advance in Wales and North Britain was continued, for after 69 and the Batavian revolt their cohorts will no longer have been commanded by their own countrymen. *Histories* 4.12, then, refers to the pre-Boudiccan period, and either has no connection at all with the eight Batavian cohorts withdrawn by Nero in 67 but relates to other units present in Britain before 61, or, if it *does* refer to the units withdrawn in 67, they are not identical with the eight cohorts sent in 61. A third possibility is just conceivable: the eight cohorts of Batavians took part in the invasion but were withdrawn before the Boudiccan revolt; after it had been crushed Nero sent them again to Britain.[18]

It seems certain, therefore, that *Histories* 4.12 must refer to the pre-Boudiccan period, and it is even possible that we can name one of the chiefs whom Tacitus there says commanded the Batavian cohorts in Britain. Julius Civilis was of noble birth[19] and commanded a cohort.[20] In AD 69, he had seen 25 years service with Rome,[21] which sounds like a round figure, but should mean that he had been enrolled about the time of the Claudian invasion of 43. He and his cohort could have been recruited by Gaius, who probably enrolled two new legions, XV and XII Primigenia, if Gaius' enlistment of Batavians in AD 40 extended beyond those for his own bodyguard.[22] This suggestion even finds some slight support in Civilis' *nomen*, Julius, which hints at a grant of citizenship made to him on enlistment by Gaius. The Batavian Julius Briganticus' father (Civilis' brother-in-law) could have received citizenship at the same time, while others such as Claudius Labeo and Claudius Victor will have received it from Gaius' successor. Above all, Civilis claimed before Petillius Cerealis that he had been a friend of Vespasian before he became emperor.[23] Such an association was a potential embarrassment to the Flavian party, whom Civilis had claimed to support during the early stages of his rebellion, and a tie with Vespasian himself was unlikely to have been invented by a pro-Flavian historian like Pliny (Tacitus' presumed source).[24] If Vespasian and Civilis had really been friends, when could they have become acquainted? Vespasian had been put in charge of Legion II by Claudius through the influence of Narcissus, and in 43 had accompanied it from Germany to Britain where he had fought with distinction.[25] And Civilis will most likely have met him during this period.[26] This would fit extremely well. For it was Vespasian who, with his brother Sabinus, was sent to reinforce the bridgehead formed by the 'Batavians' during the 'Battle of the Medway'.[27]

There is a hint of one other theatre of operations for Batavian forces in Britain during the early conquest period. Tacitus, when recounting the feud between Venutius and queen Cartimandua and its subsequent consequences for Rome, tells us that Venutius, whose Brigantian extraction he has already mentioned (this will be in one of the lost books of the *Annals*), had long been loyal and had received the protection of Roman arms during his married life with queen Cartimandua.[28] This can only mean that, in the words of E. Birley, 'within the four years when Plautius was in Britain (43–7) there were Roman troops operating in Brigantian territory in support of its ruling house'.[29] Now, Civilis had a nephew, Julius Briganticus, his sister's son, who loyally supported the Romans against his uncle during the Batavian revolt. The *cognomen* could well derive from the name of the North British tribe,[30] and if Briganticus was in his mid-twenties in 69, he should have been born during the early years of the Claudian invasion of Britain. It does not seem impossible that Briganticus' father, like his brother-in-law Civilis, commanded a cohort of Batavians in Britain, and that his son's name recalls some successful operation in Brigantian territory. In giving his son such a name he would not lack famous precedents. The practice of coining a *cognomen* from a conquered barbarian people was common under the republic and continued under the empire, when it was not restricted to the imperial house. Thus, Cossus Cornelius Lentulus, after his North African victory in AD 5/6, bestowed the name Gaetulicus, derived from that of the Gaetulians, upon his son,[31] while of particular relevance both as regards date and geographical setting is the case of Gabinius Secundus, legate of Lower Germany in 41, whom Claudius allowed to assume the name 'Cauchius' because of his conquest of the 'Cauchi' (= Chauci).[32] The clearest precedent, however, would have been the imperial one, for the Senate not only gave Claudius the title Britannicus in 43, but gave the same name to the emperor's son.[33] That more humble folk could coin such exotic cognomina for themselves is shown by the *cognomen* Actiacus, derived from Octavian's great naval victory, borne by veterans of Legion XI settled at Ateste, and that they did so for their children can be demonstrated, to cite but two examples, by the name borne by the son of a chief pilot of the *Classis Britannica* under the Flavians – Oceanus! – and that of Arminius' nephew, who was called Italicus by his pro-Roman father, Flavus.[34] Vespasian's own presence with the Batavians in Brigantian territory is not entirely out of the question either – at all events, Flavian propagandists later linked Vespasian's name with operations in the far north.[35]

To summarise: it seems likely that there were Batavians from the year 43 onwards serving in Britain, and that *Histories* 4.12, which describes their coming under the command of their own chiefs, refers to this period. Further, that Civilis may have been one of these chiefs and his brother-in-law another, and that the latter saw action in the north of the island connected with the operations hinted at by Tacitus, in his back-reference to a previous mention of the Brigantes in a lost book of the *Annals*.

What part, finally, did Batavians play in Britain after their revolt was crushed in 70? We know that Agricola employed four cohorts of Batavians at Mons Graupius,[36] and, as already suggested, it is morally certain that some at least of the '*lectissimi auxilarium quibus nota vada et patrius nandi usus quo simul seque et arma et equos regunt*'[37] used by him during the second Roman invasion of Anglesey were Batavians also. The only problem concerns the exact identity of the units involved. The eight cohorts which revolted in 69 will have been disbanded (a ninth – *Cohors IX Batavorum equitata milliaria exploratorum* – was not).[38] I.A. Richmond[39] believed that Agricola's Batavian cohorts were milliary and are to be identified with Cohorts I, II and III milliariae, which by the end of the first century or later were in other provinces.[40] If this view is correct, it may be that the eight quingenary (?) cohorts of the Batavian revolt were disbanded only to be reformed as four milliary cohorts and quickly sent back to Britain. There is, however, some doubt as to the strength of the original eight Batavian cohorts. If *Cohors IX* was milliary, they *should* have been milliary also, despite the apparent rareness of milliary cohorts during this period. That Agricola's Batavian cohorts included at least some veterans is suggested by the phrase '*vetustas militiae*' applied to them at the time of Mons Graupius. The quingenary *Cohors I Batavorum*, attested in Britain for the first time in 122,[41] will then belong to a different series, and this is perhaps the most likely explanation though others are possible.[42] The subsequent history of *Cohors I Batavorum quingenaria*, the only Batavian unit to remain in Britain, is not here relevant. It has left epigraphic records at Carvoran on Hadrian's Wall, possibly Castlecary on the Antonine Wall, and most notably at Carrawburgh on the former, where it is also stationed in the *Notitia Dignitatum*.[43]

[1]   The initial stage of the conquest probably came at the end of *Annals* 9, subsequent events down to AD 47 in the first half of *Annals* 11. See Syme 1958, 260.

[2]   Dio 60.19–21.

[3]   I would like to thank a number of colleagues and friends for reading this short article in typescript and making valuable suggestions.

[4]   Tac. *Hist.* 1.6 with 1.59, 2.27, cf. 4.15.

[5]   Tac. *Ann.* 2.8.

[6]   Tac. *Hist.* 2.17.

[7]   Tac. *Hist.* 4.12.

[8]   Dio 69.9.6; cf. *ILS* 2558, under Hadrian.

[9]   Dio 60.20.

[10] Tac. *Germ.* 29, where the Batavians are included among tribes of German origin.

[11] Riese 1889, 14 n. 4: 'Κελτική ist für Dio Germanien. Die Gallier nennt er Γαλάται, die Germanen Κελτόι, Γερμάνια ist ein Ausdruck, der für ihn mit den rheinischen Legionen verbunden ist. Dies ist sein stetiger Sprachgebruch' (with supporting references).

[12] Tac. *Ann.* 14.29.

[13] Tac. *Hist.* 4.19.

[14] Tac. *Ann.* 14.38.

[15] *RE* IV.1, 250.

[16] Frere 1967, 61 n. 1.

[17] Tac. *Agric.* 16.

[18] The view of M. Bang, for whose discussion of the history of Batavian auxiliary units see Bang 1906, 32–9.

[19] Tac. *Hist.* 1.13, *regia stirpe*.

[20] Tac. *Hist.* 4.16, 4.32.

[21] Tac. *Hist.* 4.32.

[22] Suet. *Gaius* 43, where Suetonius says that Gaius undertook his expedition to Germany in order to get new recruits for his Batavian bodyguard. The immediate reason, in fact, was to suppress the revolt of Gaetulicus in *Upper* Germany. However, Bicknell (1968) argues persuasively that Gaius did at least visit Lower Germany in AD 40, and that the army of the Lower Rhine carried out minor operations against the Canninefates from the Insula Batavorum; cf. especially Tac. *Hist.* 4.15.

23 Tac. *Hist.* 5.26.
24 cf. Brunt 1960, 510.
25 Suet. *Vesp.* 4; Tac. *Hist.* 3.44.
26 cf. Walser 1951, 91: 'Vermutlich bestanden zwischen den batavischen Truppen und Vespasian alte Beziehungen aus der Zeit, als Vespasian Legionslegat in Germanien und Britannien war'.
27 Dio 60.20.
28 Tac. *Ann.* 12.40.
29 Birley 1953a, 47.
30 Not discussed by Kajanto (1965, 52), cognomina from conquered towns, peoples, etc. Lewis and Short (L&S) derive Briganticus from Brigantes, v. sub *Brigantes*. A derivation from the Brigantii of the Lake Constance region is also theoretically possible.
31 Velleius 2.116.
32 Suet. *Claud.* 24.
33 Dio 60.22.
34 e.g. *ILS* 2243: *M. Billienus M. f. Rom(ilia) Actiacus legione XI proelio navali facto in coloniam deductus*, with the other examples quoted in the article by Ensslin (1943/4) cited below. *Dig.* 36.1.48 (Oceanus); Tac. *Ann.* 11.16 (Italicus). The name of Arminius himself may be a geographical *cognomen*, 'Armenius' – the Armenian – given him as one of the companions of C. Caesar to the east and Armenia in AD 1. See the discussion of the suggestion of Hohl by Ensslin (1943/4, 64 ff.). Ensslin, however, tentatively supported a Teutonic derivation. Examples of cognomina used by the aristocracy and derived from some special geographical connection could be multiplied under the empire.
35 Momigliano 1950, 41 f.
36 Tac. *Agric.* 36, *quattuor* – so the best MS. See Ogilvie and Richmond 1967, introduction, 78.
37 Tac. *Agric.* 18.
38 Stein 1932, 167.
39 Ogilvie and Richmond 1967, 78.
40 For these units, see most conveniently Cichorius in *RE* IV, 249 f. and the indexes of *CIL* XVI.
41 *CIL* XVI, 69.
42 Bang (1906) thought that Agricola's Batavian cohorts were quingenary and that the *Cohors I Batavorum* later attested in Britain was one of them. After their withdrawal to the continent, Cohorts II and III were made up to milliary strength and a new milliary Cohort I was added to complete the series.
43 *Not. Dig. Occ.* 40.39. It has recently been suggested by Bogaers (1967a, 75) that finds of North British trumpet *fibulae* and of a late La Tène mirror of British type from Nijmegen are to be connected with the presence of Legion IX there in the early years of the second century. This is perhaps true of those trumpet *fibulae* whose provenance is adequately recorded, since these came from the legionary cemetery. But the mirror came from the Gräberfeld

unter Hees, which belongs to the civil settlement of Ulpia Noviomagus, and this, at least, could equally well have been brought back by a returning Batavian veteran.

Part II

Frontier: AD 122–207

3
INSCRIPTIONS AND HADRIAN'S WALL

Originally published:
'Inscriptions and Hadrian's Wall', in M.F.A. Symonds and D.J.P.
Mason (eds), *Frontiers of Knowledge: a Research Framework for Hadrian's Wall, Part of the Frontiers of the Roman Empire World Heritage Site. Volume I: Resource Assessment*, 2009, Durham, 152–4

THE OBJECT OF this survey is to present the different ways in which inscriptions on stone, wood, pottery and metal have contributed and continue to contribute to our understanding of Hadrian's Wall. Something shall also be said about the ways in which future discoveries may be expected some day to extend our knowledge. Where appropriate, the lines that future work might take have been indicated. It is worth noting that literary documents provide an outline history of Hadrian's Wall, supplemented by coins, which provide dates for archaeological contexts. The Vindolanda writing tablets shed considerable light on life on the northern frontier, but nearly all date to the period before the construction of the Wall.

EVIDENCE FOR THE BUILDING OF HADRIAN'S WALL
Inscriptions from the milecastle gateways show unequivocally that the structure that we know today as Hadrian's Wall was built during the reign of that emperor and under the direction of the governor Aulus Platorius Nepos (AD 122–5/6), whose arrival in Britain shortly before 17 July 122 is demonstrated by a diploma, a certificate of privileges issued to a veteran. Further, the so-called 'centurial stones' found built into the fabric of the Wall demonstrate that the building of the frontier was divided amongst the Legions II Augusta, VI Victrix and XX Valeria Victrix, and their constituent cohorts and centuries. As a by-product

of the discovery of these stones, we have partial rolls of the centurions serving in the three legions during the reign of Hadrian.[1]

Only one fragmentary timber inscription survives from the turf stretch of the Wall,[2] and it will be a matter of extreme chance if any more are discovered.

Two inscriptions found at Benwell and Halton Chesters[3] indicate that a major change in plan, the 'fort decision', took place during the governorship of Aulus Platorius Nepos, and others that work continued on the frontier almost until the end of Hadrian's reign in 138.

Finally, inscriptions found on the *Vallum* indicate that this was created by auxiliary soldiers, rather than the legionaries who built the Wall and its forts.

EVIDENCE FOR THE LATER HISTORY OF HADRIAN'S WALL

Epigraphic evidence for the building of the Antonine Wall comes from that frontier rather than the Wall of Hadrian, though inscriptions from the latter may indicate continuing occupation of some forts. A lost inscription[4] records building work undertaken on the curtain in AD 158, thereby indicating an intention to return to Hadrian's Wall. A second inscription records building work at Birrens, an outpost fort, in the same year.[5] Many inscriptions indicate building work continuing through the second century and well into the third. Some of the later inscriptions are more informative and provide details of the buildings then being erected. They also provide information on the rebuilding of the turf section of Hadrian's Wall in stone.

Two newly-discovered diplomas[6] cast light on the British war of 180. They show that the governor Ulpius Marcellus who led the campaign was already in Britain in 178. This solves a local problem as it can now be seen that the altar inscription from Benwell, which mentions Ulpius by name, is dated to the joint reign of Marcus Aurelius and Commodus (plural emperors are mentioned), i.e. before the death of Marcus on 17 March 180, at the very latest.[7]

Fourth-century inscriptions are rare on Hadrian's Wall. It has been suggested that the building inscriptions set up by *corvées* drafted from the southern *civitates*, e.g. the *Civitas Catuvellaunorum*,[8] the *Civitas Dumnoniorum*,[9] and the *Civitas Durotrigum Lendiniensis*,[10] found along the line of the Wall, date to this time.

THE UNITS ON THE WALL

The present state of knowledge of the units attested at the forts on the Wall and the Cumbrian coast from Wallsend to Ravenglass is conveniently summarised by David Breeze and Brian Dobson.[11] There are some 23 forts concerned, and of these the garrisons of only 5 are known for certain in the Hadrianic period, though the identity of some others can be postulated. The presence of the *Ala Augusta ob virtutem appellata* at Chesters during this period was established following the discovery of an altar there in 1978,[12] and it seems reasonable to suppose that future discoveries will provide the names of some of the units in the remaining forts. For the later second century, after the abandonment of the Antonine Wall in the 160s when Hadrian's Wall once more became the frontier, 7 of the 23 units in garrison are known, while for the third century the figure is 18. This figure can be increased by 3 if one extrapolates back from the evidence of the *Notitia Dignitatum*, which lists the fourth-century units. This seems reasonable since all the *Notitia* units are identical to the third-century units where these are known, with only one exception. To sum up, there are considerable gaps in our knowledge of the army dispositions in the forts of Hadrian's Wall and the Cumbrian coast, especially during the earlier periods, but it is probable that some at least of these will be slowly filled by new discoveries, in particular chance finds, though no dramatic increase in our knowledge is likely.

Lead sealings can be stamped with the names of units, but as they sealed items in transit, they are not as informative about specific units' bases as might be hoped.

Inscriptions also provide information on the officers and soldiers of the Roman army, their ages, origins and careers, their social arrangements and their religious beliefs. Of particular importance is the collection of altars to Jupiter from Maryport dating to the reign of Hadrian. The annual dedications indicate that the average length of service of a commanding officer was three years.

PLACE-NAMES

Our knowledge of the place-names of the forts along the line of Hadrian's Wall and the Cumbrian coast, up to the time of its publication, has been conveniently summarised by Breeze and Dobson.[13] It is based on four types of evidence:

The Rudge Cup, the Amiens Patera and the newly-discovered Staffordshire Moorlands Pan (Ilam Pan) are all vessels inscribed with the names of forts along the line of approximately the western third of the Wall;

The *Notitia Dignitatum*, which lists by name units in garrison in the forts, and the names of the forts themselves, from east to west along the line of the Wall and then southwards down the Cumbrian coast;

The *Ravenna Cosmography*, which lists over 300 place-names in Britain including some 20 in the area under consideration. The names are listed in geographical 'clusters', which do not always make identification easy;

Inscriptions found at various fort sites. These sometimes provide the name of a unit listed in the *Notitia* and thus enable a name to be assigned to a fort. Alternatively, they may provide direct evidence of a site name. The derivation of the place-names of Arbeia (South Shields) and Cilurnum (Chesters) has recently been debated.[14]

The recent discovery of the Staffordshire Moorlands Pan,[15] which confirms the name Congavata (or similar) for the fort at Drumburgh, and a fragment of a military diploma from Ravenglass issued to a veteran in *Cohors I Aelia Classica*,[16] demonstrates the possibility of more such valuable discoveries.

CIVILIANS ON THE WALL

This is a subject covered by Peter Salway,[17] who made full use of the epigraphic evidence such as tombstones, building inscriptions and religious dedications, sometimes set up corporately such as the dedication to Vulcan made by the villagers at Vindolanda (*vicani Vindolandesses*).[18] This and other inscriptions demonstrate that people living in the civil settlements outside forts had self-governing rights.

Salway's study appeared in the same year that *The Roman Inscriptions of Britain* (*RIB*) was published (1965), and a review of the evidence that has accrued in the last 40 years, perhaps covering both Hadrian's Wall and the Antonine frontier and including the evidence from the Vindolanda tablets, could appropriately be undertaken after the publication of *RIB* III, which will cover new epigraphic material discovered during the past 50 years.

CULTS ON THE WALL

Inscriptions provide a large body of evidence for deities and religious practices on Hadrian's Wall. There were dedications to the official gods of the Roman pantheon, other Roman and Greek gods, foreign gods and apparently local deities.[19] Dividing the material in this way is natural, but an inscription recently found at Vindolanda[20] cannot be so neatly categorised. It is a dedication to the goddess Gallia, by the Gallic citizens (*cives Galli*) – presumably serving in the known third-century garrison *Cohors IV Gallorum*, along with 'like-minded Britons' (*concordesque Britanni*), British recruits in their unit. Altars are the main continuing sources of new inscriptions. A general survey of religion in the frontier area of Roman Britain was carried out relatively recently but there is scope for further study.[21]

CONCLUSIONS

From the brief survey given above, it is clear that inscriptions provide unique insights into the way in which Hadrian's Wall was initially constructed and manned, and into its subsequent history, the careers of the officers and soldiers who were based on it, and their religious beliefs. Some of the gaps in our knowledge have also been indicated, and these are likely to be filled both by chance finds and by discoveries made as a result of systematic excavation. It is hard to see how a specific programme of excavation or fieldwork could be designed to produce more inscriptions, in the way that planned work at Vindolanda, say, could be designed to recover more writing tablets. The single most important requirement is the publication of the third volume of *The Roman Inscriptions of Britain*, since with this the discoveries made during the last 50 years would be made readily accessible in a standard work of reference. This would facilitate surveys on such topics as military dispositions, religion, or the evidence for civilians in the frontier region to be readily updated.

Illustration note: This article was originally published with illustrations of four inscriptions, not included in the present collection, but referred to in the notes below.

Addendum: Since this article was written, the third volume of *The Roman Inscriptions of Britain*, encompassing inscriptions on stone and referred to above, has been published.[22] A recent study of the Rudge Cup, the Amiens Patera and notably the newly-discovered Staffordshire Moorlands Pan (Ilam Pan) has also been published.[23]

[1]   See Article 7, Table 1 in the present collection, centurions attested in Legion XX.

[2]   *RIB* 1935.

3   *RIB* 1340, 1427.
4   *RIB* 1389; Hassall 2009, fig. 142.
5   *RIB* 2110.
6   *RMD* III, 184; *RMD* IV, 293.
7   *RIB* 1329.
8   *RIB* 1962.
9   *RIB* 1843–4.
10 *RIB* 1672–3; Hassall 2009, fig. 143.
11 Breeze and Dobson 2000, appendix 2.
12 *Britannia* 10 (1979), 346, no. 7.
13 Breeze and Dobson 2000, appendix 4.
14 Breeze 2001; 2004; Hodgson 2002.
15 *Britannia* 35 (2004), 326, no. 8, 344–5, no. 24; Hassall 2009, fig. 144.
16 *Britannia* 26 (1995), 389–90, item f.
17 Salway 1965.
18 *RIB* 1700.
19 Henig 2009, 157–8; Webster 2009, 158–9.
20 *CA* 205 (2006), 4–5; *Britannia* 38 (2007), 346–7, no. 2; Hassall 2009, fig. 145.
21 Birley 1986.
22 *RIB* III.
23 Breeze 2012.

4
THE BUILDING OF THE ANTONINE WALL

Originally published:
'The Building of the Antonine Wall', *Britannia* 14, 1983, 262–4

THE APPEARANCE OF Lawrence Keppie's admirable survey of work in the last twenty years in the last *Britannia*[1] has prompted the writer to submit this short article: somewhat hesitantly because Dr Keppie did not much like an earlier draft of it.[2]

The speculations that follow originated in the idea that Lollius Urbicus, whose conquest in the north had been won by AD 142, did not start work on the Antonine Wall until the beginning of 143 and then had two full seasons, 143–4, to complete it before his second *triennium* ran out. This presupposes that he came to Britain early in 139 and that the Wall was actually completed during his governorship, as the author of the *Augustan Histories* implies in the *Life of Pius*. However, if, as is perhaps more likely, Urbicus was succeeded in 142 or 143, and the work was completed in 144 under a successor, it would not affect the argument that follows.[3]

The end of the campaigning season of AD 142 may have been taken up with the construction of six forts to hold the line of the isthmus, five of them later incorporated into the line of the Wall. When the total combined length of the northern defences of these forts is subtracted from the estimated total of 40,642 paces,[4] the length of Wall still to be constructed must have been very close to 40 Roman miles (40,000 paces) – or 20 Roman miles (20,000 paces) per season. We know from the distance slabs that three legions, II, VI and XX, were employed, so it might be supposed that each legion was responsible for a third of 20 Roman miles in each season, 6.6˙ miles, or 6,666.6˙ paces. In the section of the Antonine Wall eastward from Castlehill, we know from the distance slabs that Legion II completed 3,666.5 paces, Legion VI 3,666.5 paces and Legion XX 3,660.8 paces, figures that have been called by Gordon Maxwell 'curious, not to say awkward', and 'distinctly odd' by Keppie, and 'curious' and 'peculiar' by Sir George Macdonald.[5] These numbers, however, assume new significance when it is recalled that somewhere eastward again, Legion XX completed 3,000 paces.[6] If Legions II and VI completed a similar 3,000 paces (which seems not unreasonable), the added totals for each legion between Castlehill and a point a little to the east of Castlecary would be for Legion XX 6,660.8 paces or 6.6608 Roman miles, and for Legions II and VI 6,666.5 paces or 6.6665 Roman miles. In other words, it looks as if this 20 mile, 20,000 pace, central section – henceforth referred to as Section C – was being rigidly divided between the three legions into lengths equivalent to one-sixth the total length of the Wall, the division being taken to four places of decimals!

Assuming for the moment that Section C was laid out and perhaps completed first, there would remain two sections to complete in the following year: a short western Section (W) from Castlehill westward to the terminal fort at Old Kilpatrick, and a long eastern Section (E) from the eastern end of Section C to the eastern terminal at Bridgeness. Added together, Sections W and E would, of course, come to 20 Roman miles. There is only one distance slab from Section E, but many from Section W. Section W was split into six stretches, as we have hypothesised for Section C, two for each legion. They were measured in feet. Combining its two sections, Legion VI completed 7,381 feet, Legion XX 7,411 feet and Legion II 7,411 feet.

It is possible that Section E was also divided into six stretches. Three very short stretches, one for each legion, which, when added to the figures of 7,381, 7,411 and 7,411 feet in Section W, make grand totals of 10,000 feet (2,000 paces, 2 Roman miles) for each of the three, or 6 miles altogether. There remained 14 miles to complete in Section E. This distance will now have been divided into three – 4,666.6˙ paces for each legion. As it happens, the only distance slab from Section E, the famous terminal slab from Bridgeness, actually records a distance constructed of 4,652 paces, a shortfall of 14.6 paces.[7] Despite the shortfall, reminiscent of similar shortfalls of 5.7 paces in the work of Legion XX in Section C and of 30 feet, 6 paces, in the work of Legion VI in Section W, this slab goes some way towards confirming the proposed allocation of work in Section E.

If the interpretation of the Antonine Wall distance slabs is correct, then the *suovetaurilia* portrayed on the Bridgeness slab will have been performed on the completion of the Wall at its dedication, just as we know from Trajan's Column a similar sacrifice was performed on the completion of Trajan's Bridge across the Danube.[8] But even if, as is perhaps more likely and most people would probably accept, the order of construction was eastern section first, followed by central and western, and if the work took three rather than two years, the division of the work into three main sections each subdivided into six blocks equitably between the three legions is not thereby invalidated.

ACKNOWLEDGEMENTS

I would like to thank Lawrence Keppie, Valerie Maxfield, John Wilkes and David Breeze for advice after reading this short article in draft, without in any way committing them to the views expressed.

[1]   Keppie 1982.
[2]   See 'Acknowledgements' above.
[3]   For the chronology of the governorships of Urbicus and that of his unknown successor, see Birley 1981, 112–16.
[4]   This figure is based on Macdonald's (1934, 343) estimate of 37 miles, 599 yards, and a value of the Roman *passus* of 1.617 yards. Macdonald's measurements (which include the northern fort defences) were taken from a map. The distance on the ground will have been somewhat greater: cf. Macdonald 1934, 364.
[5]   Maxwell 1974, 330; Keppie 1975, 154; Macdonald 1934, 370, 374.
[6]   *RIB* 2173.
[7]   The shortfall could be explained by supposing that the Avon crossing was *included* in the 4,666.5 paces allocated to Legion II, but was *excluded* from the total when the legion actually came to record the work done. However, it is perhaps more likely that recorded distances are those that were originally allocated in which case it may have been felt sensible simply to terminate this stretch at the Avon.
[8]   Actually the column shows two sacrifices: that of an ox shown with the bridge in the background and a little later, and not, therefore, necessarily connected with the dedication of the bridge, a *suovetaurilia*.

1 Architectural setting: the Hutcheson Hill distance slab

2 Architectural setting: the Arch of Augustus in the Roman Forum

5
WINGLESS VICTORIES

Originally published:
'Wingless Victories', in J. Munby and M. Henig (eds), *Roman Life and Art in Britain: a celebration in honour of the eightieth birthday of Jocelyn Toynbee*, BAR British Series 41 (2), 1977, Oxford, 327–40

S TUDENTS OF ROMAN art and students of Roman Britain owe Professor Toynbee an immense debt. For many, including the writer, the debt is a very personal one, and it is therefore a particular pleasure to offer her this short article.

In 1969, a new 'distance slab' was discovered at Hutcheson Hill, just west of Bearsden on the Antonine Wall (Fig. 1).[1] The slab, which is now in the Hunterian Museum, Glasgow, is large, just under a metre in length, and carries the following inscription: *Imp(eratori) C(aesari) T(ito) Ae(lio) Hadriano Antonino Aug(usto) Pio P(atri) P(atriae) vex(illatio) leg(ionis) XX V(aleriae) V(ictricis) fec(it) p(er) p(edum) III (milia)*, 'To the Emperor Caesar Titus Aelius Hadrianus Antoninus Augustus Pius, a vexillation of the Twentieth Legion Valeria Victrix constructed 3,000 feet'. The text itself presents no problems, although it is of interest in that it shows that some building sections were commemorated by two slabs at each end, possibly set up on both the north and the south face of the rampart. The carvings with which the slab is also adorned, however, have provoked discussion – by Jocelyn Toynbee herself, Anne Robertson, Richard Wright, and Kenneth Steer and E.A. Cormack[2] – and it is to the interpretation of these that I wish to turn.

The first aspect of the carving to which I would like to draw attention is the general composition, and in particular the architectural framework within which the various details are set (Fig. 1).[3] Kenneth Steer has made the attractive suggestion that the architectural framework recalls the form of a triumphal arch, with central carriageway and two flanking side passages. One's first reaction is that this analogy should not be pressed too closely for the side openings have flat architraves and are not vaulted as would normally be the case. However, there is one exception to this rule, an exception which provides an exact parallel for the scheme of the 'Hutcheson Hill Arch', and I am grateful to John Ward-Perkins for pointing it out to me. The Arch of Augustus in the Roman Forum as originally erected in 29 BC consisted of a single arch but was reconstructed ten years later with side passages, on the inside of which were inscribed the consular *fasti*.[4] The form of the side passages is known from a contemporary coin, on which they are shown with flat entablatures and triangular pediments (Fig. 2).[5] The parallel is a striking one, although it is unlikely that the man who carved the distance slab from Hutcheson Hill had the Arch of Augustus in mind: indeed he may not have been thinking of an arch at all. Similar architectural schemes occur in two dimensions in Pompeian wall paintings, and Susan Walker draws to my attention, among other three-dimensional examples, the portico of the distribution reservoir of Hadrian's aqueduct at Athens.[6]

Beneath the side openings are two inscribed *tabulae ansatae*, and, beneath the central 'arch', the figure of a running boar – the symbol of the Twentieth Legion by whom the slab was set up. Within the side openings are two kneeling bound captives, compared by Lawrence Keppie to a kneeling captive on what was probably another distance slab of the Twentieth Legion found at Hag Knowe.[7] The captives on the Hutcheson Hill piece support circular medallions, or perhaps shields, which carry part of the inscription. Within the central opening are two figures. On the left the *aquilifer* of the legion stands, facing right with bowed head. In his hands he grasps the shaft of the eagle standard, which rests on his left shoulder. On the right stands a human figure portrayed frontally (Fig. 1). She is of more than human size. Over her left shoulder falls a cloak. In her left hand she holds a *patera* and in her right a wreath, which she places in the beak of the eagle. There are a number of possible interpretations as to the identity of this figure. She might be Victory, the most obvious theory, only she lacks wings, and for all other commentators this has been a vital objection. She might be, as Professor Toynbee has suggested, Britannia; or, finally, we could believe with Anne Robertson that she is the deified elder Faustina, the wife of Antoninus Pius, who died prematurely in AD 141, a year or possibly two before work on the Wall commenced. I shall consider the three possibilities in turn.

First: Victory. Both Victoria and her Greek equivalent are normally portrayed with wings. Nevertheless, Nike was sometimes represented as wingless. We know from Pausanias[8] that there was at Athens a temple of Nike Apteros on the right of the gateway to the Acropolis and that 'the Athenians think that Nike having no wings will always remain where she is'. Elsewhere he tells us that the image was made of wood and that the Mantineans had made a wingless figure of Nike in imitation of it.[9] Nike Apteros may, in origin, have been none other than the goddess Athena: Athena, as a warrior goddess, sometimes took on the attributes of the goddess of Victory and representations of Nike Athena (or Minerva Victrix) will certainly have been shown wingless, though normally she will have retained her shield and helmet, and is not therefore in question here.[10] What will Hellenistic representatives of Nike Apteros have looked like? Presumably very much like regular representatives of Nike, only lacking wings. Sculptures of the goddess, both winged and wingless, are known from the north-western provinces of the Roman Empire, for example from the port and temple site of Domburg in Holland where both are executed in a purely classical style, the wingless Nike being closely comparable to a figure in the Naples Museum also identified as Nike Apteros.[11]

It is obviously very difficult to be sure about the real identity of many of these wind-swept ladies – thus, to take an example from near home, the marble statuette from Woodchester,[12] very similar in general appearance, is probably to be identified as Diana-Luna in view of the head of the bull beside her right foot, since that deity is often shown riding in a bull-drawn chariot. We are on safer ground, however, where attributes such as wreaths and palm branches or globes are present. Figures accompanied by two out of three of these attributes must surely be Victory. There are a fair number of such figures, and where these are crudely executed we will probably be correct in thinking that there is no more significance in the occasional absence of wings than there is in that of any other symbol. Such inexpertly rendered wingless Victories include an example (Fig. 3) flanking a building inscription found at Brough-by-Bainbridge, set up in the early third century under the governorship of Valerius Pudens,[13] and several central Gaulish samian figure types (Figs 4–5).[14]

There are, however, two certain cases known to me, both, possibly significantly, from the eastern empire, where *carefully* executed representations of Victory are

3 Wingless Victory: Brough-by-Bainbridge relief

4 (top left) Wingless Victory: samian figure type 821
5 (bottom left) Wingless Victory: samian figure type 810
6 (right) Wingless Victory: Victory on the Fayum flag

rendered without wings and where we may be dealing with Romanised
versions of Nike Apteros. The first is found on a religious relief from
Dura Europos and is dated AD 159.[15] It shows the guardian spirit of
Palmyra flanked on one side by the priestly donor and on the other by
a wingless Victory complete with wreath and palm branch. The second
(Fig. 6) is on the flag of an auxiliary unit found in the Fayum and now
in Moscow.[16] A third Victory, apparently wingless, was excavated by
Richard Harper at the third-century Roman fort of Dibsi Faraj, North
Syria,[17] but is shown on closer inspection to have had wings carved in
very low relief. If the carving had originally been painted, their presence
would have been much more visible. This example shows how difficult
it can sometimes be to decide whether or not some representations of

Victory were provided with wings.

The lack of wings, then, does not absolutely preclude the identification of the Hutcheson Hill figure as Victory. Nor does the fact that she holds a *patera*, for a *patera* was held in the outstretched hand of Victoria Virgo in the shrine built by the elder Cato on the Palatine in 193 BC as we know from coins struck by a descendant, the mintmaster M. Cato.[18] It is true that Victory is rarely shown associated with standards, although the British Museum does possess a lamp with a scene showing Victory returning one of the Parthian standards.[19] Yet representations of eagles with wreaths in their beaks are extremely common, as on the slab previously mentioned from Brough-by-Bainbridge (Fig. 3), and who more reasonable to put them there than Victory?

Nevertheless, though the case for Victory being shown on the Hutcheson Hill slab is not, as I hope I have shown, impossible, on the whole I agree with those who do not think that the figure is Victory. The main reason is that, unlike the examples I have noted from Syria and Egypt, she not only lacks wings but also the other identifying symbols such as a globe or palm branch. It may be also that intentionally wingless Victories, rare enough in the east where the Greek Nike Apteros nevertheless did provide some sort of precedent, were almost unknown in the west (although there may be an example flanking the fragmentary gateway inscription from Carpow[20]). Western Victories – and this is certainly true of the Victories on the Antonine Wall distance slabs[21] and other military sculptures from the north of Britain – usually fall into clearly defined iconographic types. Thus the twin Victories on the distance slab found east of Duntocher both have raised arms (Fig. 7),[22] which recall Tonio Hölscher's Victory with shield type 5, of which one of the best examples (Fig. 8) is the famous statuette of Victory from Augst, who holds above her head a medallion with a bust of Jupiter set over a flower calyx.[23] In origin this was a Hellenistic type.

The Victories set as corner akroteria on the temple of Pius and Faustina in the Roman Forum were of the same type, and she recurs twice in a painted tomb at Palmyra (Fig. 9), an example not noted by Hölscher.[24] The seated Victory on the terminal distance slab from Old Kilpatrick at the west end of the Antonine Wall,[25] who has been described as 'resting after

7 Winged Victory: detail of the Duntocher relief

8 Winged Victory: Augst bronze figurine

her labours', is reminiscent of Hölscher's Victory with shield type 4, only here the inscribed shield is replaced by a wreath which encircles an inscription.[26] Again, twin Victories supporting ansate panels are common in Britain, and this is a motif that has republican antecedents.[27] The standard of some of these pieces could be remarkably high.[28] Small figurines of Victory, usually in bronze but in one case of silver, are not uncommonly found in Britain, and again are sometimes of competent workmanship.[29] Fragments of stone Victories carved in the round, are also known. If we are to believe Tacitus, there was at least one large statue, appropriately in Colchester (*Colonia Claudia Victricensis*), while winged Victories flanked the central shield with its gorgon head on the pediment of the temple of Sulis Minerva at Bath.[30] There is no hint that any of them (except possibly one of the bronzes) were other than winged, and even one of our rare pieces of epigraphic verse from the province alludes to golden Victory flying through the air on her wings.[31]

A second reason for doubting that we have here a scene of Victory presenting a wreath to the legionary eagle is that under the empire, Victory is never shown crowning anyone other than a member of the imperial house, or rarely, as at Dura, another divine being. Victory was often specifically called *Victoria Augusti* or *Victoria Augusta*, and if under the empire a commander won a victory, the credit and the triumph went to the emperor – the holder of *imperium* under whose auspices he – the commander – was fighting. This 'constitutional objection' would not be so strong in the present case where it is the legionary eagle who receives the wreath; nevertheless, such an action would be an infringement of the monopolisation of Victory by the imperial house.[32]

9 (left) Winged Victory: Palmyra wall painting (restored)
10 (right) Wreath-giver: the goddess Libya and the nymph Cyrene

Professor Toynbee has suggested that the figure is Britannia and is based on the reverse type of a *sestertius* of Hadrian showing the emperor togate facing a female figure who pours a libation from a *patera* over an altar, whom she identifies as the personification of the province in conformity with the associated legend *Adventui Aug(usti) Britanniae*.[33] The similarity between the Hutcheson Hill figure and that on the coin is striking. If Britannia can, on coinage of the mid-150s, grieve for the military losses sustained by the Romans during a revolt in the north of the province,[34] there can be no reason why she should not congratulate the legions of Britain for their successes a dozen years earlier. A parallel of sorts would be the relief, now in the British Museum, showing the nymph Cyrene being crowned by the goddess Libya as she strangles a lion (Fig. 10). Yet although the theory is an attractive one, Britannia is, on the coinage of the second century, normally shown armed with shield and spear (or sometimes standard, or occasionally both). It is true that early third-century coins and a relief on the back of a third-century inscription from Ribchester probably depict Britannia in flowing garments and with neither spear nor shield,[35] but for the contemporary second-century

Roman the armed female figure was the usual iconographic type. Without some sort of label as on the Hadrianic coin, it is unlikely that he would associate the Hutcheson Hill figure with Britannia.

There remains Dr Anne Robertson's interpretation – that she is the elder Faustina, the wife of Antoninus Pius, who had died only a year or two previously.[36] The regard in which she was held after her death is not in doubt: coins struck during the rest of Pius' reign name her and bear her effigy more often than is the case with any other member of the imperial family after death, while the temple with its Victories mentioned above, erected in her honour in AD 141, and subsequently dedicated jointly to her and Pius, still survives as the church of San Lorenzo in Miranda in the Roman Forum.[37] The association between imperial women and the army is generally thought to be a feature of the early third century, but it was her daughter, the younger Faustina, the wife of Marcus Aurelius, who in fact first bore the title *Mater Castrorum*.[38] In the early third century, Julia Domna, besides bearing this title, could also be portrayed as Victory, both winged as on a cameo found in Kassel,[39] or wingless as on an unprovenanced relief (Fig. 11) now in Poland.[40] Such representations were anticipated by a cameo from Cologne (Fig. 12)

11 *Wreath-giver: Julia Domna and Caracalla*

12 *Wreath-giver: the younger Agrippina and*
Claudius

which shows Claudius crowned by the
younger Agrippina, but perhaps here in
the guise of Fortuna, Tellus or Ceres.[41]

If the Hutcheson Hill relief does
represent the elder Faustina, is she
also, like Julia Domna, to be identified
as Victory? Since she is neither winged
nor bears a palm, this is on the whole
unlikely. The Roman military sculptors
of North Britain seem normally to have
made their iconographic intentions
clear enough. On occasion when some doubt may have arisen in the
viewer's mind they even went to the trouble of providing actual labels
to help in the interpretations of figures or scenes. Examples are the
vexillum inscribed LEG II on the right-hand panel of the Bridgeness
slab,[42] or the *vexillum* borne by the right-hand figure on the distance
slab from Duntocher inscribed *Virtus Aug(usti)*;[43] *Virtus Aug(ustorum)* is
similarly labelled at Chesters.[44] We are given no such help in the present
case, perhaps because, at the time when the carving was set up, none
was felt to be required. In the absence of a clear label, iconographic
or verbal, certainty is probably impossible, but for the present writer
Diva Faustina, as suggested by Professor Robertson, is the most likely
candidate for the Hutcheson Hill wreath-giver.

I have primarily been concerned with the Hutcheson Hill slab,
but in trying to interpret it I have touched on the whole question of
wingless Victories in Roman art. To draw together the threads of the
argument, it seems that if Victory lacks wings there will normally be
three explanations. First, through ignorance or carelessness on the
part of the artist; second, perhaps mainly in the eastern empire, as a
genuinely Roman 'interpretation' of the Greek Nike Apteros; thirdly, she
may not really be Victory at all, but a Roman empress who has usurped
the wreath-giving function of the goddess, and sometimes, as with Julia
Domna, other of her attributes as well. In the context of art and the
Roman army all three of these explanations may be possible. Finally,
it appears that even on the remote northern frontier of the empire, the
iconography of 'Victory', with or without wings, could be surprisingly
sophisticated.

Illustration note: This article was originally published with halftone illustrations of five reliefs, not included in the present collection, but referred to in the notes below.

1 Hassall 1977a, pl. 13.I; Keppie 1979, no. 11 with line drawing, pls 4–5.
2 Robertson 1969; *CA* 18 (1970), 196–7; *Britannia* 1 (1970), 309–10, no. 19; Steer and Cormack 1971.
3 Hassall 1977a, pl. 13.I; Keppie 1979, no. 11 with line drawing, pls 4–5.
4 Crema 1959, 209, fig. 205, on which Fig. 2 above is based.
5 *RIC* 149 = *BMC* I, pl. 3.4.
6 Stuart and Revett 1794, ch. 4, pl. 2.
7 Keppie 1975, 154.
8 Pausanias, *Description of Greece* 3.15.7.
9 Pausanias, *Description of Greece* 5.26.6.
10 Daremberg and Saglio 1912, 831–5.
11 Hondius-Crone 1955, 110–11, 77 pl. A (winged), 79 pl. B (wingless), 78 pl. A (wingless, Naples).
12 Toynbee 1964, 84; Brailsford 1958, 55, no. 11, pl. 20.
13 Hartley 1966, 19 with fig. = *JRS* 51 (1961), 192, no. 4, with correction *JRS* 59 (1969), 246, items b–d.
14 Oswald 1936/7, especially type nos 810, 821.
15 Colledge 1976, 227, pl. 146; Hassall 1977a, pl. 13.IIa.
16 Rostovtzeff 1942, pl. 4 (no mention of the fact that Victory is wingless).
17 Harper 1975, for the site; Hassall 1977a, pl. 13.IIb.
18 Crawford 1974a, 351–2, no. 343; 1974b, pl. 45; 1974a, 473; 1974b, pl. 54; Hölscher 1967, pl. 16.1.
19 Hölscher 1967, 109 with fig.
20 *JRS* 56 (1966), pl. 10.1.
21 Keppie 1979, nos 6, 10–11, 16–17 with line drawings.
22 Hassall 1977a, pl. 13.IIIa; Keppie 1979, no. 12 with line drawing.
23 Hölscher 1967, 128–30 (the type), pl. 4.3, the Augst statuette, pl. 14.3, early Hellenistic earring in the British Museum.
24 Hölscher 1967, 128; see also n. 37 below (temple of Pius and Faustina); Colledge 1976, 84–7, pl. 116 (Palmyra).
25 Hassall 1977a, pl. 13.IIIb; Keppie 1979, no. 17 with line drawing, pl. 3.
26 Hölscher 1967, 126–8 (the type).
27 e.g. *RIB* 1093, pl. 14 (a splendid example from Lanchester); cf. Hölscher 1967, pl. 14 (Rome).
28 In addition to the examples already cited from Britain, cf. the well-known dedication slab from Risingham with its flanking figures of Mars and Victory: *RIB* 1227, pl. 17.
29 Figurines: Alcock 1976, pls 37–42. Alcock 1976, pl. 38 is of an unpublished example from Brough-on-Fosse, Notts., where the drapery suggests Victory although the figurine lacks wings. Silver statuette: *RIB* 582, only the arm survives. A plaque attached to the wrist shows that it was the Victory of Legion VI Victrix.

[30] Colchester: Tac. *Ann*. 14.32. Bath: Toynbee 1962, 161–4 with fig. on 162.

[31] *RIB* 1954.

[32] The imperial monopolisation of Victory may not have been quite so rigid as I have suggested. The silver figure of Victory mentioned above, n. 29, was specifically thought of as the Victory of Legion VI, while on the distance slab from Summerston, *RIB* 2193, Victory is shown in close association with – if not actually crowning – a triumphant Roman cavalryman, as Laurence Keppie points out to me.

[33] *RIC* 882; *CA* 18 (1970), 197; *Britannia* 1 (1970), 310, no. 19; Toynbee 1924, 147, pl. 24.3.

[34] *RIC* 930. Alternatively, as Professor Toynbee (1924, 152, pl. 24.7) has suggested, she is a representation of *Britannia Capta*.

[35] *RIB* 583 = *JRS* 35 (1945), pl. 1.1–2. She is probably also represented with a mural crown and unarmed on coins of Caracalla and Geta: *RIC* 464, 483; Toynbee 1924, 156, pl. 24.9.

[36] *CA* 18 (1970), 196; Steer and Cormack 1971, 123; *Britannia* 1 (1970), 310, no. 19.

[37] Boëthius and Ward-Perkins 1970, 267–9, fig. 103.

[38] Hölscher 1967, 169. The title appears on coins but not apparently on inscriptions.

[39] Möbius 1948/9, 102–12, pl. 1.

[40] Sadurska 1972, no. 57, pl. 45.

[41] Möbius 1948/9, 112–18.

[42] *RIB* 2139, pl. 18; Keppie 1979, no. 1 with line drawing, pls 1–2.

[43] Hassall 1977a, pl. 13.IIIa; Keppie 1979, no. 12 with line drawing.

[44] *RIB* 1466.

6
THE DATE OF THE REBUILDING OF HADRIAN'S TURF WALL IN STONE

Originally published:
'The Date of the Rebuilding of Hadrian's Turf Wall in Stone', *Britannia*
15, 1984, 242–4

THIS SHORT ARTICLE is concerned with one of the outstanding questions raised by the structural history of Hadrian's Wall: 'When was the rest of the turf wall, beyond the section converted to narrow gauge under Hadrian, rebuilt in stone?'.[1] There are two ways of approaching the problem, depending on the type of evidence used, archaeological or historical, and since what follows is based primarily on the meagre historical and epigraphic evidence, it will be as well to deal briefly with the archaeological first.

When the western section of the Turf Wall was converted to stone, the milecastles were rebuilt also, and it was recognised by F.G. Simpson and I.A. Richmond[2] that the latest material from a Turf Wall milecastle would provide a *terminus post quem* for the construction of its stone successor. Research excavations were, therefore, undertaken by Richmond and J.P. Gillam at the site of Milecastle 79.[3] Material from the Turf Wall milecastle was dated by them to *c.* AD 130–40, and Richmond concluded that the Stone Wall milecastle was, therefore, built either at the very end of Hadrian's reign, or at some later date, *but before any significant re-occupation of the Turf Wall milecastle had taken place.* For Richmond, this meant the period immediately after the first Antonine re-occupation of Scotland: i.e. the late 150s, when we know that work was going on on Hadrian's Wall.[4] Fairly recently, Charles Daniels[5] has linked the rebuilding with the final withdrawal from Scotland, accepting the theory of a short re-occupation of the Antonine Wall, which was finally abandoned with the death of Pius

(AD 161). As Daniels says when discussing the evidence specifically from Turf Wall Milecastle 79:[6]

> The date of the replacement of the Turf Wall milecastle was clear. Hadrianic-Antonine pottery types were found, showing that the early structure had continued throughout the reign of Hadrian. Antonine pottery was absent; and as a rebuilding is unlikely at the very moment of abandonment of Hadrian's Wall it must have occurred as part of the re-occupation under Marcus, that is, about 162/3.

The writer of this short article is not competent to discuss the pottery found, but it is rather misleading to say that Antonine pottery was absent: the pottery included Gillam types 65 and 129, both of which are said by him to start c. AD 140, while examples of several other types, e.g. 64 and 128, could be as late as the 190s or 180s, though they made a first appearance in the later Hadrianic period.[7] Of the three sherds of samian recovered, one was thought by Grace Simpson, who contributed to the report,[8] to date to the second half of the second century. The pottery anyway strictly only provides a *terminus post quem* for the construction of the stone milecastle, and does not preclude a date later than Richmond suggested.

To turn to the literary and epigraphic evidence,[9] in the *Augustan Histories*[10] it is stated that Hadrian built a wall of 80 miles to divide the barbarians from the Romans, and a glance at, say, the second edition of the Ordnance Survey *Map of Hadrian's Wall* shows the distance to be precisely correct. The western terminal fort at Bowness-on-Solway occupies what would have been the site of Milecastle 80. Originally, Milecastles 49–80 and the Wall that connected them were built in turf. These 32 milecastles, lying west of the Irthing bridge, do not correspond to precisely 32 Wall-miles but only slightly over 31, unless, as some have thought,[11] the Wall continued for some distance beyond Milecastle 80. The existence of Hadrian's 'Turf Wall' is not recorded in any surviving ancient source, though it may be implied by the phrase *alio muro caespiticio ducto* used in describing the Wall of Pius,[12] and it is possible that some mention was made in the lost work of Marius Maximus and, more especially, Hadrian's own autobiography. For what follows, it will be necessary to assume – and this may be two assumptions too many! – that, firstly, contemporary sources *did* mention the division between an original Stone Wall with its 48 stone milecastles and an original Turf Wall with its 32 milecastles, and, secondly, that they did *not* record the fact that the first five or six miles of the Turf Wall sector had been converted to stone by the end of Hadrian's reign.[13]

Now there is a group of late Roman sources, including the *Historia Augusta, Severus*,[14] and Aurelius Victor, *De Caesaribus*,[15] which credit Severus with the construction of a wall from sea to sea. To an earlier generation of antiquaries, their combined testimony seemed so impressive that they assigned to Severus the structure that we now know as Hadrian's Wall, attributing to the latter the construction of the earthwork that we still call the '*Vallum*', which was taken to be a frontier work in its own right. Some of these sources, namely the so-called *Epitome de Caesaribus*,[16] once attributed to Aurelius Victor and printed at the end of the Teubner edition of that author, and the *Breviarium* of Eutropius,[17] add that the wall was 32 miles long.[18] Somewhat later, Jerome (*Chronicle* under the fourteenth regnal year of Severus, AD 207) talks of the wall as being 132 miles long, and he is followed by subsequent writers, for example Cassiodorus,[19] who names Aper and Maximus as the consuls for AD 207 and records Severus' work of wall-building, *his cons(ulibu)s*. The figure 32 – for which 132 must simply be a mistake – has not been explained, and it seems at least possible that it corresponds – more or less! – to the length of the original Turf Wall of Hadrian, which Severus in some lost intermediate source was recorded as replacing. Possible confirmation may come from the consular date *Apro et Maximo*,[20] cut with other quarry inscriptions on the Written Rock of Gelt near Brampton, in an area which certainly supplied stone for the replacement Wall.[21] If this short article, highly speculative as it is, helps to re-open the debate on this particular 'mural problem', it will have served its purpose.

ACKNOWLEDGEMENTS

I am grateful to Professor E. Birley for discussing the above in September 1983 during the thirteenth Congress of Frontier Studies in Aalen, and in particular for directing me to the article by Collingwood (1921) and for drawing the attention of an outsider to Wall studies to the significance of the excavations at Milecastle 79. My thanks to him should not be construed as necessarily implying his agreement with the above.

Addendum: Since this article was written, two further relevant ancient sources have been identified by the writer.[22] To those already quoted should be added the statements in Bede's *Ecclesiastical History*, ch. 5, and *The Anglo Saxon Chronicle* for the year AD 188, which will derive from earlier texts. Two of the versions of the *Chronicle* refer to Severus building a rampart of turf and a broad wall thereon. Bede also talks of a wall of stone and a rampart of turves.

1   Breeze and Dobson 1978, 235.
2   Simpson and Richmond 1935.
3   Richmond and Gillam 1953.
4   *RIB* 1389.
5   Daniels 1978, 19, cf. 5.
6   Daniels 1978, 253; cf. Richmond 1966, 207.
7   Gillam 1970. The pottery from the Turf Wall Milecastle 79 is dated group number 37.
8   Richmond and Gillam 1953, 38–40.
9   The sources are conveniently collected by Collingwood (1921, 39–45) and by Mann (1971).
10 *SHA, Hadrian* 11.
11 Breeze and Dobson (1978) assume without question that the Wall ended at Turret 80b. The second edition of the Ordnance Survey map marks a hypothetical Turret 80a.
12 *SHA, Pius* 5. Usually translated nowadays as 'after another wall, a turf one had been built', but the Latin is more naturally translated as 'after another turf wall had been built', though the point should not be pressed; cf. Collingwood 1921, n. on 43.
13 cf. Breeze and Dobson 1978, 52–3; Birley 1961, 125.
14 *SHA, Severus* 18.
15 *De Caesaribus* 20.18.
16 *Epitome de Caesaribus* 20.4.
17 *Breviarium* 8.19.
18 The Teubner text of Eutropius prints CXXXIII (*sic*). For the actual MSS readings, see Droysen 1879/1961. One of the MS reads R XXX II M.P. which could account for the confusion. In Paianios' translation, printed in a parallel text by Droysen, it is already described as being 132 miles long. Paianios' is thought to have been used by Jerome for his expanded translation of Eusebius' *Chronicle*. At all events, Jerome gives the distance also as CXXXII M.P.
19 Mommsen 1894/1961, 145.
20 *RIB* 1009.
21 Though of course the consular date could refer to later work at the quarry than that undertaken for the initial reconstruction of the Turf Wall in stone. For an illustration of these quarry inscriptions, see Daniels 1978, 42. Birley (1961, 126) draws attention to the single 'centurial stone' from the west end of the Wall (Wall-mile 79–80), *RIB* 2054, recording work by the Third Cohort of Legion II, and its similarity to building records of the legion in Wall-miles 6–8, e.g. *RIB* 1341–4, 1358–60. If the former *is* Severan, this should indicate extensive repairs towards the east end of the Wall.
22 Hassall 2008, 37 n. 57.

Part III

The Province

The Army – Administration – Towns
Religion – Education – Trade

7
EPIGRAPHY AND THE ROMAN ARMY IN BRITAIN

Originally published:
'Epigraphy and the Roman Army in Britain', in T.F.C. Blagg and
A.C. King (eds), *Military and Civilian in Roman Britain: Cultural
Relationships in a Frontier Province*, BAR British Series 136, 1984,
Oxford, 265–77

THIS ARTICLE IS primarily concerned with epigraphy and the Roman army in Roman Britain, for which inscriptions and other inscribed material provide a particularly rich source. It touches briefly, however, on the 'interface' between military and civilian, where, except in the field of recruitment, inscriptions provide far less information.

Roman Britain was above all a military province. With four legions stationed in the island for most of the first century and thereafter a permanent establishment of three legions, and an auxiliary garrison of 50 or more regiments, the governor of the province had under his command something of the order of a *tenth* of Rome's *total* legionary forces and an amazing *seventh* of her total auxiliary strength. The reason for this enormous concentration of troops was the direct result of the failure of Domitian to round off the conquest of Scotland effected by the governor Agricola in the AD 80s. Thereafter Britain was a 'frontier province' – unlike Spain, for example, where the total conquest of the peninsula under Augustus had made the withdrawal of all but a single legion and a handful of auxiliary units possible. The requirements of this frontier province involved the commitment of a substantial proportion of the Roman army for defence and, in the wilder regions, for internal security.

As a professional standing army, the day-to-day running of the Roman army involved the labours of a professional body of clerks and

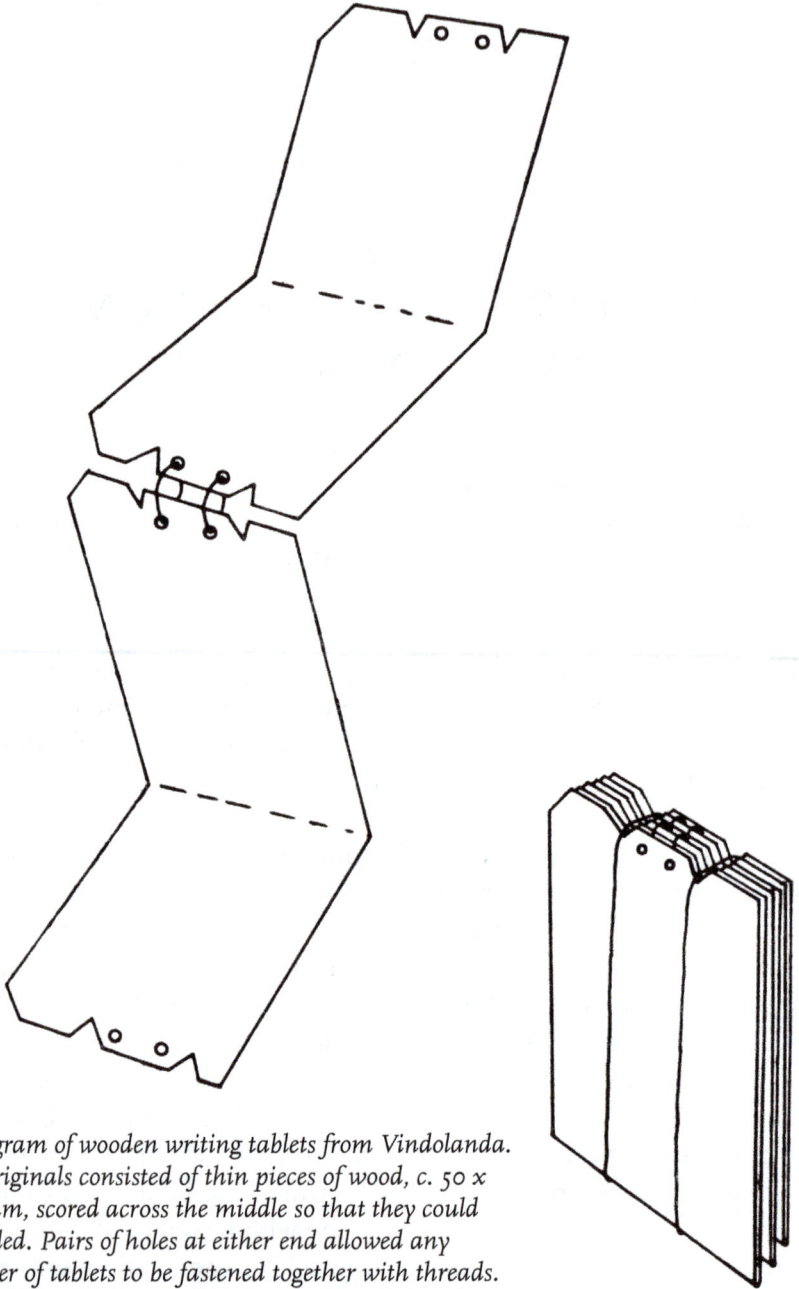

1 *Diagram of wooden writing tablets from Vindolanda.
The originals consisted of thin pieces of wood, c. 50 x
160 mm, scored across the middle so that they could
be folded. Pairs of holes at either end allowed any
number of tablets to be fastened together with threads.
The series could then be folded concertina-fashion. 'V'-
shaped nicks allowed cords to pass round the complete
packet. These unique documents partly resemble the
traditional scroll and partly the codex, of which they
may be the forerunner*

accountants. Of the mountains of papyrus that they employed over a period of, say, four centuries, a tiny fraction only survives,[1] but it was an organisation in which literacy at all levels was prized, and the evidence for this comes from a whole range of inscribed objects. Thus, individual soldiers were required to buy their own weapons and equipment on enlistment, and often inscribed the items with their own names,[2] just as one might scratch his name on a favourite samian cup.[3] From the Neronian fortress of Usk comes a series of lead luggage tags inscribed with the contents, weight, value and bag number, presumably corresponding to a separate checklist, and such tags have been found at various other sites both in Britain and abroad.[4] From Brough under Stainmore[5] come lead sealings affixed to goods sent from the military zone in the north for distribution or despatch to the south, where similar seals marked, like the Brough examples, with the names of the units responsible for their despatch have also been recovered – notably from Leicester.[6] Tiles were stamped with the name of the legion or auxiliary unit that had produced them,[7] and were sometimes inscribed with records of output or idle comments by the soldiers detached to work in the kilns.[8] And, if no fragment of papyrus survives from either a military or civilian context in the island, the remarkable Vindolanda writing tablets[9] show that the letters, official and private, written by military personnel, and the whole range of military records kept by military clerks, were not confined to the medium of papyrus, but that on Rome's north-western frontier at least a local substitute was employed. The tablets consist of thin slivers of wood on which pen and ink could be employed. Their importance for the study of Latin palaeography and language, quite apart from the extreme interest of their contents, can hardly be exaggerated (Fig. 1).

The indication of ownership and contents, the stamped tiles and sealings, the graffiti, and above all the wooden writing tablets from Vindolanda, all contribute to our understanding of the Roman army in Britain. Much of this material is either extremely fragile or else, as in the case of the tiles and inscribed potsherds, of little intrinsic interest, and it is only comparatively recently that archaeologists have had either the skill to recover the former or the wit to preserve the latter. Not so for the hundreds of inscriptions on stone that have been recorded and sometimes put in safekeeping from the seventeenth century to the present day. These are the tombstones, building records, altars and religious dedications, milestones, etc., that form the major part of the epigraphic record from the province. They tell us little of the

more dramatic aspects of the Roman army's activities in the island –
inscriptions like *RIB* 2034 set up 'because of successes won north of the
Wall', or 'after the slaughter of a band of Corionototae',[10] are extremely
rare – but much about other activities of the legions and auxiliaries
stationed in the province.

One of the most informative types of inscription is the epitaph.
These texts normally give, for legionaries who were exclusively Roman
citizens, the deceased's names (often but not always the *tria nomina*,
the three names: *praenomen*, *nomen* (family name) and *cognomen*, which
were the hallmark of a Roman citizen), his Roman voting tribe, his
place of origin (*origo*), his unit, his rank, his years of service and his age
at death. One may note in passing that by subtracting the number of
years served from the age at death of a serving soldier, it is possible to
establish his age at recruitment. Though legionary tombstones are not
provided with absolute dates, as epitaphs of civilians occasionally were,[11]
they can often be quite closely dated, particularly in the fluid conditions
of the first century AD, when the cemeteries outside legionary fortresses
would be in use for the relatively short periods in which the legion was
in residence. Similarly, certain legions remained in the province only for
relatively short periods – Legion XIV from AD 43–67 returning briefly
in 69, II Adiutrix from 70–*c.* 86, IX Hispana from 43 to a time early
in the second century – and all tombstones recording personnel from
these legions must have been set up within these chronological limits.

Occasionally even closer precision is possible. Thus, on a
tombstone from Wroxeter,[12] Legion XIV is given the title *Gem(ina)* but
lacks the further titles *Martia Victrix*, awarded for its role in crushing
the Boudiccan revolt in AD 61, and a *terminus ante quem* for the cutting
of the inscription is thereby provided. The number of such early-dated
legionary tombstones from Britain on which the deceased's place of
origin is given is not large but it does illustrate a pattern of recruitment
observable from other provinces, with legionaries being drawn at first
from the Roman colonial settlements of northern Italy and southern
Gaul, and gradually from a wider area including Spain and the Danube
provinces. One interesting phenomenon is the group of four men[13]
serving in Legion II Adiutrix, whose *origo* is given as the Roman colony
of Aprus in Thrace and who, as Sir Ronald Syme has suggested to the
writer, were native Thracians given Roman citizenship on enlistment
and the pseudo-*origo* of the sole Roman colony in the province. The
tombstones of soldiers in Legion II Augusta from Caerleon, Legion XX

from Chester and Legion VI Victrix can only be given a *terminus post quem* – of *c*. AD 75, *c*. 86 and *c*. 122. On many of these monuments, the *origo* of the deceased is not given, and there is a strong presumption that the tombstones were of men recruited locally, the sons of veterans or of serving soldiers. If the latter, they will have had the status of their mothers, since serving soldiers were technically not allowed to marry. In most cases this will have meant that they were peregrines (non-Romans), but, like the men from Aprus cited above, that they were given Roman citizenship on enlistment.

A similar pattern is observable with recruitment into the auxiliary regiments – when *origines* are given, they are normally on first-century monuments and they show how recruits were, during the first decades in the history of the province, either drawn from the original area in which the unit was raised[14] or from the area in which it was previously stationed.[15] Inscriptions like that from Mumrills, of the soldier in yet another Thracian unit, on the Antonine Wall, where the deceased is described as a Brigantian by race,[16] are rare, yet again the presumption is that on the numerous tombstones from the military cemeteries along Hadrian's Wall where no indication of origin is given, the deceased will in fact have been born locally, as has been suggested above from the epitaphs lacking *origines* from the permanent legionary fortresses.[17]

Besides the tombstones of auxiliary cavalrymen, another class of document also has a bearing on recruitment to the auxiliary unit, as well as much else. These are the so-called military diplomas, inscribed in duplicate on the inside and outside faces of a pair of bronze tablets. The diplomas are certificates of Roman citizenship issued, normally, to time-expired auxiliary veterans after 25 years service. On these documents the recipient's name is given, as well as his unit, its commanding officer, and his ethnic affiliations. Besides Roman citizenship, the diplomas also record the grant of *conubium*, legal marriage, with a woman of peregrine status; this was important because it meant that the veteran's sons would also receive Roman citizenship. If the recipient had already contracted a marriage in accordance with local law or custom, the grant of *conubium* was made retrospective and any children who existed at the time of the grant would automatically be accorded Roman citizenship. To avoid abuses of the system, the children's and the wife's names would be given alongside the veteran's own. Thus on a diploma[18] issued to a Briton serving in Dacia we find mention of the veteran himself, Lucco the son of Trenus, a tribesman of the Dobunni, his local wife Tutula daughter of Breucus, a tribesman of the Azali, his son Similis and daughters Lucca and Pacata. In AD 140, the grant of *conubium* ceased to be made retrospective, a diploma of 13 December 140 incidentally having the new formula on the inner text, while retaining the old in error on the outer.[19] This change would bring the auxiliaries into line with the legionaries, whose sons did not get the prized Roman citizenship on their fathers' discharge. As far as the auxiliaries were concerned, this change for the worse may have been made more palatable by linking it with the granting of Roman citizenship to auxiliary recruits – perhaps just the sons of auxiliary veterans – on enlistment, thus once again bringing the auxiliary units into line with the legions. This second change is suggested by the sudden fall in the number of diplomas issued in the late 160s.[20]

Besides details of the grants of Roman citizenship to a veteran and his family, diplomas give us much additional information. Each document was an extract from an imperial decree, whereby citizenship was given to large numbers of eligible veterans in a particular province. Curiously the diplomas include *in extenso* the preamble to the decrees, listing all the units concerned in the grant by name and the fact that they were serving in a particular province under a specific governor. For Britain, we have in whole or part fourteen diplomas, twelve found in this country and two found abroad including the most useful of all, a diploma issued in AD 122,[21] found at the Roman site of Brigetio in Hungary. This lists no less than 50 auxiliary units serving in Britain at the time – perhaps the total auxiliary establishment of the province. By comparing the diploma lists from different years and from different provinces, it is possible to tell much about the movements of units from one section of the imperial frontier to another in response to military requirements.

Finally, diplomas on occasion also give us some idea of the order of battle of auxiliary units within a province,[22] and attempts have been made to assign some of the British diplomas, which normally list far fewer units than the Brigetio diploma, to groups of auxiliaries stationed in specific areas or 'commands', for administrative – and possibly tactical – purposes, dependent on the three legions stationed at York, Chester and Caerleon.[23] Such attempts depend on the location of the various regiments at specific fort sites through the discovery of inscriptions naming them. Unfortunately, the comparative lack of inscriptions in some areas still leaves a number of questions unanswered, although the situation in the areas held under permanent military occupation in the north and west is better than in the Midlands and south of Britain, where the handful of early auxiliary tombstones serves only to indicate what could be achieved in defining troop dispositions given a state of epigraphic abundance.

If such a utopian situation is unlikely ever to arise, military inscriptions from specific fort sites can help us to understand the organisation and function of the Roman army in a number of ways. Where we have complete and reconstructable fort plans and an epigraphically-attested garrison, much can be deduced about the internal organisation of the type of unit concerned by an examination of the barrack accommodation.[24] Where we have a series of the annual new-year dedications made by the commanders of auxiliary units, as at Birdoswald and especially Maryport, it is possible to estimate the normal length of service in the province of individual auxiliary commanders as three or four years.[25] The auxiliary officers as a body are the subject of a recent important prosopographical study.[26]

Epigraphy has also much to tell of the way in which the two greatest monuments of the Roman army in Britain, Hadrian's Wall and the Antonine Wall, were constructed and garrisoned.

In the case of Hadrian's Wall, the construction of major structures such as forts and milecastles were recorded on inscriptions of conventional type. The inscriptions from the forts can often be dated by the precise titles accorded to Hadrian, such as the grant of tribunician power renewed annually. Those from the milecastles were simpler, mentioning only the names of Hadrian, the governor Aulus Platorius Nepos, and the legion responsible. There were at least two inscriptions for each of an original 80 milecastles,[27] and so a total of 160, of which those for the westernmost 32 milecastles built in turf were cut on wood.[28] Particular idiosyncrasies in milecastle design, especially as regards their gates, occur regularly with the work of specific legions,[29] and demonstrate that, while the overall specifications were laid down by Nepos and his architects, the detailed plans were drawn up by the architects attached to the different legions. It is possible that the turrets too may have had simple inscriptions which mentioned only the legion concerned without naming Hadrian or Nepos.[30] Work on the Wall itself was divided between the legions, and the differences in construction, taken together with the evidence of epigraphy, allow a reconstruction of the original allocation of the work to the three legions involved, each legion being assigned a number of five- or six-mile lengths.[31] Inscriptions were set up at each end of these legionary lengths naming both the legion involved and the relevant cohort engaged in the work at this point.[32] The legion seems not to have been simultaneously engaged over the whole of its legionary length but probably worked as a unit on each third of a Wall-mile allocated to it, i.e. the distance between a milecastle and an adjacent turret or between a pair of turrets. Within each third of a mile, the ten cohorts into which the legion was subdivided were assigned their own stretches. Again they 'signed' their work at each end. The inscriptions do not mention the parent legion, but do mention the century engaged at each end of their stretch.[33] Finally, each of the six constituent centuries of the cohorts was allocated surprisingly small stretches, of the order of 5 Roman paces (25 Roman feet). These building inscriptions, 'centurial stones' as they are often called, were set up at each end of the century's length. They record only the name of the centurion,[34] unless they happen to come at the end of the parent cohort length in which case the relevant cohort number is mentioned too. If this theoretical scheme is near the truth, the 45 miles of Hadrian's Wall from the Tyne to the Irthing, from which point westwards the structure was first of all built in turf, should originally have been furnished with something of the order of 15,000 centurial stones. In fact, the number may be several times greater, for when the section of turf wall built on the steep hill from the crossing of the river Irthing up to Birdoswald fort was constructed, centurial lengths averaging only sixteen feet were employed, and the work was also divided horizontally, each century constructing 9 courses only out of a total of 18 or 27.

The destruction of so much of Hadrian's Wall and the complexity of the problem[35] may mean that a final explanation in detail of how the work was allocated to the legions and its constituent parts may never be forthcoming. In the meantime, however, the general significance of the building inscriptions is clear – unlike the building records at forts and milecastles, they were not intended as a permanent record of work done, but as a means of indicating who had been responsible for the work during construction and thus potentially for controlling its quality. Similarly the so-called *Vallum*, the great earthwork that accompanies the Wall to the south, was provided with building records set up by the auxiliary regiments engaged in the work.[36] Auxiliaries were also apparently engaged in building the parapet and crenellations of the Wall.[37]

Coh. I	Coh. VI
Serenus (primus pilus)	(Decimus)
Flavius Civilis	7 Decimiana
Flavius Crescens	(Lepidus)
Iulius Candidus	7 Lepidiana
Nas. Bassus	Liberalis
———	Lousius Suavis
Opsilius	Gellius Philippus
Valerius Sabinus	
Pompeius Rufus	
Olc. Libo	
Coh. II	**Coh. VII**
Olc. Libo ?	Maximianus?
Laetianus	
Coh. III	**Coh. VIII**
(Socellius)	(Sabinus)
7 Socelliana	7 Sabiniana
Claudius Augustanus*	Seccius
Ferronius Vegetus*	Valerius Verus
Senilis	Iulius Pri(scus/mus)
Sentius Priscus	
Max. Tern.	
———	
Maximus	
Coh. IV	**Coh. IX**
Liburnius Fronto	Paulius Aper
Terentius Magnus	Flavius Noricus
Coh. V	**Coh. X**
Caecilius	Flavius Noricus
Iulius Valenus	Aelius Aelianus
Iulius Iuv(enalis?)	Iulius Florentinus
Ostorianus	Iunius Rufus
Valerius Maximus	Matellius(?) Ursus
Maximus	Munatius Maximus
Sextius Proculus	———
———	Sempronius
Valerius Rufinus	Vesuvius Rufus

Table 1 Legion XX centurions building Hadrian's Wall

Arrows indicate promotions N.B. 20+ centurions of Legion XX are unassigned to cohorts, while 40+ centurions are unassigned to legions (but probably XX or II).
* Attested also at Chester

In addition to the information they yield on the way in which the Wall was constructed, these humble building records also provide us with the names of many of the centurions in the three legions employed. The best represented in this respect is Legion XX. At any one time, this legion will have had a theoretical establishment of 59 centuries engaged on the work, 6 in each of the nine 'ordinary cohorts' (numbers two–ten) and 5 in the first cohort, where however each centurion was in charge of a double century of 160 rather than 80 men as was normal. In Table 1, the centurions who can be allocated to cohorts in Legion XX are listed. The names below the horizontal lines in Cohorts I, III, V and X are supernumerary to the theoretical requirements. The reason for their presence is that the Wall took a number of years to construct, and promotions, for example of Flavius Noricus from Cohort X to Cohort IX, left a vacancy which had to be filled. In some cases the post remained vacant for a while, either through death or promotion, and this fact is indicated by the adjectival form of the centurion's name, e.g. Socellius and the *centuria Socelliana* of Cohort III. This practice allows us to posit the existence of the centurions Decimus and Lepidus in Cohort VI, and Sabinus in Cohort VIII. In some of the cohorts, we lack the names of even the minimum number of six centurions. This is probably not because the cohorts were not so heavily engaged in the work, as is usually assumed, but because we do not have the 'cohort stones' which alone would have enabled us to assign centurions to their cohorts.

Inscriptions have a great bearing on the subsequent history of Hadrian's Wall, for example a quarry inscription from near Brampton[38] with a consular date of AD 207 which, it has recently been suggested, may support an inference from the meagre literary sources that this was the date of the conversion to stone of the western section of the Wall originally built in turf.[39] But none form so impressive a group as the series relating to its original construction discussed above, or the building inscriptions from the Antonine Wall to be examined below.

On the Wall constructed by Hadrian's successor, Antoninus Pius, in Scotland, the building inscriptions were intended to be permanent records of the work undertaken, unlike the numerically impressive but visually unimposing centurial stones of Hadrian's Wall. They were magnificent pieces of work set up at each end of the legionary lengths and on both the north and south faces of the Wall.[40] Neither cohorts nor centuries within the legions record their presence, which simplifies matters, and this and the relatively large proportion of surviving stones makes possible tentative reconstructions of the way the work was allocated between the legions.[41] Inscriptions also suggest answers to the problems of how the forts on the Antonine Wall were garrisoned, since many were clearly too small to contain complete units, and suggest that the *cohortes equitatae*, in which part of the strength were cavalrymen and part infantry, were often subdivided. Thus, *Cohors I Fida Vardullorum equitata*, a milliary unit – i.e. nominally consisting of 1,000 men and normally commanded by a tribune – is recorded on an inscription[42] from Castlecary on the Wall as being there under the command of an officer of lower rank, a prefect, possibly because part of his unit was detached. Against this, however, the unit does retain the milliary symbol, though this could have been an error. Similarly, perhaps, on an inscription of *Cohors IV Gallorum* from Castlehill,[43] the unit lacks the usual indication of its part-mounted status, the title *eq(uitata)*, though this may be simply because the stone-cutters had insufficient space on the die to include it, rather than that the cavalry element was absent. The idea that part-mounted units were divided into their cavalry and infantry elements to help provide garrisons for the Wall forts is hardly proved by such meagre evidence, but is *a priori* likely. To the six regular types of auxiliary unit would be added, in effect, two extra types of cavalry detachment, about a quarter and a half the size of a regular cavalry *ala* of 500 men (and possibly two extra types of infantry detachment, though this depends on the strength of the infantry element in the two sizes of mixed units).

Something of the wealth of epigraphic material for a study of the Roman army in Britain should be clear from the above. In contrast, the evidence for the civilian side of the province is poor, particularly in the field of local administration, where the evidence consists of a pathetic handful of inscriptions. Excluding the *coloniae*, we know of only *one* office-holder at *civitas* level, an ex-*quaestor* from the *civitas* of the Carvetii in Cumbria,[44] and one magistrate, an *aedile*, in one of the constituent *vici* of a *civitas* – the Parisi.[45] The council (*ordo*) of the *civitas* of the Silures is attested on a statue base found at Caerwent,[46] and there are two fine inscriptions from the *fora* at Wroxeter and St Albans.[47] On other topics, such as religion, we are better informed, and civilian evidence complementary to that of the Vindolanda tablets for language and palaeography is provided by the increasing number of curse tablets from southern Britain recovered on excavations, notably at the religious sites of Bath and Uley, but also as chance finds often made by metal detectorists.

Inscriptions relating to civilians in the frontier areas were studied by Peter Salway twenty years ago in his *The Frontier People of Roman Britain*. This work includes an appendix listing 112 inscriptions mentioning people who were unequivocally 'civilians',[48] to which about 10 inscriptions found subsequently can be added. Salway's list also includes four dedications made by *vicani* in the settlements that sprang up outside forts on and behind the Hadrianic frontiers and on the Antonine Wall, from Old Carlisle,[49] Housesteads,[50] Vindolanda[51] and Carriden.[52] The inscription from Housesteads was set up, by decree of the *vicani*, *decreto Vicanorum*, while the Old Carlisle inscription has, wrongly in the present writer's opinion, been thought to include a reference to *magistri*,[53] though the phrase *curam agente*, which occurs on the inscriptions from both Vindolanda and Carriden, may be a periphrasis for *curator*. Two of the four, the stones from Old Carlisle and Vindolanda, are dedications to Vulcan, and Salway points out[54] that he is the common object of devotion on the part of *vicani* elsewhere, and we might compare the special regard in which Marsyas seems to have been held by chartered towns.[55] Another administrative or religious grouping, the *curia Textoverdorum* of *RIB* 1695 found near Vindolanda, has, along with parallels from the Rhineland, been the subject of a recent study.[56] The only piece of actual new evidence from the northern frontier zone relating to the administration of the local populace, in this case direct rather than local administration, is the mention of a *centurio regionarius*, sometimes, if rather vaguely, translated as 'district officer', at Carlisle, in one of the Vindolanda tablets.[57]

If inscriptions from northern Britain have little to say about the civilian tail of the army, the families of soldiers, and the traders who lived in the *vici*, they have virtually nothing to tell us about the native population outside the *vici*. It has been suggested above that auxiliary troops who formed the frontier garrisons, no less than the legions stationed behind the frontiers at the three great military bases of York, Caerleon and Chester, recruited locally. But how far the requirements could be met by the *vici* alone is a question that is unanswerable. Between the military in the forts and the civilian in the *vici* outside their walls will have existed the strongest ties. And no doubt in the *vici* there will have been a strong native element, even if it is usually disguised by the colourless Roman names that men of native or half-native birth will have affected. But what relations existed between the fort and *vicus* on the one hand, and the Brigantian hill farmers on the other, is a question that is, epigraphically at least, unanswerable, since as far as the written word is concerned, the latter simply do not exist.

[1] Fink 1971.
[2] Breeze 1976.
[3] e.g. Hassall 1982.
[4] Hassall 1982.
[5] Richmond 1936.
[6] Clay 1980.
[7] Hassall 1979a; McWhirr 1979b for earlier references; and subsequently Brodribb 1980; Philp 1981, 123–42; Boon 1984.
[8] Tomlin 1979.
[9] Bowman and Thomas 1983.
[10] *RIB* 1142, cf. 946, 1051; *JRS* 53 (1963), 160, no. 4.
[11] e.g. *Britannia* 12 (1981), 369–70, no. 4, set up in AD 258 in the consulship of Tuscus and Bassus.
[12] *RIB* 94.
[13] *RIB* 475–7, 484.
[14] e.g. *RIB* 121, 201, Thracians in Thracian units.
[15] e.g. *RIB* 109, a Frisian in a Thracian unit brought to Britain from Lower Germany.
[16] i.e. A more-or-less local recruit: *RIB* 2142.
[17] cf. Dobson and Mann 1973.
[18] *CIL* XVI, 49.
[19] *RMD* 39.
[20] Roxan 1986b.
[21] *CIL* XVI, 69.
[22] Roxan 1986a.
[23] Birley 1953b; Jarrett 1966.
[24] Hassall 1983b.
[25] Wenham 1939.
[26] Devijver 1976–80.
[27] cf. *RIB* 1637–8.
[28] cf. *RIB* 1935.
[29] Breeze and Dobson 1978, 56–8, figs 10–11.
[30] *RIB* 1443.
[31] Breeze and Dobson 1978.
[32] *RIB* 1646–7.
[33] e.g. *RIB* 1646, 1649.
[34] e.g. *RIB* 1564–5.
[35] cf. Stevens 1966.
[36] e.g. *RIB* 1365.
[37] *RIB* 1445.
[38] *RIB* 1009.
[39] Hassall 1984.
[40] *RIB* 2198; *Britannia* 1 (1970), 309–10, no. 19.
[41] e.g. Hassall 1983a.
[42] *RIB* 2149.
[43] *RIB* 2195.

44 *RIB* 933.
45 *RIB* 707.
46 *RIB* 311.
47 *RIB* 288; *JRS* 46 (1956), 146–7, no. 3.
48 Salway 1965.
49 *RIB* 899.
50 *RIB* 1616.
51 *RIB* 1700.
52 *JRS* 47 (1957), 229–30, no. 18.
53 Hassall 1976.
54 Salway 1965, 25.
55 Phillip 1930, 1993.
56 Rüger 1972.
57 Bowman and Thomas 1983, no. 22, with discussion on 110.

8
MILITARY TILE-STAMPS
FROM BRITAIN

Originally published:
'Military Tile-stamps from Britain', in A. McWhirr (ed.), *Roman Brick and Tile: Studies in Manufacture, Distribution and Use in the Western Empire*, BAR International Series 68, 1979, Oxford, 261–6

A S HAS BEEN shown previously,[1] with the possible exception of Legion XI,[2] none of the legions stationed in Britain in the first century AD stamped the tiles they were producing in their tile-works. The same is almost certainly true for the auxiliary units and the *Classis Britannica*. However, from some point early in the second century, all three legions then stationed in the province are found stamping tiles, and their example is followed by the British fleet and at least two *alae* and ten cohorts of Britain's auxiliary garrison. It will be convenient to examine the evidence for all three branches of the military in Britain separately, starting with the 'senior service', the legions.

LEGIONARY TILE-STAMPS

From the time of Hadrian, the legionary dispositions in Britain were made permanent both as regards unit and location, with Legion II Augusta based at Caerleon, Legion VI Victrix at York and Legion XX Valeria Victrix at Chester. The evidence for the practice of stamping tiles by the first of these has, in effect, been reviewed by George Boon in his comprehensive study of the legion's base.[3] At Caerleon, no stamped tiles have been found in contexts securely dated to the first century, and indeed the earliest context that Boon actually cites for a stamped tile of this legion is in the auxiliary fort at Aberyscir, not constructed in stone (the time at which the buildings will have received tiled roofs) until after c. AD 140. The presumption is that the legion was already stamping tiles for its own use at this date. Aberyscir, incidentally, was just one of a number of forts in South Wales which received tiles from Caerleon (others being Usk, Abergavenny and Llandovery in the second century, and Pennal in the Dyfi estuary in the third).

In the course of the third century, the legion received various honorific titles derived from the dynastic or personal names of the current emperor, and these are included in abbreviated form on its stamps. Thus we find the title *Antoniniana* under Caracalla in *c.* AD 212, and this was retained under Elagabalus, but dropped during the reign of Severus Alexander, 222–35, in favour of *Severiana*. A single stamp of the legion carries the title *Vi(ctoriniana)* after the 'Gallic' Emperor Victorinus, 269–71, and is in fact the latest dateable evidence for the existence of the legion at Caerleon. It might be thought that tiles bearing the common *Antoniniana* title would be equally valuable as a source for dating the buildings in which they are found. Unfortunately, this is not the case, since tiles seem to have been often re-used or even stockpiled at time of manufacture for use at a later date. Thus, for example, numbers of *Antoniniana* tiles have been found from the barracks of the legion's Seventh Cohort, but the restoration to which they belong probably dates to AD 255–60 (30 years after the tiles were originally stamped), as we know from an inscription which records the rebuilding.[4]

Legion VI, like Legion II, produced tiles not only for its own use but for attached auxiliary forts, in the case of Legion VI as far north as Hadrian's Wall and including the great base at Corbridge.[5] Tiles stamped by the legion mostly carry the inscription *Leg(io) VI V(ictrix)*, and are examples of R.P. Wright's types 42–5. Besides the titles *Victrix* and *Pia Fidelis*, which the legion already bore before its transfer to Britain in 122, it was, like Legion II, given the further title *Antoniniana* and *Severiana* by Caracalla and Severus Alexander respectively, as well as *Gordiana* by Gordian II, 238–44. The legion was also, uniquely, awarded the title *Britannica*, which occurs on stamps from Carpow (occupied 208–12).

The tile-works of Legion XX have been excavated at Holt and the stamps found there have been discussed by Peter Grimes,[6] who published his report of the excavations in exemplary fashion from the notes left by the original excavators, though it should be noted that not all the known stamps of the legion have actually been attested at Holt. Legion XX, like the other two British legions, was apparently given the title *Antoniniana*, while other stamps[7] carry the letters DE, perhaps for *De(ciana)*, derived from the name of the Emperor Trajan Decius, 249–51. One stamp seems to give the name of an officer in abbreviated form and reads SUB LOGO PR, variously expanded as *sub L(...) O(...) G(...) o(ptione) pr(incipis)*, or *sub Logo pr(aefecto)*, depending on whether a subordinate officer or the actual commander of the legion is being indicated. An interesting graffito shows that a soldier in the First Cohort of Sunuci (stationed at Caernarvon under Severus[8]), Aventinus by name, was working at Holt. This suggests that although the legion might supply auxiliary units in the vicinity with tiles, the auxiliary units might, on a reciprocal basis, send unskilled labour to the works depot. The question of how labour was organised in military tile-works, however, is one about which we know all too little, though from military tile-works on the continent we have records of *magistri figlinarum*, in one case in charge of a squad of 60 men.[9] Finally, two tiles have recently been published from Chester (Fig. 1), which uniquely among all tile-stamps from Britain conclude with a consular date, AD 167. They will have read: *tegula(m) A(ulus) Viduc(ius) f(ecit) Vero III co(n)s(ule) Leg(ioni) XX V(aleriae) V(ictrici)*, 'Aulus Viducius (?) made this roof tile for the Twentieth Legion Valeria Victrix in the third consulship of Verus'.[10]

1 Composite drawing of legionary tile-stamp from Chester

TILE-STAMPS OF THE FLEET

The tile-stamps of the *Classis Britannica* have been admirably reviewed by Gerald Brodribb,[11] though his work will need revision once the very extensive material from Dover has been published. The Dover material will not, however, affect Brodribb's observations on the extremely restricted distribution of finds of stamped material. Apart from examples from the major British and continental bases at Dover and Boulogne, they are confined to a relatively short stretch of the south coast running from Pevensey to Richborough, and iron-working sites in its immediate hinterland. Lympne has also produced stamped tiles of the fleet, but the tiles themselves both here and at Dover, Pevensey and Richborough appear to belong to structures which ante-date the construction of the Shore forts which were later built at all four sites. The absence of stamped tiles of the fleet from the Shore forts does not necessarily mean that the *Classis Britannica* had been disbanded at the time of their construction, perhaps only that the tile-works operated by the fleet were not called upon to supply material (for auxiliary tile-stamps from two of the Shore forts, Reculver and Brancaster, see below).

Finally, just as we do not know when the fleet ceased to exist, let alone ceased to stamp tiles, so the date at which it first started stamping tiles is not known, though new evidence from Dover may be expected to throw light on this particular problem.

AUXILIARY TILE-STAMPS

In reviewing the evidence for tiles stamped by auxiliary units in Britain, it will be convenient to divide the country up into a series of zones.

a) Hadrian's Wall

Tile-stamps of *Cohors V Gallorum* have been found at South Shields, and the unit is known to have been in garrison there in the early third century.[12] Similarly, stamped tiles of *Ala I Asturum* come from Benwell, where an inscription[13] attests the unit as the third-century garrison (a tile stamped with the same die is also known from Wallsend). Great Chesters has produced tiles stamped *Cohors II Asturum*, and this too is known as the third-century garrison.[14] From Hare Hill comes a stray tile of *Cohors I Tungrorum*, known from numerous inscriptions to have been the garrison at Housesteads;[15] this is slightly odd since one would have expected *Cohors II Tungrorum*, the third-century garrison at Castlesteads,[16] which is closer to Hare Hill.

b) The Wall hinterland

Maryport has produced tiles of *Cohors I Hispanorum*. There certainly was a unit of this name stationed at Maryport under Hadrian.[17] But the *Notitia Dignitatum*,[18] whose information for the garrisons of the Wall and its hinterland has been shown to be valid for the third and fourth centuries, places a *Cohors I Hispanorum* (not necessarily the same unit) at a site which may or may not be identical with Maryport, so that the tile-stamp could possibly be third or fourth century in date rather than second.

From Lancaster come tiles of the *Ala Sebosiana*, and an inscription originally set up to the Gallic Emperor Postumus, 262–6, records the presence of the unit there.[19] Tiles of *Cohors III Bracaraugustanorum* have been found at both Manchester and Melandra Castle. From the fort at Slack come tiles stamped by *Cohors IIII Breucorum*, and the tile-works of this unit have been located at nearby Grimscar,[20] while a detachment probably of this unit (though possibly *Cohors III Bracaraugustanorum*, the reading of the stamp is not completely certain) was outposted at the fortlet of Castleshaw.[21] The dating at these sites is interesting: Slack was occupied from *c.* AD 80–140, being rebuilt in stone sometime after 90, while Castleshaw was only occupied from 90–125.[22] The tiles from these two sites are some of the earliest stamped by auxiliary units in Britain. *Cohors IIII Breucorum* was transferred at an uncertain date to Ebchester, where it was certainly in garrison in the third century[23] and where it continued to stamp tiles. Stamped tiles also come from two other third- or fourth-century sites in the general vicinity of Ebchester: the N CON stamps from Binchester, probably the *Numerus Concangiensium*, 'unit of men from Concangium' (= Chester-le-Street), and the ΛΒΟΛCI stamps from Chester-le-Street itself. The latter could conceivably be intended for *Abulci*, the *Numerus Abulcorum* being one of the garrisons attested by the *Notitia Dignitatum*[24] in Britain – at Pevensey, to which it could have been transferred from the north.[25]

c) Wales

Only one fort in Wales, Caersws, has produced auxiliary tile-stamps.[26] They read C·I·F | S·P·P·, of which the first line is to be expanded *C(ohors) I F(risiavonum)*, and C·I·C·F, perhaps for *C(ohortes) I C(eltiberorum*[27] *et I) F(risiavonum)*, though I can find no parallels for two auxiliary units jointly stamping tiles in this way. However, the alternative, *C(ohors) I C(eltiberorum) f(ecit)*, seems even less likely since the word *f(ecit)*, though usually to be understood, is not normally included.

d) South-eastern Britain (the Saxon Shore)

Two of the earliest Shore forts, Reculver, guarding the approaches to the Thames estuary, and Brancaster, sited in a similar position in relation to the Wash, have both produced auxiliary tile-stamps.[28] From Reculver come tiles stamped by *Cohors I Baetasiorum*, the garrison recorded in the *Notitia Dignitatum*.[29] From Brancaster, two tiles are now known stamped *C(o)h(ors) I Aq(uitanorum)* (Fig. 2), the *Notitia* garrison being the *Equites Dalmatae*.[30] This is the first time that a Shore fort has yielded evidence for a garrison other than that given in the *Notitia*. The probable explanation is that the cavalry regiment (one known to have been raised after the middle of the third century) replaced the infantry one.

2 Auxiliary tile-stamp from Brancaster

CONCLUSION

Legionary tile-stamps are clearly basically a phenomenon of the second and third centuries, though a few of the Legion IX stamps may date from the late first century. The *Classis Britannica* was probably stamping tiles more or less contemporaneously but the published dating evidence is meagre. Of the twelve auxiliary units that stamped tiles, six did so during the third century. One, *Cohors IIII Breucorum*, did so in the early second and also in the early third, while two, *Cohors III Bracaraugustanorum* and *Cohors I Hispanorum, may* have stamped tiles in the early second century but the evidence in both cases is ambiguous. For the remainder there is no evidence. The conclusion to be drawn is that in Britain auxiliary units normally stamped tiles only in the third century. This is in direct contrast to the Rhineland, where the stamping of tiles by auxiliary units was usually a century earlier, during the late first and early second century.[31]

Addendum: Since this article was written, the extensive material from Dover, relating to the *Classis Britannica* and referred to above, has been published.[32] For stamps of the *Classis Britannica* found up to December 1986, see now *RIB* II, fascicule 5 (1993),[33] and for legionary and auxiliary tile-stamps, *RIB* II, fascicule 4 (1992).[34]

[1] McWhirr 1979b.
[2] Wright 1978.
[3] Boon 1972.
[4] *RIB* 334.
[5] Wright 1976.
[6] Grimes 1930.
[7] *JRS* 45 (1955), 146, no. 8.
[8] *RIB* 430.
[9] Bogaers 1969a, 31 n. 24.
[10] *Britannia* 9 (1978), 476, no. 16.
[11] Brodribb 1969.
[12] *RIB* 1060.

13   *RIB* 1334.
14   *RIB* 1738.
15   e.g. *RIB* 1584–6.
16   *RIB* 1981–3.
17   *RIB* 823 with note.
18   *Not. Dig. Occ.* 40.49.
19   *RIB* 605.
20   McWhirr 1979a, 182.
21   Bogaers 1969a, 40.
22   Bogaers 1969a, 40.
23   *RIB* 1101.
24   *Not. Dig. Occ.* 28.20.
25   Hassall 1977b, 9.
26   Nash-Williams 1954, 107–8.
27   Or *C(ugernorum)*, if the tile-stamps are late first or very early second century, or *C(ornoviorum)*, if they are third century.
28   Hassall 1977b, 8–9.
29   *Not. Dig. Occ.* 28.18.
30   *Not. Dig. Occ.* 28.16.
31   Bogaers 1969a, 32.
32   Philp 1981, 123–42. See also Brodribb 1980.
33   *RIB* II.5, 2481.
34   *RIB* II.4, 2459–63 and 2464–80 respectively.

Sepolcro antico nella Via Appia.

1 Tomb of Quintus Veranius on the Via Appia

9
FOOTNOTES TO *THE FASTI*

Originally published:
'Footnotes to The Fasti', in H.M. Schellenberg, V.E. Hirschmann and
A. Krieckhaus (eds), *A Roman Miscellany: Essays in Honour of Anthony
R. Birley on his Seventieth Birthday*, Akanthina Monograph 3, 2008,
Gdańsk, 31–41

IN 1981, Anthony R. Birley published *The Fasti of Roman Britain*,[1] a work on the prosopography of the governors, equestrian procurators, and other officers and officials serving in the province. It was a study which the author was uniquely qualified to undertake. If students of the history of the province of Britannia were fortunate then, their good fortune was compounded with the appearance in 2005 of an updated and expanded version of *The Fasti* entitled *The Roman Government of Britain*.[2] In both works, the most valuable section is that which deals with the forty-odd governors of the undivided province from Aulus Plautius, Claudius' first governor, to the unfortunate Julius Marcus, Caracalla's first governor and arguably the last governor of the undivided province. The object of this article is to add one or two observations to the accounts of about a quarter of these forty or so governors, in particular drawing attention to new evidence where it exists. In making these comments I imply no criticism of either *The Fasti* or *The Roman Government*. Far from it! The massive importance of both works is self-evident, and so I hope that their author will not be offended if I offer these disjointed jottings merely as 'Footnotes to *The Fasti*'.[3]

AULUS PLAUTIUS = BIRLEY NO. 1

Among much else of interest, Birley[4] draws attention to the statement in the *Annals* of Tacitus[5] of how Pomponia Graecina, the wife of Plautius, practised a 'foreign religion', and refers to the interesting idea that this relates to Christianity. He does not discuss the location of the legions in Britain under Plautius, though he does so for his successor Ostorius Scapula (= Birley no. 2). For this very early period, the whole question of legionary dispositions needs rethinking in the light of the discovery of the tombstone of a veteran of Legion II at Alchester – now known to have been a legionary fortress.[6] The placement of Legion XX at Gloucester under Scapula has recently been confirmed by the discovery there of a tombstone of a soldier in that legion.[7]

QUINTUS VERANIUS = BIRLEY NO. 4

Birley refers to the famous funerary inscription of Verania, the governor's daughter, which provides details of her father's career. The inscription was studied originally by A.E. Gordon,[8] and subsequently by Eric Birley.[9] Neither mention the fact that the actual mausoleum on the Via Appia, from which the inscription presumably came, survived at least into the eighteenth century, when an illustration was published by Pietro Santi Bartoli (Fig. 1).[10]

SEXTUS JULIUS FRONTINUS = BIRLEY NO. 10

There are two 'footnotes' I would like to add to the account of the career of Frontinus given by Birley, though both concern the period after he governed Britain. The first relates to his command against the Chatti under Domitian in 83, as legate of the army of Germania Inferior. Frontinus himself refers to the strategy he adopted on that occasion, although with self-effacing modesty refraining from naming himself:

> When the Germans according to their usual custom began to attack our men from the woods and secret hiding places and had a safe escape into the depths of the forests, the Emperor Caesar Domitian Augustus, after having driven roads [or having advanced the frontier] over 120 miles (*limitibus per centum viginti milia passuum actis*), not only changed the fortunes of war, but rendered the enemy, whose refuges he had exposed, into our power.[11]

In trying to interpret the phrase *limitibus per centum viginti milia passuum actis*, the brief mention by the compiler of the *Verona List* of provinces of the loss of territory in Germania Superior in the third century must be relevant: 'The Romans once possessed territory for 80 leagues across the Rhine from the fortress at Mainz. These tribal states were taken over by the barbarians during the reign of Gallienus. One league comprises one-and-a-half miles', *Trans castellum Mogontiacense LXXX leugas trans Renum Romani possederunt. Istae civitates sub Gal(l?)ieno imperatore a barbaris occupatae sunt. Leuga una habet mille quingentos passus.*[12] That is to say, 80 leagues of the *Laterculus* is precisely the 120 miles of the *Strategemata*. Dietwulf Baatz[13] explains the 120 miles of Frontinus as the grand total made up by roadways (*limites*) driven forwards into the forests. The alternative is that it represents the total *length* of the frontier from the Caput Limitis on the east bank of the Rhine opposite Brohl to the fort of Ober Florstadt on the Nidda, which works out at about the right distance. The statement in the *Verona List* would then refer to the territory to the south and behind this line, comprising the plains formed by the River Nidda and its tributary the Wetter and the southern Taunus mountains. It was the latter that for strategic reasons Frontinus was anxious to take in.

The second 'footnote' concerns the period when Frontinus was proconsul of Asia. Birley refers to 'the inscription at Hierapolis in Phrygia dateable to AD 84–5' which mentions him. It is worth adding that this inscription formed the dedication of the north gate of the city and the text shows that it opened onto a street that was also constructed under the name of the proconsul. The gate itself was an imposing structure with three arched carriageways flanked by two round towers. It was restored by the Italian Archaeological Mission at Hierapolis between 1957–69 and can now be seen in all its glory – a fitting monument to a distinguished and dedicated servant of the Roman state.[14]

GNAEUS JULIUS AGRICOLA = BIRLEY NO. 11[15]

Here I have three comments to make on three passages in the *Agricola* discussed by Birley. The first comes where Tacitus describes his hero clamping down on sharp practices on the part of the military that had, apparently, been allowed to flourish under his predecessor (Frontinus).[16] But had such abuses really been rampant under Frontinus – the model of a conscientious and effective civil servant? A far more likely context would have been in the late 60s under Trebellius Maximus. Maximus (= Birley no. 7) had 'ruled the province with a certain decency of administration' (*comitate quadam curandi provinciam tenuit*),[17] and yet, according to the historian, Roscius Coelius, the mutinous legate of Legion XX, had claimed that Maximus had 'robbed the legions and left them poor'.[18] Were these two aspects of Maximus' administration connected? Had Maximus in reality been trying to clamp down on the sort of abuses in the collection of the *annona* described by Tacitus under Agricola's governorship? If so, as legate of Legion XX in succession to Coelius, Agricola would have been in a good position to have known about such sharp practices, and no doubt would have done what he could in implementing the policy of Maximus in trying to prevent them during the governorship of his successor, Vettius Bolanus.

The second passage is where Tacitus talks of Agricola establishing *praesidia* on the Forth–Clyde line.[19] Birley translates the word as 'forts' – but it may mean no more than garrisons. At any rate, no actual Flavian fort sites are known along the line later taken by the Antonine Wall, and perhaps the *praesidia* were housed in temporary camps, some of which survive to have been misinterpreted as 'construction camps' for the legionaries engaged on the building of the Antonine Wall over half a century later.

The third passage is a famous crux: the location of the Battle of Mons Graupius. Birley[20] puts great emphasis on Calgacus' pre-battle speech that 'there was no land beyond us'[21] – sentiments echoed in Agricola's own speech to the army[22] – and places the site of the battle beyond the Great Glen, perhaps between the dramatic peak of Ben Loyal and the sea (note his *Meall Leathal na Craoibh*, 'the hill on the north side of Ben Loyal'). Of course, it is perfectly possible that Tacitus could have heard directly from his father-in-law the gist of what Agricola himself had said to the Roman forces; however, it is an entirely different matter with the speech of Calgacus. But surely neither speech is to be taken literally as the words actually spoken by the two men.[23] The man who could confuse Cartimandua with Boudicca[24] was not as scrupulous in the *Agricola* as people assume. For his audience, it was enough that the battle took place in the far north, and if so these were the sort of things that Calgacus and Agricola would have said to their men. South of the Moray Firth is the Mountain of Benachie and the Roman marching camp of Durno, but at 58.3 ha, the largest of any temporary camp north of the Forth–Clyde line, this must be attributed to Severus, whose army is estimated to have exceeded that of Agricola.

It is my personal view that there is only one reliable clue as to the location of the battle, the mention by Ptolemy of a place called 'Victoria' in the territory of the Damnonii of central Scotland. Alastair Strang[25] locates Victoria at the Agricolan fort of Fendoch, which, although it lies some 25 miles due east of the formal location of Victoria as calculated on Ptolemy's co-ordinates, is still within the margins of error found in Ptolemy.[26] A further 19 miles to the east lies Mon Crieff Hill. This would seem to be too far away from the calculated position of Victoria to make it a possible candidate for the site of Mons Graupius, though the formal resemblance of the names[27] might otherwise make this an attractive suggestion.[28]

SALLUSTIUS LUCULLUS = BIRLEY NO. 12

The suggestion has recently been made by Miles Russell[29] that the inscription set up by this governor on a dedication made at Chichester, and previously regarded as a forgery,[30] may be genuine after all, and further that a second dedication from the same place made by one Lucullus Ammini fil.[31] relates to the same man. From this starting point, Russell has elaborated the theory that Sallustius Lucullus was in fact the son of the British prince Adminios, whose flight to Caligula is recorded by Suetonius.[32] His child would then have been formally adopted by Gaius Sallustius Passienus Crispus and entered a normal senatorial career, ending up as governor of Britain! According to this theory, the fact that both dedications were found in Chichester is in itself significant, for Chichester, Noviomagus Regnensium, was the capital of the client king Tiberius Claudius Togidubnus,[33] who, some have proposed,[34] may have been the same as the Togodubnus, brother of Adminios, who had at first opposed the Roman invasion of 43, but then, it is argued, joined the Romans.[35] A sort of parallel to the proposed career of Lucullus, a couple of generations earlier, would be that of M. Julius Cottius, equestrian governor of the Cottian Alps and son of the last client king Donnus,[36] or C. Iulius Antiochus Epiphanes Philopappus, suffect consul in 109 and descendant of the kings of Commagene.[37]

Q. LOLLIUS URBICUS = BIRLEY NO. 24

From the inscription giving his career before the governorship of Britain,[38] we know that he was a *fetialis*, the priests who traditionally performed the ritual of declaring war, appropriate enough for the man who, as governor, initiated hostilities against the tribes north of Hadrian's Wall. One of the legionary legates serving under him will have been Claudius Charax from Pergamum, commander of Legion II Augusta,[39] who is presumably shown sacrificing in front of the men of his legion in a carved panel on the famous building inscription from Bridgeness on the Antonine Wall.[40] Incidentally, the family of Lollia Bodicca, the wife

of the centurion Flavius Virilis, who had served in Legion XX, stationed
at Chester, but finished his career in Africa with Legion III Augusta,[41]
surely owed its citizenship to Urbicus,[42] just as Q. Neratius Proxsimus,[43]
'from Lincoln', as Birley suggests, 'may have owed his franchise to the
governor L. Neratius Marcellus' (= Birley no. 15).

Q. ANTISTIUS ADVENTUS = BIRLEY NO. 31

Birley suggests that 'the governor may have been the Adventus to whom
C. Julius Solinus dedicated his *collectanea rerum memorabilium*'. This
is an attractive idea since a case can be made for arguing that Solinus
was a Briton. Not only does he mention the shrine of Sulis Minerva at
Bath (Aquae Sulis),[44] but he also appears to have a theophoric *cognomen*,
Solinus, referring to the goddess herself, a name also borne by two other
Britons from the Bath area.[45]

THE INTERREGNUM FOLLOWING THE DEPARTURE OF ULPIUS MARCELLUS = BIRLEY NO. 33

'Those [sc. the soldiers] in Britain then, when they had been rebuked
for their mutinous conduct (for they did not in fact quieten down
until Pertinax quelled them), having chosen out of their number 1,500
javelin-men, sent them to Italy'. This statement comes from Xiphilinus'
epitome of Dio,[46] and it is just possible that Dio himself (or his source)
actually said that they sent chosen i.e. 'picked' men, that is the *singulares*
or guards of the (absent) governor.[47]

PUBLIUS HELVIUS PERTINAX = BIRLEY NO. 35

Pertinax, the grandson of a slave and a future emperor, is one of the
most interesting men to have governed the province. He and his father
are also the subject of a fascinating article by Richard de Kind on the
Roman marble portraits from the villa of Lullingstone in Kent.[48] I can do
no better than quote the summary by Martin Henig:[49]

> Richard de Kind points to the very striking resemblance between the
> second deliberately damaged Lullingstone portrait and a portrait head in
> Aquileia generally held to be a portrait of Pertinax before his succession
> to the imperial throne in AD 193. Pertinax served as Legatus Augusti
> after Ulpius Marcellus, and it is possible that Lullingstone served as a
> luxurious retreat for the governor during his brief sojourn. The bust was
> damaged as a result of an unofficial *damnatio memoriae* by soldiers who

resented his firm discipline and were unable to find the fleeing governor. The other portrait is explained as probably that of his father, P. Helvius Successus, and is mid-second century in date. If this highly plausible paper is correct, we have here a very important marble portrait, one of only a handful from Britain to portray an emperor.

ALFENUS SENECIO = BIRLEY NO. 39

Birley states that 'More British inscriptions name Senecio than any other governor' – formally true if one discounts the inscriptions once set up under his near successor, Julius Marcus, whose name has been erased. Birley points out that he was a native of Cuicul in Numidia, but does not discuss the name which shows that his was descended from an old Italic, or perhaps Etruscan, family whose *nomen* ended with the suffix *-enus* rather than the more usual *-ius*.[50] His *cognomen*, Senecio ('Groundsel'), is perhaps one of a class of nicknames derived from plants, like Cicero from *cicer*, 'chick-pea', that was favoured under the republic.[51]

Senecio should have been 'the governor of Britain who appealed for assistance to Severus following a barbarian invasion'[52] – a statement regarded by Birley with caution as a rhetorical *topos*. What we can say about him is that the inscriptions show Senecio carrying out work on Hadrian's Wall,[53] the forts of the Wall hinterland,[54] and at least one outpost fort.[55] All this activity shows that there was at the time 'no thought of moving into Scotland again' – and yet, in an extraordinary *volte-face*, this is precisely what Severus did. His long-term objective is clear: this was to be no mere punitive expedition, albeit carried out in overwhelming force, but the prelude to permanent occupation, as is shown by building the east gateway at the legionary base at Carpow in stone,[56] and the construction of the principia and bath building attached to the praetorium in similar durable materials, including roof tiles stamped LEG VI VIC B P F.[57] It was of course not to be. On becoming sole emperor, Caracalla withdrew from Scotland, and the frontier once more reverted to the line of Hadrian's Wall. Here the work carried out under Senecio had been so extensive that later generations credited Severus with the construction of a new frontier wall. The relevant passages are discussed by Birley in the course of his general treatment of the Severan expedition (195–203). In one case, the *Augustan Histories, Life of Severus*, the simple statement is made that the emperor constructed a wall from sea to sea (*muro per transversam insulam ducto, utrimque ad finem Oceani munivit*).[58] Other sources also describe the wall as running from sea to

sea, but, in addition, specify its length – as 32 or 132 miles,[59] or, in one
case, 133 miles.[60]

These texts clearly derive from the same source, a source which
Birley suggests gave the distance as LXXXII(I) miles – with the comment
that '82 miles for the whole length of the Wall is more or less correct'.
Another explanation has been put forward by the present writer,[61] that
the lost text recorded the conversion of the western section of the Wall
from turf, in which it had originally been constructed, to stone. This
was originally precisely 32 miles in length. The *Life of Hadrian* in the
Historia Augusta[62] only gives the total length of the wall – stone and
turf – as 80 miles. This is correct: as originally built, since there were
precisely 80 milecastles and 80 'Wall-miles'. There is no mention of a
turf wall here at all, but such a reference to it in at least one source used
by the compiler(s) of the *HA* is perhaps implied by the passage in the
Life of Pius,[63] where it is recorded that the emperor built *another* turf wall
(the translation of the phrase *alio muro caespiticio ducto* as 'another wall,
a turf one' is not what the Latin says). The date of the conversion of the
major part of the turf wall to stone is not known – despite the belief that
this took place under the governor Gnaeus Julius Verus (= Birley no.
27), attested in Britain in AD 158. In fact, we know that the easternmost
four miles of the turf wall had already been converted to stone under
Hadrian.[64] Accordingly, if the theory outlined above is correct, it would
mean that the author of the lost source attributing the work to Severus
knew that Severus had replaced Hadrian's turf wall in stone, and knew
that this was 32 miles long, but did not know that part had already been
rebuilt in stone before his time.

GAIUS JULIUS MARCUS = BIRLEY NO. 41

Birley thinks Julius Marcus was appointed by Caracalla and Geta before
their departure from Britain in spring 211 or at latest by Caracalla in
211/12, perhaps as the last consular governor of an undivided Britain or
one of the first praetorian governors of Britannia Inferior. The governor
is remarkable because there are more than a dozen inscriptions set up
on his initiative for the safety of the Emperor Caracalla, usually alone
but sometimes associated with his mother Julia Domna. Most of these
inscriptions were erected by the personnel of units serving on the
northern frontier and include the phrase *pro pietate ac devotione communi*,
that is they were set up 'out of their common loyalty and devotion'. On all
of these 'loyalty inscriptions' where the space once occupied by the name

of the governor survives, it has been deliberately erased and can only be restored because, uniquely, it survives on a contemporary milestone.[65] It is clear that Marcus suffered *damnatio memoriae*. What was the context for the erection of these 'loyalty inscriptions', and why was the name of Marcus erased? After discussing this matter, Birley concludes that after the murder of Geta (December 211), news of which the army in Britain can be presumed to have received badly, 'Julius Marcus clearly needed to affirm the army's and his own loyalty. However... clearly his action failed to convince and he incurred *damnatio*'.

It seems to me that there may be an extra dimension to the erection of the loyalty inscriptions and the death and disgrace of Julius Marcus. A remarkable inscription found in the early nineteenth century at the fort Housesteads on Hadrian's Wall is the dedication *Dis Deabusque*, set up by the First Cohort of Tungrians, *secundum interpretationem Oraculi Clari Apollinis*[66] – 'in accordance with the interpretation of the oracle of Apollo at Claros'. Claros lies in western Asia Minor, and the dedication turns out to be one of a series of half a dozen similar inscriptions found at various sites in the Roman world. The most recent of these discoveries was made at Volubilis.[67] Many years ago, Eric Birley had suggested a general context for the inscriptions and a date – 213.[68] In that year, Caracalla was not only physically ill but suffered from some sort of mental breakdown brought on by feelings of guilt towards his father and brother. In his distress, he appealed to Aesculapius and Serapis, and specifically Apollo Grannus,[69] and perhaps indirectly to Apollo of Claros.[70]

What were the instructions that he received from the Oracle of Apollo at Claros? That he, Caracalla, should proclaim his piety by making sacrifices and dedications to the gods and goddesses throughout the known world? It was all to no avail. One recourse perhaps remained: the willing exchange of a life for a life by the act of *devotio*. *Devotio* was, literally, the self-sacrifice of a suppliant to a deity for the health or wellbeing of another. The practice had an ancient pedigree. From the early days of the republic were the stories of Marcus Curtius who, mounted on his horse and fully armed, sprang into a mysterious hole that had appeared in the Forum, thus fulfilling the oracle that Rome's 'greatest treasure' should be thrown into the Abyss. Then there was the Roman consul, Decius Mus, who devoted himself before engaging in battle with the Latins, rushed into the thickest of the enemy and was slain, thus ensuring the Roman victory. As late as 49/8 BC at Dyrrachium, Crastinus, a *primipilaris* of Legion X, and 120 soldiers, in effect devoted themselves before the battle. They all perished and Caesar won a famous victory.[71] A possible example of *devotio* is the mysterious death of Antinous in the Nile, 'for some say he had devoted himself to death for Hadrian...',[72] but the clearest parallel would come in the account of the illness of Caligula in Suetonius, 'when... some even vowed to fight as gladiators, and others who vowed their lives put up inscriptions for the safety of the ill prince (*pro salute aegri... capita sua, titulo proposito, voverent*). From a later passage in Suetonius, we know that Caligula recovered and pay-back time arrived for those who once had been foolish enough or, more probably, unfortunate enough to be coerced into this rash act of 'devotion'.[73]

Was Marcus, whose loyalty was already suspect, somehow prevailed upon to make some ritual bargain, reflected in the series of 'loyalty dedications'? Caracalla, like Caligula, recovered, but Julius Marcus may have rejected the curt instruction to fulfil his vow. If so, compulsion was used, and to the imposed act of *devotio* was added the ignominy of *damnatio memoriae*. To the warped mind of Caracalla, who put to death four innocent Vestal Virgins by burying them alive in the traditional manner – it would have been five if his fifth intended victim had not cheated murder by suicide[74] – the removal of one suspect general might have seemed no great thing, and even an act of piety and gratitude to the gods for his safe recovery.

In concluding my contribution to this Festschrift for Tony, I discussed the series of dedications made for the welfare of the Emperor Caracalla by the troops stationed in Britain under the governor Julius Marcus, *pro pietate ac devotione communi*. I, too, make my offering *pro pietate ac devotione*, but in the sure confidence that I shall not suffer the same fate as my namesake, the governor Marcus! No, Anthony is no Antoninus, and even if he does not agree with all I have written, our shared memories of Oxford in the early 1960s, and of various Roman Frontier Congresses and Pilgrimages of Hadrian's Wall, far from being the objects of *damnatio*, are recollections to be cherished.

POSTSCRIPT OR 'FOOTNOTES TO THE FOOTNOTES'

After I had sent off the last corrections to the text of 'Footnotes to the Fasti' to Hans Michael Schellenberg early in September 2007, I attended the 13th International Congress of Greek and Latin Epigraphy at Oxford. Sadly, Tony could not be there, but many old friends were, and in conversations with them I heard about a number of things that are relevant to some of the points that I made in my article, and these I give below.

Aulus Plautius = Birley no. 1

Legionary dispositions: Dennis Saddington reminded me about the fragmentary inscription set up by a soldier in Legion IX from the temple at Hayling Island,[75] found during excavations there directed by an old pupil of mine, Tony King. This could have been made by a soldier while he was stationed at nearby Chichester, which Graham Webster long ago suggested may have been the site of a legionary base. If this were the case, the legions under Plautius could have been stationed at Colchester, where Legion XX is attested by the tombstone of a centurion,[76] and then in an arc running from Chichester in the south (Legion IX), through Alchester in the centre (Legion II), to a site further north, conceivably at Irchester (Legion XIV).

Quintus Veranius = Birley no. 4

To Benet Salway I am grateful for knowledge of the interesting monument from Patara, briefly alluded to by Birley.[77] The full publication of this extraordinary structure has just appeared and was shown to me by Mustafa Adak, one of the joint authors.[78]

Gaius Julius Marcus = Birley no. 41

Gil Renberg told me about the article by C.P. Jones,[79] and the follow-up.[80] So far from there being half a dozen dedications, there are now eleven such inscriptions known, the most recent discovery, from Cosa, found during excavations directed by another old student of mine, Lisa Fentress. Jones argues that these dedications were set up in response to the crisis created by the Antonine Plague. If so, it does not affect the main thrust of the argument that I have presented, that the death of Julius Marcus was the result of *dedicatio*. On the appeal to Apollo Grannus, Wolfgang Spickermann and a third old pupil of mine, Ralph Häussler, told me about the important but fragmentary inscription set up to Apollo Grannus at the sanctuary at Grand (Gallia Belgica), apparently mentioning Caracalla (Antoninus).[81] It seems to me still possible that the suggested mission from the priests of the sanctuary of Apollo Grannus at Faimingen[82] to Claros took place under Caracalla rather than Marcus.

Illustration note: This article was originally published with a halftone illustration of the author at the 18th International Congress of Roman Frontier Studies (Limes Congress) in Amman, Jordan (September 2000), not included in the present collection.

[1] Birley 1981.
[2] Birley 2005.
[3] In citing the literary sources, I have followed the practice of Birley (1981) himself in normally not referring to specific editions.
[4] Birley 1981, 23 n. 35.
[5] Tac. *Ann.* 12.22.
[6] *Britannia* 36 (2005), 478, no. 4.
[7] *Britannia* 36 (2005), 476, no. 3.
[8] Gordon 1952.
[9] Birley 1952; republished with a brief postscript in Birley 1953a, 1–9.
[10] Bartoli 1704, no. 42 (copy in the Library of the Society of Antiquaries of London, reproduced here with permission). Versions of the engraving were later used by de Montfaucon (1719, vol. 5, pl. 29, and subsequent editions and translations (into French and English)). Quintus Veranius is the only governor of the province, apart from those who subsequently became emperor, whose portrait – admittedly very schematic – survives, on a coin of Kibyra in Lycia Pamphylia: *RPC* I, 2889, with discussion on 473–4.
[11] Frontinus *Strategems* 1.3.10.
[12] *Laterculus Veronensis* 15.7 = Seeck 1876/1962.
[13] Baatz 2000, 15.
[14] d'Andria 2003, 70–3 (section 4: 'The Frontinus Gate'), figs 43–5.
[15] I have always had a soft spot for Agricola: not only do we share the same birthday (13 June), but I was also born in 1940, the nineteenth centenary of his birth (Tac. *Agric.* 44.1)!
[16] Tac. *Agric.* 19.1; discussed by Birley (1981, 80).
[17] Tac. *Agric.* 16.3.
[18] Tac. *Hist.* 1.60.
[19] Tac. *Agric.* 23; discussed by Birley (1981, 84).
[20] Birley 1981, 88 ff.
[21] Tac. *Agric.* 30.1.
[22] Tac. *Agric.* 33.3, 33.6.
[23] cf. Thucydides and his comment on the speeches he puts into the mouths of his protagonists – that they were not the words that were actually spoken but that they advanced the sort of arguments and exhortations that might have been used in the circumstances.
[24] Tac. *Agric.* 31.7.
[25] Strang 1998.
[26] A. Strang, pers. comm.
[27] Johnston (1934) derives the name from the Celtic *Monadh Craoibh*, 'Hill of the Tree'. It was the scene of a battle in AD 728: Watson 1926.
[28] Victoria is also listed in the *Ravenna Cosmography* as on the Forth–Clyde,

along with an unidentified place, Colanica, also in the territory of the Damnonii, which supports this reading (as opposed to Colania in Ptolemy). For both names, see Rivet and Smith 1979, 311, 499. A wild explanation for the name Colanica is that it is not in fact a place at all, but a transcription into Latin letters, VICTORIA [... AGRI]KOLA NIKA (or similar), of a gloss in an original Greek source. If so, the missing letters had already dropped out by the time this source was used by Ptolemy.

29 Russell 2006a; 2006b. Rejected by A.R. Birley, pers. comm.

30 *RIB* 2334*.

31 *RIB* 90.

32 Suet. *Gaius* 44.2.

33 Birley 1981, 466–8, appendix; *RIB* 91 + add.

34 Hind 2007.

35 Dio 60.20–1.

36 *ILS* 94.

37 C. Iulius Antiochus Epiphanes Philopappus: *PIR*² I, 151.

38 *ILS* 1065.

39 Birley 1981, legionary legates, no. 26.

40 *RIB* 2139; *CSIR* I.4, 68.

41 *ILS* 2653.

42 Burn 1969, no. 74, with commentary.

43 *JRS* 52 (1962), 192, no. 8.

44 C. Julius Solinus *Collectanea rerum memorabilium*, ch. 22.

45 Sulinus Bruceti filius, *RIB* 105 (Cirencester) and *RIB* 151 (Bath); Sulinus Maturi filius, *RIB* 150; perhaps also Svlicena = Svligena?, *RIB* 134 (Gloucestershire).

46 Dio 72(73).2²–4 = Loeb edn, vol. 9, 88.

47 Hassall 1973, 235, appendix 1, with references to the Greek equivalents for *pedites* and *equites singulares*.

48 de Kind 2005.

49 Henig 2006.

50 Schulze 1904/66, 120.

51 Senecio is given in the *OLD* as either an old man or a plant, probably groundsel. Kajanto (1965, 301) prefers the former meaning. For Cicero, see Kajanto 1965, 335.

52 Herodian 3.14.1.

53 At Chesters, *RIB* 1462; Birdoswald, *RIB* 1909. There is also a dedication from Benwell to the Victory of the Emperors set up while he was governor, *RIB* 1337 + add.

54 Bainbridge, *RIB* 722–3; Bowes, *RIB* 740; and Greta Bridge, *RIB* 746.

55 Risingham, *RIB* 1234 + add.

56 *JRS* 55 (1965), 223–4, no. 10; cf. Wright 1974. Unless Carpow was founded by Commodus and abandoned *c.* 206, a possibility suggested by the coin series: P.J. Casey, pers. comm.

57 *RIB* II.4, 2460.71–4.

58 *SHA, Severus* 18.2.

59   32 miles: *Epitome de Caesaribus* 20.4. 132 miles: Jerome *Chronicle* 212i, 213a; Orosius 7.17, also mentioning the ditch, wall and turrets.

60   Eutropius 8.19.1–2.

61   Hassall 1984. To the ancient sources there quoted should be added the statements in Bede's *Ecclesiastical History*, ch. 5, and *The Anglo Saxon Chronicle* for the year AD 188, which will derive from earlier texts. Two of the versions of the *Chronicle* refer to Severus building a rampart of turf and a broad wall thereon. Bede also talks of a wall of stone and a rampart of turves.

62   *SHA, Hadrian* 11.

63   *SHA, Pius* 5.

64   e.g. Breeze and Dobson 2000, 85.

65   *RIB* 298, found near Hadrian's Wall Milecastle 17 and dated 213.

66   *RIB* 1579.

67   Euzennat 1976.

68   Birley 1974.

69   Dio 77(78).15.6 = Loeb edn, vol. 9, 318.

70   A fragmentary inscription from Ephesus, *AE* 1971, 455, mentions Apollo Grannus, and Euzennat (1976) suggests that this indicates contact between the priests of the cult of Apollo Grannus at Faimingen in Rhaetia, where there was a major sanctuary to the god, with the area of Ephesus, specifically Claros to the south. The mission from Faimingen will have been to enlist the help of the priestly administration at Claros in responding to Caracalla's request for divine aid.

71   Marcus Curtius: Livy 7.6; Decius Mus: Livy 8.3, 8.6, 8.9–10; Crastinus: Caesar *Bellum Civile* 3.9.

72   *SHA, Hadrian* 14.5; cf. Birley 1997, 247.

73   Suet. *Gaius* 14.2, 27.2.

74   Dio 77(78).16 = Loeb edn, vol. 9, 318–20.

75   *Britannia* 12 (1981), 369, no. 3.

76   *RIB* 200.

77   Birley 1981, n. 89. See Salway 2007, 194–201 (section 2.5: 'The Claudian Monument from Patara') = *SEG* 51 (2001), no. 1832.

78   Şahin and Adak 2007.

79   Jones 2005.

80   Jones 2006.

81   See most recently *AE* 1983, 716.

82   See n. 70 above.

10

ROMAN SOLDIERS IN ROMAN LONDON

Originally published:
'Roman Soldiers in Roman London', in D.E. Strong (ed.), *Archaeological Theory and Practice: Essays Presented to Professor William Francis Grimes,* 1973, London, 231–7

IN THE FIELD of Romano-British studies, Peter Grimes has played a full and distinguished role, from the publication of the important military tile-works at Holt[1] to the excavation of the London Mithraeum and fort in the 1950s.[2] The first two are almost type-sites of their kind – a legionary industrial establishment, and the shrine of a group of wealthy Mithraic worshippers in the most cosmopolitan city of the province. Both are presented complete and entire to students of Roman military antiquities on the one hand and to those of Roman religion and art on the other. But the surprising discovery of the fort prompts further speculation: Professor Grimes has given us its size, eleven acres, and the approximate date of its foundation, about AD 100, but who were the troops who were stationed within its walls and what was their function? This short article, offered to a distinguished scholar and a good friend, reviews the possible answers.

Ralph Merrifield[3] suggested that the fort was garrisoned by men seconded from the different British legions – the presence of men from all three, II, VI and XX, is attested by their tombstones – while Professor Frere[4] thinks of an urban cohort – 'the police force of a provincial capital'. Which explanation is likely to be correct – or can a third hypothesis be advanced?

THE 'URBAN COHORT'
The question of urban cohorts is a complicated one but since it has been studied fully by H. Freis,[5] no prolonged treatment is given here.

It is enough to say that the absence of such a unit at London in the historical or epigraphic record need not in itself be significant. Only a handful of tombstones survive from Roman London, and the unit itself would not be included in the lists of *alae* and cohorts given in the half dozen or so military diplomas that survive from Roman Britain. These were issued to veterans of auxiliary units who received citizenship on discharge. Each diploma gives in its preamble a list of *all* units from which discharges were being made at a particular time, not only the unit to which the veteran actually receiving the document belonged. But the soldiers in urban cohorts were already Roman citizens and will have been treated differently on completing their military service. Though they did receive a diploma on discharge, as the surviving diploma issued to a veteran in Cohort XIII Urbana at Lyons shows,[6] these merely confirmed, if necessary retrospectively, the legality of marriages they might contract or have contracted with citizens (female) and peregrines. The chances of finding a diploma issued to a veteran in any particular unit are very remote. If veterans in a hypothetical London urban cohort had special diplomas issued to them, one would be fortunate indeed to find one. However, though this negative evidence is hardly significant, there are strong *a priori* grounds for thinking it extremely unlikely that a unit of this type was ever stationed in London, or indeed that an urban cohort was the normal 'police force' of any provincial capital. Apart from Rome, and occasionally other places in Italy, such as Puteoli and Ostia, urban cohorts are known only to have been stationed at Lyons (variously XIII, XVII, XVIII and I) and Carthage (XIII and I). Lyons was not only the capital of Gallia Lugdunensis, but the venue for the annual meeting of the *Concilium Galliarum*, the provincial council representing all three Gallic provinces. It was also the centre of the road system in Roman Gaul, and in the first century housed an imperial mint. Carthage was, after Rome, one of the most important cities in the west and the seat of the proconsul of Africa, one of the two most senior governors of senatorial provinces. However, Gallia Lugdunensis had no permanent military establishment, while Africa, after the creation of a separate command in Numidia under Caius, was likewise devoid of troops. In both cases, the importance of the towns concerned, coupled with absence of troops in the vicinity, entailed taking special measures, and the posting of urban cohorts was the solution adopted. This was not just a matter of prestige: the Lyons cohort also provided the personnel for the governor's staff (normally seconded from legions stationed in the province), and that

at Carthage a proportion of the staff of the proconsul of Africa, the rest
being supplied by men from III Augusta in Numidia. London did not
compare in status with either Lyons or Carthage, and Britain, with three
or four legions, was not short of men for the governor's staff, while
the shadowy existence of a mint, which may on occasion have been
temporarily set up in the province under the Flavians[7] or during the
reign of Antoninus Pius,[8] will hardly have been permanent or important
enough to warrant the creation of a special British urban cohort. The
only possible candidate for such a unit is Cohort XVI, attested before
AD 66,[9] whose whereabouts is unknown. The unit, however, is not
mentioned again, and probably only existed under Claudius and Nero,
long before the construction of the Cripplegate fort.

SECONDED LEGIONARIES

On the analogy of other provinces, soldiers will have been supplied by
all three British legions for service at the provincial capital. The ranks
and functions performed by these soldiers serving on the *officium* of
the governor have been reconstructed by A. von Domaszewski[10] and
summarised by A.H.M. Jones,[11] and it would be out of place to reiterate
their conclusions here. It is enough to say that the total number of such
men must have been very large – 200 or more for the *officium* of the
governor of a three-legion province[12] – though scarcely large enough to
form the major element in the garrison of the Cripplegate fort, and that
they ranged in their duties from clerks and grooms to prison guards and
executioners. The largest group were known collectively as *beneficiarii
consularis*, 60, or perhaps 30, being detached from each legion for service
with the governor. None are known from Roman London and many will
have been detached for service elsewhere in the province where they
are in fact attested. There will have been a considerable number of
stratores too, nominally grooms. However, like the *beneficiarii*, some at
least may have been outposted, performing minor local administrative
functions, at any rate the sole *strator consularis* known from the province
was buried at Irchester (Northants.).[13] Another significantly large group
were the *speculatores*, ten from each of the three legions. They were
normally concerned with the custody and execution of prisoners, but like
another group, the *frumentarii*, had wider duties as government agents
which might take them to Rome. The Ashmolean Museum possesses
a fine tombstone[14] set up by a *frumentarius* of Legion XX V.V., as other
inscriptions[15] show to a *speculator exercitus Britannici*. For their existence

in London, we have direct epigraphic evidence too,[16] while a reference
in Justinian's *Digest*[17] may relate to one of the more ghoulish aspects of
their duties in the provincial capital (Appendix 1).

Before leaving the question of legionaries at London, it is worth
noting that several do not have a specific function attributed to them
on the tombstones, and there thus remains the possibility that a small
legionary detachment was stationed there, quite apart from those
'specialists' who served on the governor's staff.

Some may have been under the command of the procurator. In
an often-quoted passage, Tacitus[18] describes how, at the time of the
Boudiccan revolt, the procurator Decianus Catus sent 200 soldiers
to Colchester, and it has usually been assumed that they came from
London.

THE GOVERNOR'S GUARD

The guard of a governor of an imperial province consisted of both
cavalry and infantry, known respectively as *equites singulares* and *pedites
singulares*. Both sections were formed from 'picked' men (hence the name
'*singulares*'), drawn from the cavalry *alae* and infantry cohorts serving in
the province (Appendix 2). The *equites* were commanded by a seconded
legionary centurion known as an *exercitator equitum singularium*,[19] and
according to Ernst Stein[20] had a nominal strength of 500. The *pedites*
were also commanded by a legionary centurion, who at least on occasion
doubled up as commander of the *stratores*.[21] Inscriptions[22] suggest that
guardsmen of both groups remained enrolled on the strength of the
auxiliary units from which they were detached, for they are described on
them as being an *eques* or *pedes* of such and such a unit, followed by the
words *sing(ularis) co(n)s(ularis)*. In fact, we have direct proof that this was
so. The annual status report of *Cohors I Hispanorum Veterana* stationed
in Moesia, which lists a whole series of men who were out-posted
though still on the rolls of the unit, includes one or more men detached
for service with the legate as *singulares*.[23] A consequence of this is that on
completing terms of service, men would be discharged from their own
units, not from the guard, in contrast to the imperial *Equites Singulares
Augusti* stationed at Rome, who had an independent establishment and
received diplomas on retirement.[24] This explains why units of provincial
equites and *pedites* are never found on the diploma lists. The exception
that proves the rule is the unit of *Pedites Singulares Britannici* who, as
their name shows, originally served in Britain, and who are found on a

number of second-century diplomas from Moesia and Dacia. They will have been despatched from Britain under exceptional circumstances, and henceforth developed an identity of their own, independent of the units from which the individual soldiers were drawn. Professor E. Birley, who draws attention to this unit and its significance, suggests[25] that it may have been removed as a consequence of Domitian's purge of Sallustius Lucullus, a governor of Britain suspected of tampering with the loyalty of the troops. At all events, after its removal from the province, it is inconceivable that it was not replaced, while an inscription from Ribchester[26] proves that the *equites singulares* certainly survived.

The permanent quarters of the *equites* and *pedites singulares* must have been London, in succession to Colchester, the capital of the province. Since the cohort of *Pedites Singulares Britannici* is not described on the diplomas as milliary, it presumably numbered 500, thus corresponding to the *equites*, making a total of 1,000 in all. In the relatively cramped conditions of the northern frontiers,[27] the 1,000-strong *Ala Petriana*, admittedly all cavalry, occupied an area of just over 9¼ acres at Stanwix. If, at 11 acres, the Cripplegate fort is considered still too large for the governor's guard alone, it may also have housed some of the detached legionaries serving at the capital – especially perhaps the *stratores*, who as we have seen were sometimes at least commanded by the same centurion as the *pedites singulares*. However, that the guard formed the major part of the fort's garrison seems on present evidence to be the most likely explanation of its existence.

APPENDIX I: *DIGEST* 48.20.6

As shown above, among the legionaries seconded to the provincial capital of London were the 30 *speculatores* or military policemen. The text discussed here concerns the function of *speculatores* as military police and probably relates specifically to the province, although not dealt with by E. Birley in his study of Roman law and Roman Britain.[28]

The passage in question contains a rescript of Hadrian, with the early third-century jurist Ulpian's comments upon it, sent to a certain provincial governor, Aquilius Bradua. He had been identified with M. Appius Bradua, whose family name was Atilius for which the Aquilius of the *Digest* is almost certainly a corruption.[29] He is known from a broken inscription set up at Olympia[30] to have been governor of (Lower) Germany and Britain. A.R. Birley[31] suggests that these posts were held under Trajan, and that he received the rescript later as proconsul of

Africa under Hadrian. Such a post would have been mentioned on the inscription which, since it describes Hadrian as *divus*, was set up after that emperor's death. The only possible place for such a mention is in the lost second line together with Bradua's consulship, and the fact that he was *comes*(?) of Hadrian. However, its inclusion here is unlikely since this would mean that the sequence of posts held by Bradua, given in chronological order on the inscription, would be broken. Bradua's governorship of Lower Germany will have followed shortly after his consulship in 108 and before he went on to govern Britain (the British governorship regularly follows that of Lower Germany in the second century). He should then have received Hadrian's rescript while serving in Britain as one of that emperor's first governors.

The rescript – a legal ruling in answer to a question raised by a provincial governor in his capacity as judge – concerns *pannicularia*, literally 'rags', a technical term for the clothes that a condemned man wore which were often considered as the 'perks' of the *speculatores*. The soldiers in the gospels who drew lots for Jesus' clothes after his crucifixion were, in the eyes of the law, disposing of *pannicularia*. Bradua, who presumably had sentenced men to death in the province, was concerned with the precise definition of the term and Hadrian wrote back to say that it included, besides the prisoners' clothes, any petty cash or cheap rings less than five *aurei* in worth, but excluded rings set with a sardonyx or other precious stones, or bonds for large sums of money. Ulpian, in his commentary, says that nobody, from the *speculatores* to the governor, should appropriate these trifles which, like the more valuable property, belonged to the imperial treasury. But since it was not worth sending the price fetched for them to the emperor, as over-scrupulous governors frequently did, it was enough that any money realised should go to the Parchment Fund of the governor's *officium*, or pay for other minor expenses.

Appendix 2: Dio 73 (Xiphilinus' epitome)

There is one possible literary reference to the London garrison which should be mentioned. In Xiphilinus' epitome of Dio[32] we read how the legates in Britain, in the absence of the governor (οἱ ἐν Βρεττανίᾳ τοίνυν ὑπάρχοντες) during a period of anarchy towards the end of Commodus' reign, having picked a force of 1,500 javelin-men (χιλίους καὶ πεντακοσίους ἀκοντιστὰς ἀπὸ σφῶν ἀπολέξαντες), sent them to Italy to enforce their demands. Dio's original text could conceivably have referred to the *equites* and *pedites singulares, stratores,* and others of the London garrison, all of whom would have been 'picked'. The regular Greek term for *pedites singulares* was ἐπίλεκτοι πεζοί,[33] and *equites singulares,* ἐπίλεκτοι ἱππεῖς.[34]

[1] Grimes 1930.
[2] Grimes 1968.
[3] Merrifield 1969.
[4] Frere 1967.
[5] Freis 1965; 1967.
[6] *CIL* XVI, 133.
[7] Mattingly 1967.
[8] Askew 1951; Todd 1966.
[9] *ILS* 2648.
[10] von Domaszewski 1967.
[11] Jones 1960, 151–75.
[12] Stein 1932.
[13] *RIB* 233.
[14] *ILS* 2372.
[15] *CIL* VI, 3357, 3359.
[16] *RIB* 19.
[17] *Dig.* 48.20.6.
[18] Tac. *Ann.* 14.32.
[19] *ILS* 2417.
[20] Stein 1932.
[21] *ILS* 2418.
[22] *CIL* XIII, 8185, 8223, 8188, 6270.
[23] Fink 1971, no. 63.
[24] *CIL* XVI, 144, 146; Speidel 1965, 110.
[25] Birley 1953a, 20–30.
[26] *RIB* 594, cf. also 725, 1266, 1713.
[27] Jarrett 1969, 150–2.
[28] Birley 1953a, 48–58.
[29] *PIR*² A, 1298; Thomasson 1960.
[30] *ILS* 8824a; Dittenberger and Purgold 1896, no. 620 with drawing.
[31] Birley 1967.
[32] Dio 73 = Loeb edn, vol. 9, 88.
[33] cf. Josephus *Bellum Judaicum* 3.5.5.
[34] cf. Arrian *Contra Alanos* 4.24.

II

LONDON AS A PROVINCIAL CAPITAL

Originally published:
'London as a Provincial Capital', in J. Bird, M.W.C. Hassall and H.
Sheldon (eds), *Interpreting Roman London: Papers in Memory of Hugh
Chapman*, Oxbow Monograph 58, 1996, Oxford, 19–26

THE GENESIS OF this contribution lies in a paper originally presented at a conference on 'The Archaeology of the London Region to 1500', organised by the London and Middlesex Archaeological Society and held in the Museum of London in October 1986. I am glad to think that Hugh himself will have heard the original version, and it seemed an appropriate tribute to offer to someone who was, of course, intimately connected to both the Society, of which he was president, and the Museum, where he began his professional working life. It is also a small token of affection to a warm-hearted and generous friend.

The title of this article begs a question: is one justified in using the term 'provincial capital' in the context of Roman provincial administration at all? After all, it might be argued that the capital of a province was simply the place where the governor happened to be at a given moment, just as the capital of the empire was simply the place where the emperor happened to be at the time when, for example, he promulgated the imperial rescripts that were preserved and collected in the *Theodosian Code*. Thus, according to this view, when Tiberius Claudius Paulinus, governor of Lower Britain, wrote to his friend Sennius Sollemnis in Gaul offering him a post on his staff from the as yet unlocated fort or settlement of Tampium,¹ Tampium, rather than York, the provincial capital, had become, in effect, the 'capital' of Britannia Inferior, through the mere presence of Paulinus. The post, incidentally, was probably that of *assessor*, literally 'advisor', and the salary was 250 gold pieces (*aurei*).

Though there is a certain amount of validity in this line of reasoning, the fact remains that there would, nevertheless, be a permanent seat of administration: the governor would, no doubt, take key personnel with him when he went on campaign in the summer, or in his judicial capacity toured his province on circuit, visiting the centres of the assize districts (*conventus*) into which the province was presumably divided, but the administrative 'tail' would, so to speak, remain behind. It is the permanent location of the seat of government in this sense that can reasonably be called the provincial capital. In fact, we know what in the later imperial period the correct name for the capital of a province was. In the *Notitia Galliarum*, where the constituent *civitates* are listed for each of the fourth-century provinces of Gaul (no less than seventeen of them), each section is headed by the name of the relevant *metropolis*, and these 'mother cities' would have been the provincial capitals.[2]

The case for the concept of provincial capitals is even stronger when one is dealing with alien political units which became incorporated into the empire as new provinces, such as the Carthaginian state or the Kingdom of Pergamum, which became the provinces of Africa and Asia respectively. When this happened, the existing centres of administration naturally retained their role under the new regime. In Britain, Camulodunum (Colchester) had held a pre-eminent position prior to the Claudian invasion in AD 43 as the capital of Cunobelin, the major dynast in south-eastern Britain. Camulodunum – or *Camulodunon*, to give it its Celtic form, 'The High Place of Camulos', the Celtic war god – was the strategic objective after the initial landings had been effected, and it was into Camulodunum that Claudius was to ride in triumph at the head of his victorious troops during his brief stay in Britain. In AD 49, the legion that had been based there, probably ever since Claudius' visit, was removed for service on the western front, and a colony of retired veterans was established on the site. When the emperor himself died half a dozen years later, his successor, Nero, decreed that a temple be constructed in his honour there.[3] Major temples for the imperial cult were established in provincial capitals, as, to cite but two examples from the western provinces, at Tarraco (Tarragona) and Lugdunum (Lyons), the capitals respectively of Hispania Tarraconensis and Gallia Lugdunensis. Such cult centres were closely linked with the institution of the Provincial Council. This was a body to which the provincial communities, in Britain the tribal cantons or *civitates*, sent annually-appointed delegates who met under the presidency of the priest

(*sacerdos*) of the imperial cult. This dignitary was expected to underwrite
the costs of the Council and of the festivals and games that accompanied
its meetings, and Tacitus[4] comments on the heavy expenses that fell to
the lot of the priests at Colchester. Colchester, then, was not only the sole
Roman colony in Britain at this period, but was also the home of the
imperial cult and the seat of the Provincial Council, and there can be no
serious doubt that it, rather than London, was the capital of Britannia in
the first years of the new province's existence.

After the destruction of the Temple of Claudius during the
Boudiccan revolt of AD 60 or 61, it appears that the great edifice was
rebuilt, and so, in a sense, Colchester may have remained the 'religious
capital' of the province down to the time that it was divided in the early
third century. The problem of the precise date of the division, and of the
way in which this was carried out, will be touched upon below. Here it
is enough to note that the Provincial Council, though it too presumably
continued to meet at Colchester, may also have maintained an office
in London. This is suggested by the tombstone set up by a slave of the
province (*provincialis*) to his young wife – a free woman, incidentally[5] –
which has been found there.[6] Again, the Council appears to have made
at least one dedication at London to the Divine Spirit (*numen*) of the
Emperor.[7]

If, in the early days of the history of the province, the 'administrative
capital' was at Colchester in addition to the 'religious capital', there are
reasons for arguing (as indeed is universally assumed) that the former
was soon moved to London. Indeed, the move may have been anticipated
by the staff (*officium*) of the other imperial appointee, the procurator,
if this was not from the outset based in London. The procurator was
the emperor's chief financial agent in the province, and, among his
principal duties, will have been the collection of the land tax (*tributum
soli*) and property tax (*tributum capitis*) from provincial communities.
At the outset of the Boudiccan revolt, the then procurator, Decianus
Catus, whose high-handed actions towards the Iceni and their queen
had precipitated the rebellion, was clearly not in Colchester, since he
sent 200 half-armed men to the city, and then made good his escape
to the continent. Tacitus, to whom we owe this information,[8] does not
say that he was in London at the time, but it is a strong possibility.
Again, his successor, Julius Classicianus, was buried in London, as
we know from the discovery there of the inscription from his funerary
monument.[9] His death almost certainly occurred during his period of

office, and this certainly suggests that London was the 'financial capital', whether the permanent offices of the governor's staff were there or not. Other supporting pieces of evidence are cited elsewhere,[10] such as the well-known series of tile-stamps emanating from a kiln or kilns operating under procuratorial control.[11] These stamps read PP.BRI. LON or variants, and stand for *P(rocuratores) P(rovinciae) Bri(tanniae) Lon(dini)*, 'the Procurators of the Province of Britain at London'. Less explicit but most evocative of all is the remarkable find of the single leaf from a diptych, or folded wooden writing tablet, branded on the outside with the official procuratorial stamp – *Proc(uratores) Aug(usti) Prov(inciae) Dederunt Brit(anniae)*, 'the Procurators of the Emperor in the Province of Britain issued this'.[12] This piece of 'official stationery' will have originated in the procurator's *tabularium* or record office. Here the census returns from provincial communities will have been stored, and a small army of freedmen and slaves laboured to ensure the smooth running of the financial administration of the province.

It is, however, the activities of the governor and his staff, rather than those of the procurator, that form the main subject of this article. The governor himself was both the commander-in-chief of the provincial garrison of four legions (later reduced to three) and over 50 auxiliary units, and the chief judicial official in the island, though some of his legal functions were carried out by an official known as the *legatus iuridicus*, another high-ranking senatorial appointment. The governor's own official title was *legatus Augusti pro praetore*, 'legate of the Emperor with the rank of pro praetor'. In constitutional theory the emperor ruled the so-called 'imperial' provinces directly through the grant of *imperium* that he received on his accession, but in practice governed them through deputies or legates selected by himself. In the case of Britain, these *legati* had all previously held the consulship, hence the alternative title *consularis*, 'man of consular status', that is sometimes accorded them. For Britain, the first dated use of the term *consularis* for the governor occurs in a fairly informal context in a personal letter found at Vindolanda,[13] *c*. AD 100, and indeed it seems to be the normal term in the tablets discovered there. It does not occur in the more official texts of inscriptions till after the middle of the second century.[14] However, the term does occur in the titles of two classes of men on the governor's staff who are discussed below, the *stratores consularis*, literally 'grooms of the consular (governor)', and *beneficiarii consularis*, literally 'beneficiaries of the consular (governor)', hence the extended discussion here. By the fourth century, the consular legate as such no longer existed, being, in effect, replaced by an official known as the *Vicarius* of Britain, but the term *consularis* survived, as we shall see, as the title of a subordinate official based in London, the governor of the sub-province of Maxima Caesariensis.

In the first two centuries AD, there is no direct evidence for the presence of the governor himself in London, though there is for that of his staff (*officium*). This consists mostly of tombstones of deceased members that have been found there, such as the monument erected to a colleague by a group of *speculatores* on secondment from Legion II Augusta.[15] The *speculatores* were military policemen, who numbered among their other duties the execution of criminals, itself a reminder that the governor was not only the commander-in-chief of the province but also the highest legal authority. Roman citizens, it is true, had the right of appeal to a higher court – that of the emperor – but with respect to provincials who lacked Roman citizenship, the legate possessed the *ius gladii* ('right of the sword'), and could impose the supreme sanction on those convicted of a capital offence. It was normal practice for ten *speculatores* to be seconded from each legion stationed in the province, so there would have been initially 40 such 'military policemen', as they are sometimes termed, when the standing garrison stood at four legions, but subsequently 30 when the garrison was reduced to three.

The *officium* will have had at its head another military man, a legionary centurion on secondment, known as the *princeps praetorii*. This may have been the position held by Vivius Marcianus, who had been seconded for service at London from Legion II Augusta based at Caerleon in South Wales. Known from his tombstone, he is probably to be identified as a centurion on the basis of the staff that he holds, which could well be the centurion's *vitis*, staff, literally vine stock, and the presence of what is probably the conventional epigraphic sign shaped like a '7' used to indicate centurial rank.[16] However, there are other possible explanations for the presence of a seconded legionary centurion in London, such as the commander of the governor's foot guards (see below), so we cannot be certain what duties Vivius Marcianus performed at the provincial capital. Another funerary monument, the famous sculpture depicting a soldier in 'undress' uniform, wearing a loose-fitting overgarment known as the *paenula*, was found in 1876 reused in the foundations of one of the bastions of the Roman city encountered in Camomile Street.[17] It gives as clear a picture as one could wish of the appearance of a soldier detached from his legion to serve on the governor's staff – though the legion itself is unfortunately unknown since the inscribed part of the tombstone is missing. In one hand the deceased carries a small rectangular object by a strap, probably to be interpreted as a packet of writing tablets, appropriate enough when one considers the bureaucratic duties of many members of the governor's *officium*. This will have, theoretically, included three *cornicularii* and *adiutores* (administrative officers and assistants), three *commentarienses* (accountants and assistants), *librarii* (clerks) and *exceptores* (shorthand writers), not to mention *exacti* and *quaestionarii* (tax collectors and torturers). A.H.M. Jones,[18] in a fundamental study, reckons the governor's *officium* to have numbered more than 200 men.

It is easy to assume that the governor's staff was composed only of his military *officium*, but this was not the case. In addition to the military establishment was the *tabularium* (registry) under a *scriba* (literally 'clerk'), whose importance is reflected by the fact that he was of equestrian status, that is to say that he was selected from the second order of Roman society, the so-called Roman Knights. One such, Gaius Julius Justus, died in Britain, though the monument recording the fact was actually found in Rome.[19] Presumably the death of Justus occurred in London, where the *tabularium* will normally have been located, but as emphasised at the beginning of this article, the governor himself was mobile and would certainly take key members of his staff with him. One such may have been the *scrib(a)*, Demetrius, who made a dedication in Greek to Ocean and Tethys and – significantly in this context – the gods of the *praetorium* (official residence or headquarters), inscribed on a pair of inscribed bronze tablets found at York.[20] Demetrius has been identified with a man of the same name who met the Greek essayist and biographer Plutarch at Delphi in AD 83/4, after having just completed a tour of duty in Britain, during which he was employed on a mission to explore the Western Isles of Scotland. The identification is perhaps unlikely, but if correct would mean that his tenure as head of the *tabularium* occurred at a time when it was situated in London. Alternatively, the dedication could date to the third century after the division of Britain. In that case, Demetrius will simply have been in charge of the *tabularium* at York, the capital of the northern province, Britannia Inferior, and so will not be relevant to a consideration of London as a provincial capital.

As a pro-magistrate of the Roman people, the governor will have had the right of being attended by five lictors, the 'policemen' who bore the ceremonial bundle of rods (*fasces*) and axes before the higher republican magistrates at Rome. Indeed, a colloquial way of referring to the provincial legate was as a *quinquefascalis*, 'a five-fasces man', as an ex-governor of Gallia Lugdunensis referred to himself in one of the letters preserved on the Marble of Thorigny mentioned above.[21] There is, hardly surprisingly, no evidence for this small group of men from the city, though a recent but unconfirmed report of the find of part of an inscribed tombstone from one of the Roman cemeteries east of the city, in what is now Whitechapel, may mention the *antecursores Britannici*, literally 'those who go in front', i.e. the foot-boys of the governor. Finally, while considering such lowly grades on the governor's staff, mention may be made of the governor's groom (*equisio consularis*) based at London, attested in one of the recently-discovered Vindolanda tablets.[22]

The Latin word *strator* is a synonym for *equisio*, but the 'grooms of the consular governor', *stratores consularis*, who are mentioned on a couple of inscriptions from the province, fulfilled more responsible functions than simply mucking out and cleaning tack. From literary sources such as the fourth-century historian Ammianus Marcellinus and his account of the doings of a corrupt *strator* called Constantianus,[23] and legal documents like the *Theodosian Code*,[24] we know that the *stratores* were concerned with the supply of horses for the Roman army. One such 'remount officer' is attested on an inscription found at Irchester, Northants.,[25] but the presence of another *strator* at the port of Dover[26] suggests that, like the *strator* Constantianus mentioned above, they sometimes drew on sources for suitable mounts outside the province in which they were based.

One other significant group on the governor's staff, though perhaps additional to the governor's *officium* in the narrow sense, were the *beneficiarii consularis*, 'the beneficiaries of the consular governor', legionaries who, through the patronage of the governor, enjoyed a status just below the rank of centurion. As many as 60 are thought to have been detached from Legion III Augusta to serve either with the legate of the legion in his capacity of governor of Numidia or with the proconsul of Africa at Carthage.[27] In a province with more than one legion, each may have supplied a quota of 60 *beneficiarii* to serve the governor. If this is correct, then the governor of Britain will have had at his disposal 180 of them, or 240 before the legionary establishment in the province was reduced from four to three. A number of these men are known, but none from Roman London itself. Though in a sense on the governor's staff, they will have been sent to serve at posts like that of Osterburken in southern Germany, the subject of a recent monograph,[28] which also reviews the evidence for *beneficiarii consularis* throughout the empire. In Britain, they are found at two places in the south of the province, the small Roman walled town of Dorchester on Thames,[29] and Winchester, Venta, the capital of the tribal canton (*civitas*) of the Belgae,[30] but their presence is mostly attested at forts, or the settlements outside them, in the northern frontier zone, though this may be due to the accident of survival since there are in general more inscriptions from the military north of Britain than from the civilian south. There is no direct evidence as to their function, though it may have been connected with the supply of foodstuffs to the frontier region. Curiously, after the division of the province into two in the third century, the *beneficiarii* of the governor of the southern province, Britannia Superior, based in London, are found operating in the northern province, Britannia Inferior, as is made clear from the qualification *Britanniae Superioris* attached to the title *beneficiarius consularis* on the inscriptions which mention them. This state of affairs could be explained simply by the fact that the governor of the Upper Province outranked the governor of the Lower Province, or else by the fact that the former had two legions under his command, including Legion XX based at Chester, and so had twice as many men available as his colleague. Whether they belonged formally to the Upper or the Lower Province, the *beneficiarii* of the two governors will have been provided with messing facilities on visits to the respective provincial capitals. An inscription, unfortunately fragmentary, from York[31] illustrates the sort of form that such support might take, for it attests the presence there of a *collegium*, guild, of the *beneficiarii* of Gordian, the later emperor, and one of the early governors of the northern province, Britannia Inferior, shortly after its creation in the early third century. Where there was a *collegium*, there will have certainly have been a club house or mess, *schola*. Such facilities presumably existed in Roman London, the capital of Britannia Superior, too (see below).

So far it has mainly been the evidence of inscriptions that has been under consideration, but the presence of the governor in London has also been linked with three major archaeological discoveries: the so-called Cannon Street palace, the Cripplegate fort, and the building on the site of old Winchester Palace in Southwark. The former is the subject of a separate study by Gustav Milne.[32] If he is correct and the foundations ascribed to the 'palace' really belong to more than one building, the notion that it was the governor's residence (*praetorium*) when in London can be dismissed. The Cripplegate fort has been identified as the permanent quarters of the 'picked' cavalry and infantrymen (*equites singulares* and *pedites singulares*) who served as the governor's bodyguard.[33] Unlike the military personnel so far discussed, who were seconded from the three or four legions based in Britain, the guardsmen were detached from the so-called Roman auxiliary units stationed in the province. Raised from men who, unlike legionaries, lacked Roman citizenship, there were at least 50 such regiments stationed in Britain under Hadrian,[34] though with a nominal strength of 500, or sometimes 1,000 men, they were a tenth or at most a fifth the size of the legions. As one of the recently-published writing tablets from Vindolanda shows, the men selected for service as the governor's bodyguard were retained on the books of their respective regiments. The document, a strength report of the First Cohort of Tungrians, records that no less than 46 men were absent as guards of the legate, as well as a centurion who had been sent to London, perhaps with them.[35] This point is worth emphasising and it may explain an anomaly in the planning of the fort at Ellingen in southern Germany,[36] where an inscription attests the presence of the *pedites singulares* of the governor of the province of Raetia in the later second century.[37] The guardsmen were under the command of a legionary centurion of Legion III Italica on secondment from its base at Regensburg, just as the governor's guard at Cologne, the capital of Germania Inferior, were under the command of a seconded legionary centurion,[38] as they very probably were at London, but it is the plan of the fort that particularly commands attention. There are two anomalies. The first concerns the barrack accommodation. As usual each century was accommodated in a row (*striga*) of paired rooms (*contubernia*), the rear room for the bunks of a section of eight men, the front room for arms and baggage. But at Ellingen, instead of the expected ten *contubernia*, there are twelve, though of course not all suites may have held a full complement of eight men. The second curiosity is to be found in the centre of the fort where the stone-built shrine of the standards (*aedes*) is clearly identifiable, but the other features to be expected in a regular military headquarters (*principia*), such as the aisled hall (*basilica*) and ranges of administrative offices, are lacking. The absence of these features has been explained by Werner Zanier[39] as possibly due to the fact that the men who composed the corps of guardsmen at Ellingen still remained 'on the books' of their original units, as the Vindolanda document cited above so clearly demonstrates. It would be interesting to know whether there was a true headquarters building, *principia*, in the centre of the Cripplegate fort – one might, on the analogy of Ellingen, suspect not.

The third discovery that might conceivably have had some connection with London's role as a provincial capital comes not from the city itself but from the site of the medieval Winchester Palace, south of the river in Southwark. Here, in 1983/4, the Department of Greater London Archaeology excavated the remains of an elaborate building, one of whose rooms had a suspended vaulted ceiling and sophisticated wall paintings thought to date from the mid-second century. Nearby, in the filling of the hypocaust stokehole of a large bath building with debris thought to date to the early fourth century, the excavation team under Brian Yule found fragments of thin sheets of marble which once carried a lengthy inscription.[40] This inscription is one of the most interesting finds from Roman London in recent years. It can be dated to the third century and lists legionaries cohort by cohort, and is similar, for example, to an inscription from the legionary base of Lambaesis in Algeria which lists centurions from the ten cohorts of Legion III Augusta.[41] Only a few letters of the preamble of the London inscription survive so that neither the identity of the legion concerned nor the reason for the erection of the inscription can be ascertained, though, given the date, only Legions II Augusta or XX Valeria Victrix, both in Upper Britain, should be in question, since Legion VI was stationed at York in the Lower Province. It has occurred to the present writer that the men could all have been *beneficiarii*, and, if so, that they were all members of a guild as existed for the *beneficiarii* of Legion VI at York (see above). In this case, the elaborately decorated building in which it was found could possibly have been used as the guild's club house (*schola*), though not necessarily originally built for this purpose. The number of men – between 60 and 70, if all cohorts contributed an equal amount – is about correct for the *beneficiarii* contributed by a single legion, if the analogy of the number of *beneficiarii* drawn from Legion III Augusta is valid. Even if the men recorded were not in fact *beneficiarii*, the general reasoning may be correct, that is that the men listed belonged to a military guild such as Severus sanctioned for the first time in the early third century. But whether or not the elaborate Winchester Palace building served as a *schola* for such a guild, the existence of legionaries in Southwark in the third century is an undoubted fact, and is surely to be connected with London's status as a provincial capital.

A provincial capital certainly, but at the date when the Winchester Palace inscription was set up, London will no longer have been the capital of Britannia, a united Britain, but of Britannia Superior, 'Upper Britain', the southern of the two provinces into which the unitary province had, at some time in the third century, been divided. The division had occurred before 217, since, in a general review of the legionary dispositions throughout the empire, written at the latest in that year by the historian Dio,[42] we learn that Legion VI (at York) was in the province of Britannia Inferior, while Legions XX Valeria Victrix (at Chester) and II Augusta (at Caerleon in South Wales) were in Britannia Superior. The legate of Britannia Superior was always, as the governor of united Britain had been, an ex-consul, as befitted the governor of a 'two-legion' province, while the governor of Inferior, with only one legion under his command, was a man who had held the praetorship only and would only go on to become consul after relinquishing office in Britain.

If the division took place before 217, its exact date is, nevertheless, a matter of considerable controversy.[43] The difficulty lies in the fact that the near-contemporary author Herodian[44] states unequivocally that the division took place immediately after the Battle of Lyons in 197, while we know that *consular* legates – who should either be the governors of an undivided Britain or of Britannia Superior – were acting in the northern military zone, an area which naturally fell with the command of Britannia Inferior, a dozen years after that date. All sorts of explanations have been proposed to get over the crux, and it would be tedious to rehearse them. A.R. Birley[45] has, however, drawn attention to one vital piece of information that has otherwise been generally ignored: in 212, the Provincial Council, acting on behalf of the Province of Britain (*in the singular*), set up an inscription at Tusculum[46] in honour of Julius Asper, 'patron' of the province, and one of the two 'ordinary' or regular consuls (his father was the other) who held office at the beginning of that year. Indeed, the inscription was set up probably just because he had been accorded the honour of an 'ordinary' consulship. The division of Britain clearly had not yet happened, and Herodian therefore must simply have made a mistake.

If a context for the division of the province need be sought, it may have lain in the events that followed the death of the Emperor Severus in 211. Severus had left the throne to his two sons, Caracalla and Geta, but Caracalla had murdered his brother. The news seems to have been taken badly in Britain, and the loyalty of the legions there was suspect.

The governor, Julius Marcus, instructed the units under his command to make protestations of loyalty to the new emperor but in vain, and his fate can be inferred from the fact that his name is erased on most of the inscriptions in the province that once bore his name.[47] The division of Britain at this juncture would have rendered any further attempt to tamper with the loyalty of the troops difficult if not impossible. As if to confirm this idea, a second inscription, found in Rome,[48] unfortunately incomplete, was set up by the Provinces (in the plural) of Britain protesting their loyalty and devotion. If, as seems not improbable, the erection of this inscription belongs to the same general context as those 'loyalty' inscriptions set up on the orders of the unfortunate Julius Marcus, then it should be possible to date the division of Britain to sometime during the year 212.

Whenever precisely the division took place, London and York became the capitals of the provinces of Britannia Superior and Inferior respectively, and Martiannius Pulcher, the third-century governor who is recorded on an inscribed altar as restoring a temple of Isis somewhere in London, will certainly have been one of the governors of the southern province, Britannia Superior.[49] The course of the boundary between the two new provinces will never be known precisely, but something can be inferred from the meagre evidence available. From the passage in Dio already cited we know that Legion XX was stationed in the southern province, while Legion VI lay in the northern, Britannia Inferior. Further, an inscription dated to 237 found at Bordeaux[50] shows that not only York, the base of Legion VI, but Lincoln too, lay in Britannia Inferior. Now Lincoln was a *colonia*, a 'colony' or settlement of retired legionary veterans who worked the surrounding agricultural land, but this land, the *territorium* of the *colonia*, will itself have been carved out of the territory of the Corieltauvi. Since it is reasonable to assume that the provincial boundary respected the boundaries between tribes, it is pretty certain that the whole of the tribal territory of the Corieltauvi, together with its 'cantonal capital' at Leicester, lay in Britannia Inferior.[51] Similar reasoning would suggest that Britannia Superior included not only Chester, the base of Legion XX, but also the territory of the tribe in which it was situated, which, according to Ptolemy was the Cornovii.[52] The boundary, therefore, will have run from east to west in a sort of zig-zag, including the territory of the Corieltauvi in the Lower province and that of the Cornovii in the Upper (Fig. 1).

By 312/14 at the latest, the date of an early fourth-century list of provinces, the so-called *Verona List*,[53] further subdivision had taken place. There were now four provinces: Britannia Prima, Britannia Secunda, Maxima Caesariensis and Flavia Caesariensis. These four could, in theory, have been created by simply subdividing Britannia Superior and Britannia Inferior,[54] but in such a way as to respect pre-existing tribal boundaries. On the analogy of similar provincial subdivisions elsewhere in the empire, Britannia Prima will have been part of the old province of Britannia Superior, and Britannia Secunda part of the old province of Britannia Inferior. But an alternative suggestion,[55] or variants of it, has attracted a certain amount of support. According to J.B. Bury, Maxima Caesariensis and Flavia Caesariensis were subdivisions of a hypothetical province, 'Maxima Caesariensis'. This was formed by detaching the southern part of Britannia Inferior (the 'York Province') and adding to it the northern part of Britannia Superior (the 'London Province'). On the analogy of the province of Mauretania Caesariensis, which derived its title from the name of the provincial capital, Caesarea (Cherchel, Algeria), Bury reasoned that Maxima Caesarieinsis owed the second part of its name to that of its capital, another Caesarea. Since, however, there was no known Roman city in Britain so called, he suggested that it was an alternative name for Verulamium (St Albans), given it by its Catuvellaunian rulers in the period prior to the conquest of AD 43, as a compliment to Caesar Augustus. The title Maxima he took to be a contraction of Maximiana, named after Maximian, whom Diocletian co-opted as joint emperor, and ruler of the western provinces in 285. For the contracted form Maxima, rather than the expected Maximiana, he cited as a parallel the later fourth-century British province of Valentia, rather than the expected Valentiniana, named after the Emperor Valentinian. With the creation of the new province, so the theory went, there were three provinces: Maxima Caesariensis, what remained of the old province of Britannia Inferior, now called Britannia Secunda, and what remained of Britannia Superior, now named Britannia Prima. Within a few years, however, Diocletian created the 'tetrarchy'. In this system, the empire was to be ruled by four men. Diocletian himself remained emperor ('Augustus') of the eastern empire, but was now assisted by a junior colleague (or 'Caesar'), Galerius. In the west, Maximian also continued as 'Augustus', where he was supported by his own 'Caesar', Flavius Constantius. Britain at this period was in the hands of the usurpers (Carausius succeeded by Allectus), but when it was recovered for the western empire by Constantius in 296, Maxima Caesariensis, argued Bury, was itself subdivided. One half retained the old title, Maxima Caesariensis, while the other was called Flavia Caesariensis in honour of (Flavius) Constantius. There were now the four provinces of the *Verona List*: Maxima Caesariensis, Flavia Caesariensis, Britannia Prima and Britannia Secunda.

A simpler variant of this theory[56] has found greater acceptance (Fig. 2). Eric Birley suggested that Caesarea was a new name for London, awarded after its recovery of the island by the Caesar Constantius and named in his honour, just as he was celebrated in a contemporary panegyric and commemorated by the issue of the famous Arras medallion. According to this theory, the hypothetical third province was created soon after 296 and named after its capital, Londinium/ Caesarea, Britannia Caesariensis. Before 312/14 (the date of the *Verona List* of provinces), the new province was subdivided to form the new provinces of Maxima and Flavia, named after Maximian and (Flavius) Constantius. After the resignation of Maximian along with his colleague Diocletian, the two senior tetrarchs, in 305, and the elevation of the Caesar Constantius in 305 to become western Augustus, the Caesarea name of London was changed to Augusta, the title that we know it officially bore in the fourth century,[57] but this change did not affect the designations of the provinces. Birley's version of Bury's 'Caesarea' theory is attractive and is, accordingly, accepted here.

If Birley is correct, London, once the capital of an undivided Britain, then of the third-century province of Britannia Superior and of the shadowy Britannia Caesariensis, was now the capital of either Maxima Caesariensis or Flavia Caesariensis. To decide which it is likely to have been, it is necessary to trace the subsequent administrative history of Roman Britain. For this there are two pieces of evidence: the writings of the Roman historian Ammianus Marcellinus, who wrote in the second half of the fourth century, and that enigmatic document, the *Notitia Dignitatum*, a crucial source for the study for the organisation of the later Roman Empire, compiled in the early fifth. In Ammianus Marcellinus,[58] we read that shortly after 367 a new province had been created, Valentia, named after the Emperor Valentinian, carved out of one or more of the existing four sub-provinces. From the *Notitia*, we learn that while three of these five provinces were of relatively low status and were governed by officials called *praesides*, two, Maxima Caesariensis and Valentia, were governed by men who retained the older and more

1 *Early third-century division of Britain*

2 *Hypothetical late third-century division of Britain*

3 *Early fourth-century division of Britain*

4 *Late fourth-century division of Britain*

prestigious title of *consularis*. It is in the highest degree likely that these had London and York, the old capitals of Britannia Superior and Britannia Inferior, as their administrative centres.[39] London then will have been the capital of Maxima Caesariensis (Figs 3–4).

But we can be certain that in the fourth century, London was not merely a provincial capital, one among five, but that she far surpassed the rest. For at this period the smaller provincial units into which the empire was then divided were grouped together into larger units called dioceses, and London will surely have been the capital of the diocese of Britannia. As such, it will have been the seat of a high-ranking official called the *Vicarius*, who was responsible not directly to the emperor as the old provincial legate had been, but to a luminary called the Praetorian Prefect of the Gauls. The members of the *officium* of the *Vicarius* are listed in the *Notitia*,[60] and consisted of a Chief of Staff, *princeps*; a Principal Secretary, *cornicularius*; two accountants, *numerarii*; a secretary, *commentariensis*; registrar, *ab actis*; a secretary in charge of correspondence, *cura epistolarum*; an adjutant, *adiutor*; assistants, *subadiuvae*; shorthand writers, *exceptores*; guards, *singulares*; and an unspecified number of other members of his *officium, reliqui officiales*. The members of the *officium* of the *consularis* of Maxima Caesariensis corresponded to that of the *Vicarius*. They are not actually listed, but will have been identical to that of the *consularis* of Campania,[61] under whose section in the *Notitia* they are listed as a specimen for the staff appropriate to a governor of this status. It consisted of a Chief of Staff; two senior record office clerks, *tabularii*; an adjutant; secretary; registrar; an assistant; shorthand writers; and other members of the service, *reliqui cohortalini*.

As the diocesan capital, Londinium will presumably have also been the place where the officers who had in the course of time come to take over the functions of the old provincial procurator were located. In one case we can be certain that this was so, for the officer in charge of the diocesan treasuries, the *Praepositus* of the *Thesauri Augustenses*,[62] was surely based at Londinium/Augusta. Indeed, it is likely that we have archaeological testimony to his presence there in the discovery of silver ingots on Tower Hill.[63] Two other diocesan financial officers almost certainly had their *officia* in the city. They were the Chief Accountant of Britain, *rationalis summarum Britanniarum*, a subordinate of the Count of the Sacred Largesse, a euphemism for the imperial equivalent of the Department of Inland Revenue,[64] and the Chief Accountant of the Imperial Patrimony in the British Provinces, a subordinate of the Count of the Imperial Patrimony, *rationalis rei privatae per Britannias*.[65]

As the diocesan capital, in its buildings and general character, fourth-century London may have been hardly recognisable from its first-century predecessor, but, though the names of the high-ranking officials who lived and worked within its walls had also changed and their numbers had almost certainly increased, it was still the financial and administrative centre of Roman Britain. And as the 'capital of Roman Britain', it has attracted the attentions and energies of a band of scholars and archaeologists, not least among whom was Hugh.

1 *CIL* XIII, 3162; Pflaum 1948; cf. Lewis and Reinhold 1955, 445; 1990, 403.
2 Seeck 1876/1962, 261–4.
3 Fishwick 1972.
4 Tac. *Ann.* 14.31.
5 cf. Jones 1949, 44.
6 *RIB* 21.
7 *RIB* 5.
8 Tac. *Ann.* 14.32.
9 *RIB* 12.
10 Milne 1996.
11 *RIB* II.5, 2485.
12 *RIB* II.4, 2443.2.
13 Bowman and Thomas 1994, no. 225.
14 *RIB* 1809, referring to the governor Calpurnius Agricola.
15 *RIB* 19; Hassall 1973.
16 *RIB* 17; Birley 1966, 228.
17 RCHM, pl. 7.
18 Jones 1949.
19 *ILS* 1883; Jones 1949, 40 n. 25.
20 *RIB* 662–3, where, however, *scrib* is interpreted as part of the dedicator's name, 'Scribonius'.
21 *CIL* XIII, 3162, col. 3, lines 6–8.
22 Bowman and Thomas 1994, no. 310.
23 Amm. Marc. 29.3.5.
24 *CTh.* 6.31, an edict dated to 365.
25 *RIB* 233; cf. Richmond 1955, 77.
26 *Britannia* 8 (1977), 427–8, no. 4.
27 Jones 1949, 44.
28 Schallmayer et al. 1990.
29 *RIB* 235.
30 *RIB* 88.
31 *Britannia* 1 (1970), 307, no. 12.
32 Milne 1996.
33 Hassall 1973.
34 *CIL* XVI, 69.
35 Bowman and Thomas 1994, no. 154.
36 Zanier 1992.
37 *AE* 1983, 730.
38 *ILS* 2418.
39 Zanier 1992.
40 *Britannia* 16 (1985), 317–22, no. 1.

41 *ILS* 2452.
42 Dio 55.23.2–6.
43 Graham 1966; Mann and Jarrett 1967; Birley 1981, 168–72; Frere 1987, 162–4.
44 Herodian 3.3.2.
45 Birley 1981, 171.
46 *CIL* XIV, 2508.
47 Birley 1981, 166–8.
48 Beard 1980.
49 *Britannia* 7 (1976), 378–9, no. 1.
50 Courteault 1921; *AE* 1922, 116.
51 cf. Bury 1923, 4.
52 Rivet and Smith 1979, 142–3.
53 Seeck 1876/1962, 247–53.
54 Casey 1978, 191.
55 Bury 1923.
56 Birley 1963.
57 Amm. Marc. 27.8.7; 28.3.1.
58 Amm. Marc. 28.3.7.
59 Hassall 1976, 109.
60 *Not. Dig. Occ.* 23.17–26.
61 *Not. Dig. Occ.* 43.5–13.
62 *Not. Dig. Occ.* 11.37.
63 e.g. *RIB* II.1, 2402.4.
64 *Not. Dig. Occ.* 11.37.
65 *Not. Dig. Occ.* 12.15.

THE IMPACT OF MEDITERRANEAN URBANISM ON INDIGENOUS NUCLEATED CENTRES

Originally published:
'The Impact of Mediterranean Urbanism on Indigenous Nucleated Centres', in B.C. Burnham and H.B. Johnson (eds), *Invasion and Response: the Case of Roman Britain*, BAR British Series 73, 1979, Oxford, 241–53

INTRODUCTION

THERE ARE THREE types of evidence that are relevant to the topic under discussion. The first is that of contemporary writers, paramount among whom in this context is Tacitus who, in a famous passage in the *Life* of his father-in-law, Agricola,[1] gives what may be a rather idealised picture of the way in which a good governor might encourage urbanisation as part of a programme of pacification. The second is provided by inscriptions. Unfortunately, we possess very few 'municipal inscriptions' such as exist for certain areas of the empire, showing, for example, the survival of native magistracies in some districts, *sufetes* in North Africa or *vergobrets* in Gaul,[2] and the detailed working of municipal institutions under the empire. The third type of evidence, and potentially the most valuable for Roman Britain, comes from excavation. Excavation on 'pre-Roman nucleated centres' (for which, following the Roman author Suetonius, I shall use the term *oppida*) is possible since the sites are often unencumbered by modern building, though modern agricultural activities have in many cases caused great damage. However, though many *oppida*, whether open sites or hillforts, have been sampled by excavation, only *total* excavation of the interior, such as has never been undertaken in this country, will be able to answer all the questions we still need clarified: were specific areas reserved for specific functions, e.g. artisans' quarters or markets or meeting places; were there larger huts suggesting social stratification; and was the presence of religious sanctuaries a regular feature?

Excavation on the new Romanised towns, on the other hand, is usually hampered by modern building since the majority of sites were utilised in the medieval and modern period, though there are exceptions: Verulamium, Wroxeter, Silchester and Caistor-by-Norwich. But in most of these, little is known of the earliest Roman structures.

There are four areas which I wish to examine in this article: the first (and largest) is based largely on the documentary sources, the remaining three on the evidence of archaeology, and it is here that progress in the future is most likely to be made.

STATUS

In a famous passage in the *Life of Vespasian*,[3] Suetonius says that as commander of a legion in Britain (in fact Legion II Augusta), the future emperor defeated two powerful *civitates*, fought over thirty battles, captured twenty *oppida*, and took possession of Vectis, the Isle of Wight. This last locates the scene of his campaign in southern Britain, and the *oppida* have accordingly been identified with the hillforts of the Southern Chalk, a number of which have revealed traces of the Roman assault.[4] It seems a reasonable inference that whatever the identity of the two *civitates*, the twenty *oppida* should be attributed to them. The double question then follows: what is meant by the term *civitas* and what by the term *oppidum*?

The Latin word *civitas* can be defined as an autonomous political unit, which in the Mediterranean context usually meant a city-state, but was also used by the Romans of the tribes of north-west Europe. The Latin word *oppidum*, which Suetonius uses of the hillforts, is the general one for town, but one should resist any temptation to take the word literally in the present passage. Just as the word *civitas* normally meant a city and *civis* citizen, but were used by the Romans of tribes and tribesmen, so *oppidum* was presumably used by Suetonius simply as the nearest Latin equivalent for the Celtic word actually in use by the people who lived in the hillforts, perhaps *dunon*. Caesar[5] had also used the word *oppidum* to describe a defended British tribal capital but was clearly unhappy about it ('the Britons call it an *oppidum*...'), while in the second century Ptolemy would employ the word city (*polis*) to describe any inhabited place in Britain,[6] although his readers would certainly have objected to the usage if they could have seen the sort of settlements he was describing.

In Britain at the time of the Claudian invasion, the tribes, or most of them, as we know from the literary sources, were ruled over by kings, eleven of whom are recorded as having submitted to the emperor in the inscription on the triumphal arch erected to him in AD 54.[7] This will presumably have been true of the two tribes defeated by Vespasian. The twenty *oppida* in the territory of these two *civitates* will, in some sense, have been subject to the kings, but their defences imply that if their inhabitants chose to exercise a degree of local autonomy, it would be difficult for the king to stop them without resorting to force. Fighting and feuding between factions within at least two tribes in Britain, the Catuvellauni[8] and the Brigantes,[9] is in fact directly attested, and can be inferred in the case of one more, the Atrebates.[10] We do not know who exercised authority in the *oppida*, possibly chieftains or sub-kings. In Kent, the later *civitas* of the Cantiaci, four independent kings ruled in Caesar's day and are named by him,[11] and each may have controlled a single *oppidum*.

Turning now to the situation after the Roman conquest of southern Britain under Claudius, when the territory of half a dozen or more tribes was *in formam provinciae redacta*, the question arises how precisely was this achieved and how did the measures taken affect the status of settlements in the new province? There were two stages in the formation of the new province. The first was achieved by force of arms: Britain was brought *in dicionem populi Romani*, to quote again from the arch of Claudius. The second involved a legal process resulting in the formation of a *lex provinciae* or its equivalent, perhaps drawn up by Claudius on the spot in Britain, in consultation with a band of senators.[12] Claudius' settlement, like the *Lex Pompeia*, the *Lex Rupilia*, and the *leges provinciae* of Bithynia and Sicily,[13] may have included regulations concerned with the internal organisation of the *civitates* even if, initially, control of their affairs was to remain in the hands of their kings or possibly *praefecti civitatis*, 'district officers', appointed by Rome (see below). How the affairs of the *civitates* came to be ordered after this transitional period is hinted at by two inscriptions. The first, from the *civitas* of the Silures of southern Wales, probably organised by the Romans soon after their conquest by the governor Frontinus in the mid-70s, shows that their affairs had been entrusted to a council, *ordo*.[14] The second, from the territory of the Carvetii in Cumbria, shows that a certain Flavius Martius[15] was a *senator* (councillor) and *quaestorius*, that is ex-*quaestor*, one of the pair of financial officers in his *civitas*. There is no direct evidence for the other magistrates normal in Roman municipalities – the pair of judicial officials, *duoviri iuredicundo*, and *aediles*, who saw to the upkeep of public buildings – but they probably also existed. These three pairs of magistrates will have been annually elected by the tribesmen (*cives*).

The *ordo*, with whom all effective power lay, may have numbered 100. There is good evidence for this in the case of the settlements of Roman citizens (*coloniae*) but there is very little direct evidence for the *civitates*. In Gaul, the *ordo* of the *civitas* of the Treveri numbered 113 in AD 69,[16] although this number may have included *praetextati* (the sons of members of the council who will have been enrolled by the special *duoviri quinquennales* elected every five years, whose function was to revise the roll (*album*) of councillors and fill vacancies). On the other hand, at Tymandus, a village in Asia Minor which was given the status of a *civitas* at some time in the third century AD, there were, initially, only 50 *decuriones* (councillors), although it was hoped that later it would be possible to increase the number to 100.[17] We know that *decuriones* in the Roman *coloniae* were often required to maintain a house in the *colonia* itself (e.g. Tarentum)[18] or within a mile of it (e.g. Urso),[19] to act as security for public money that they might handle on election to magistracy. In the case of Tarentum, the size of the house is specified as 1,500 tiles (probably about 1,500 ft² or 140 m²). If a similar regulation applied in Britain, it seems likely that if a decurion did not possess a house of the modest size specified at Tarentum in the chief town of the *civitas*, it was enough that he should have a farm of comparable size anywhere in its territory. The *ordo* met in the chief town of the *civitas* (the term '*civitas* capitals' has been coined for them by John Wacher[20]), which in some cases certainly possessed its own local magistrates independent of the elected tribal ones, for example at Brough-on-Humber.[21] Brough (Petuaria), though a '*civitas* capital', ranked as a *vicus*, and this will have been the term for other towns in the territory of the *civitas* also having their own elected officers.

When did this 'municipalisation' of the *civitates* take place? In two cases we know that it was not immediate and that the monarchy was at first retained. The *civitas* of the Iceni of East Anglia had submitted voluntarily to Rome, and despite an abortive anti-Roman rebellion in

AD 47,[22] their monarchy was still in existence in 60 when the last king died and thus precipitated the Boudiccan revolt.[23] Similarly, Tacitus informs us that under the second governor, Ostorius Scapula (47–51), certain *civitates* were handed over to the British king Cogidubnus (or perhaps Togidubnus).[24] Cogidubnus ruled these *civitates* from Chichester, Noviomagus Regnensium, the 'New market of the people of the kingdom (*regnum*)'.[25] His presence inside the town is attested by a famous inscription,[26] and his palace just outside has been excavated by Professor Cunliffe.[27] It is conceivable that other *civitates* also continued to be ruled at first by kings – a case for the Dobunni has been argued by Professor Frere.[28] If the *civitates* did not at first continue to be ruled over by kings, one of two things may have happened: either the Romans 'imposed a council and magistrates' upon them as Corbulo did to the defeated Frisii in AD 47,[29] or they may have been administered for a time directly by the Romans through *praefecti civitatis*, an idea first put forward by Professor Frere,[30] and one that has found considerable favour. The kind of men selected for the post of 'district officer' were ex-soldiers, senior centurions and the like. Professor Frere[31] argued that the *praefecti* were withdrawn when the military garrisons of the original Claudian *provincia* were removed in the 70s. The fort sites were handed over for civilian use, and the *civitates* were, for the first time, allowed to run their own affairs. This conclusion was supported by the apparently Flavian date of many of the administrative buildings, the *basilicae* and the attached *fora*. Not too much weight, however, should be attached to this, since although it is certainly true that the presence of a forum and a basilica implies the possession of self-government, the opposite cannot be inferred from their absence: at Verulamium work on the forum and basilica was not completed until 79, as we know from the inscribed dedication,[32] but the town had almost certainly been self-governing for at least 20 years.[33] Again, at Wroxeter the forum and basilica were not built until AD 130,[34] although the *civitas* of the Cornovii had almost certainly had self-government since before the turn of the century.

PHYSICAL APPEARANCE AND FUNCTION

The most obvious feature of the *oppida*, in the area campaigned over by Vespasian, is their defences.[35] The fact that here at any rate their inhabitants still chose to live in what must often have been awkward and inconvenient sites should imply that the security offered by the *oppidum* was valued. After their incorporation within the province, the *civitates*

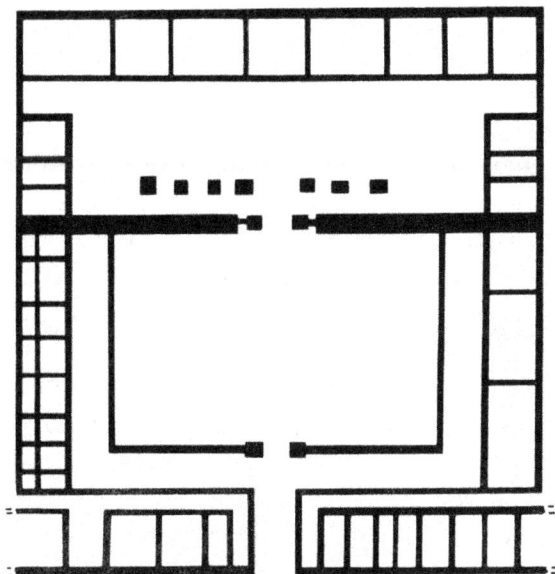

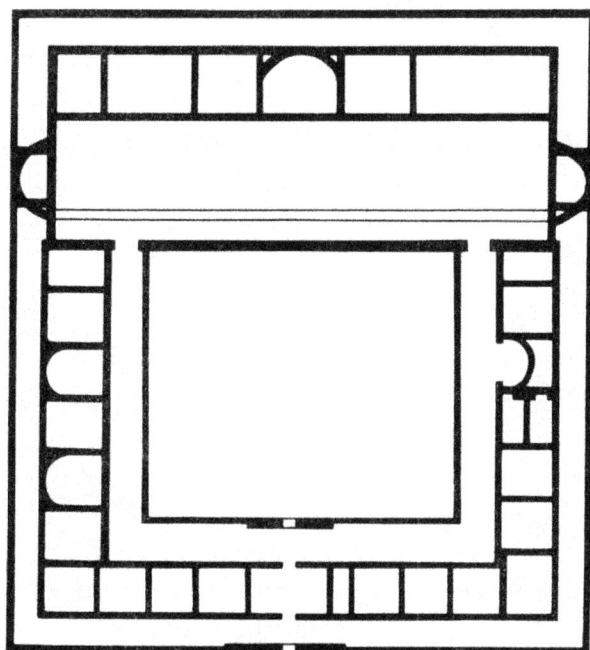

1 Headquarters building at Neuss, AD 70 (top), and forum and basilica at Silchester, late first century (bottom)

were deprived of the opportunity to make war on their neighbours, and the new tribal capitals and *vici* do not normally have defences. Winchester and Silchester are exceptions to this rule, and Wacher[36] has suggested that this may be because they were in territory added to the kingdom of Cogidubnus. When the new towns were provided with defences in the second century, they were built in turf and timber like the Roman fort defences built particularly in the preceding century. Urban defences of this type are exceedingly unusual in the empire.

It seems possible that some of the *oppida* may have functioned as markets (this, however, is something that only total excavation could prove), and they must certainly have dominated the surrounding countryside. But to call them 'administrative centres' would, presumably, be too formal a way of describing their relationship to the territory in which they lay. The new '*civitas* capitals' certainly acted as both markets and administrative centres, and to enable them to do so, they were provided with a market place and 'town hall' (forum and basilica). As Professor Atkinson long ago[37] pointed out, the standard plan of a forum and basilica in Roman Britain bears a striking resemblance to the headquarters building (*principia*) of a legionary fortress. In the case of the civic centre at Silchester and the legionary headquarters at Neuss, the comparison can be made not only between the plans but in overall dimensions also, especially if the external colonnade of the former is ignored (Fig. 1). The Romano-British forum-basilica is a distinct regional type, and its similarity to its military equivalent is not simply due to the derivation of the latter from civilian prototypes in north Italy, as has been argued.[38]

Turning to the living and working accommodation in the *oppida*, compared with that of the earliest Roman towns, circular huts were the norm and it is possible that some of these were used solely for working and others for domestic purposes. In size, the area varies from under 30 to 75 m² at Danebury,[39] while at Hod Hill huts average about 40 m².[40] As far as the new Roman towns are concerned, pride of place must still go to Professor Frere's excavations of the mid-first-century shops in *insula* XIV at Verulamium, where the comparison between the neat row of double units, with living accommodation at rear and workshop in front set behind a veranda, to a military barrack block is almost too good to be true (Fig. 2). For comparison in size with the native huts mentioned above, the rear rooms are 20 m² and the front rooms 30 m². Though the shops at Verulamium, with their heavy sleeper beams, were much more

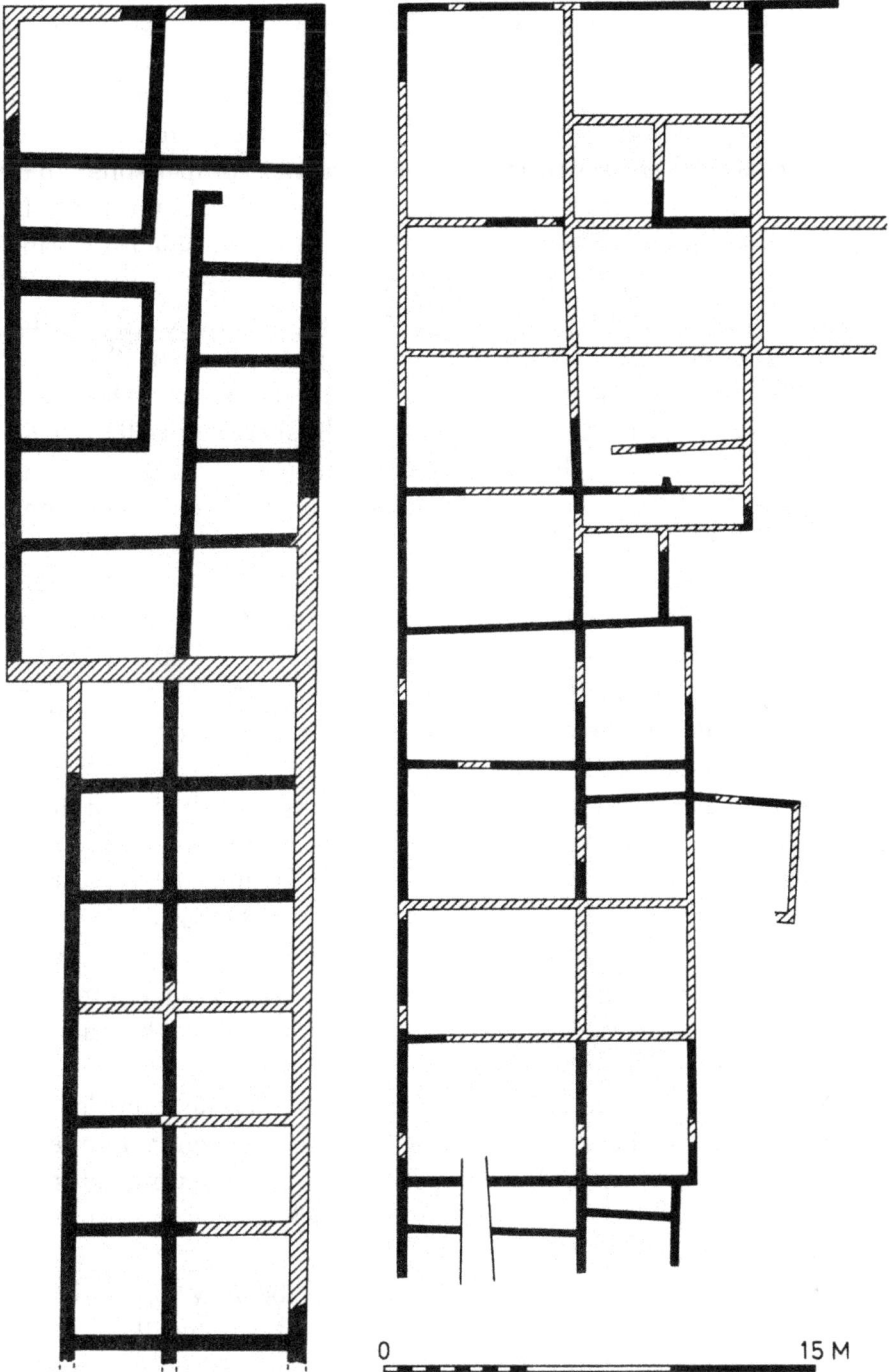

2 Barrack block at Caerleon, second century (left), and shops at Verulamium, mid-first century (right)

sturdily built than the Iron Age huts, the basic building technique in wattle and daub is the same.

Like the legionary fortresses, the new 'civitas capitals' were provided with baths and amphitheatres (rarely theatres). Though neither are particularly close to their legionary equivalents, comparisons can be made with the bath buildings regularly built for auxiliary forts and the simple amphitheatres which are occasionally found outside their walls. In the case of the baths, Roman technique and expertise must have been drawn upon, as it surely was for the construction of the gravity-fed aqueducts which supplied water to almost all the larger towns (Silchester is a rare exception). It goes without saying that no formal architectural provision was made for either bathing or public spectacles in the oppida.

We do not know whether religious sanctuaries regularly existed in the oppida, although the name Camulodunum may be taken to imply that there was a shrine of Camulos at Colchester, and the hillforts of Maiden Castle, South Cadbury and Danebury had shrines.[41] It is quite possible that religious sanctuaries existed in many other hillforts and that their sanctity survived for several centuries, so that during the pagan revival of the fourth century AD, temples to the old gods were re-established in them. The design of these temples, as of the temples built in the new Roman towns, was generally of the 'Romano-Celtic' type, with central cella surrounded by circular ambulatory, which probably goes back to a pre-Roman architectural tradition.[42] Roman religion in the 'civitas capitals' was accommodated in the small aedes, the central room in the row of offices built along one side of the basilica (see Fig. 1), the exact equivalent of the similarly-placed shrine of the standards in a legionary fortress. There was normally no capitolium, a temple of classical type built on a lofty podium, as is common in other cities in most of the western Roman provinces.

Finally, unlike the oppida, virtually all the 'civitas capitals', and some of the vici, had a street grid which must have been laid out early in the town's existence and which probably in all cases pre-dates the building of the forum-basilica complex, for which space was presumably reserved from the start.

In the surveying of the street grids of the new towns, in the planning of some of their earliest private buildings and their public buildings, in the subsequent construction of their defences, and the provision of a piped water supply, it is hard not to see the influence of military prototypes, and when we remember that there is good evidence for military expertise and assistance being employed in civil projects from the time of Marcus Aurelius,[43] it is hard not to believe too that the same thing had not already been happening in Britain from the AD 70s, if not earlier.

POPULATION

Our information here is extremely scanty, but George Boon[44] has estimated that the population of Roman Silchester, the only town in the province to have been completely excavated, was a mere 1,200. If there were originally some 300 huts in pre-Roman Hod Hill[45] with, on average, families of five per hut, one would arrive at a comparable figure of 1,500. About one in six of the huts at Hod have an 'annexe', and I.A. Richmond[46] suggests these belonged to an elite class.

SITING

The twenty *oppida* that were captured by Vespasian in southern Britain were presumably destroyed. In one case, Hod Hill, the Romans cannot have allowed the site to be reoccupied since a Roman fort was planted uncompromisingly in one corner of the hillfort. However, it would probably be going too far to claim, as R.G. Collingwood once did,[47] that the Romans deliberately moved the inhabitants down from the hill-top towns to the plain in Britain – or for that matter elsewhere. To take two classic examples of continuity: at neither Numantia in Spain or Alesia in Gaul, scenes of two bitter sieges by the Romans in the mid-second and mid-first century respectively, was there any shift in population, and at Sabora, in Spain, the inhabitants actually *petitioned* Vespasian to be allowed to move their town down from their awkward hill top and refound it on the plain.[48] Any shift in population is as likely to have been undertaken willingly by the inhabitants of the *oppida* themselves as to have been initiated by Rome. That there was a change in the sites of 'nucleated settlements' after the conquest is certain, though at Maiden Castle at least it was not immediate.[49] As Dr Webster has shown,[50] and Professor Rivet has reminded us,[51] the new settlements sprang up on the sites of abandoned auxiliary forts and legionary fortresses.

Professor Rivet,[52] elaborating the idea that for the first 30 years of their existence the *civitates* were administered by *praefecti*, has suggested that the commanders of auxiliary units doubled in this role; when the units were posted further to the west and north in the Flavian period, the fort sites, from which the *civitates* had once been administered, continued to be the seat of the tribal administration, only this was now in the hands of the tribesmen themselves. I have argued above that there is no evidence that the *civitates* remained so long under direct Roman supervision, nor is there any evidence that those *praefecti civitatis* of whom we have details elsewhere, were serving soldiers. Why then was there a shift in population to the abandoned fort sites?

The reason must surely be that the forts and their paid garrisons of men without women must have attracted civilians with an eye to the main chance. These settlements remained in existence even when the garrison moved on, and enjoyed the great advantage of being sited in a direct relationship to the Roman military road network. Their economic survival was assured as certainly as that of older *oppida* was doomed. There is no reason to suppose that the initiative to move the seat of tribal administration from one of the old *oppida* to the site of one of the new townships did not come from the tribe itself, although permission, together with the allocation of the deserted fort site to them, must have come from the governor as legate of the emperor. Where the transfer of the '*civitas* capital' was made, the opportunity was taken to give the whole site a new street grid. This only rarely happened for lesser towns. Only in a few cases does occupation of the pre-Roman native site continue, e.g. Verulamium, Silchester, and Colchester (as a Roman colony not strictly relevant here) – and in two of these, if not all three, the presence of a nearby Roman fort or fortress ensured that the site enjoyed good communications.

In conclusion, it may be instructive to look at the area between Hadrian's Wall and the Wall of Antoninus Pius in Scotland.[53] In AD 140, the governor Lollius Urbicus overran the area between the two Walls. Hill-top settlements like the *oppidum* of the Selgovae on Eildon Hill North were taken and not reoccupied, and a new fort was built on the abandoned Agricolan fort of Newstead nearby. The *civitas* of Votadini, on the other hand, may have submitted voluntarily; at all events Traprain Law, the main centre of the tribe, seems to have continued in existence. At the nearest Roman fort of Inveresk, a settlement (*vicus*) quickly sprang up outside the walls, as we know from recent excavations.[54] Inveresk may have had an administrative role, for the presence of an imperial procurator, Q. Lusius Sabinianus, is attested by finds of two inscriptions.[55] Then in *c.* 150, the first Antonine occupation of southern Scotland came abruptly to an end. Though the Roman hold on southern Scotland was re-established, it was never secure and may have been brief. But if matters had worked out differently, it seems reasonable to wonder whether the *vicus* at Velunia would not have replaced the *oppidum* at Traprain Law as the tribal centre, and whether the map of Roman Britain would not now have included an Isca Votadinorum in the far north – to match that other tribal centre, Isca of the Dumnonii, Exeter, in the south-west.

1   Tac. *Agr.* 21.
2   Hassall 1972, 861 n. 13.
3   Suet. *Vesp.* 4.
4   Branigan 1974.
5   Caes. 5.21.
6   Rivet 1977a, 45. The difficulty in finding a suitable word for native 'nucleated settlements' was felt by other classical writers: cf. Finley 1973, 123–4 referring to Strabo 3.4.13, 'In fact even those who assert that there are more than 1,000 cities in Iberia seem to be led to do so by calling the big villages cities (*poleis*)', and Pausanias 10.4.1, '... Panopus, a city of the Phocians, if one can give the name of city (*polis*) to those who possess no government offices, no gymnasium, no theatre, no market places, no water descending to a fountain, but live in shelters just like mountain cabins right on a ravine'.
7   *ILS* 216.
8   Suet. *Gaius* 44.
9   Tac. *Hist.* 3.45.
10   Allen 1944, 8.
11   Caes. 5.22.
12   Under the republic, the responsibility of organising new provinces lay with the Senate. When new territory was ceded to Rome, the Senate normally sent out a commission of ten of its members to draw up and issue a set of ordinances under which the new province was to be governed. This was known as the *lex provinciae* and was, in Roman constitutional terms, a *lex data* (i.e. a law that was 'given' or 'issued' rather than 'passed' by the Roman people on the motion of a magistrate). In some cases, the *lex provinciae* was issued not by a commission but an individual, e.g. the *Lex Pompeia* issued by Pompey to Bithynia by virtue of his proconsular *imperium*, and still technically a *lex data*: Magie 1950, 1231. Claudius may have acted in a similar way in the case of Britain. It is interesting to note (though it may be no more than coincidence) that he could have drawn on the assistance of no less than nine other senators: Frere 1978, 83 (excluding Vespasian, his brother Sabinus, Hosidius Geta and Aulus Plautius, all probably commanding legions, and Didius Gallus in command of the cavalry, but including Julius Planta, *ILS* 206, not mentioned by Frere). Alternatively, Claudius' settlement could have been ratified on his return to Rome or not drawn up until afterwards. Dio (60.23) says that in AD 44, after Claudius' British triumph, the Senate voted that 'all the agreements that Claudius or his lieutenants should make with any peoples should be binding, the

same as if made by the Senate and People', but this is more naturally taken as Frere (1978, 82) takes it, to apply to treaties with independent states including those tribes in Britain that had not yet been conquered.

13 Abbott and Johnson 1926, 48–9, 72.

14 *RIB* 311, dated to shortly before AD 220.

15 *RIB* 933.

16 Tac. *Hist.* 5.19.

17 *ARS* 270.

18 *ARS* 63, sect. 3.

19 *ARS* 114, sect. 91.

20 Wacher 1975, 22.

21 *RIB* 107.

22 Tac. *Ann.* 12.31.

23 Tac. *Ann.* 14.31.

24 Tac. *Agr.* 14; *RIB* 91 + add.

25 For the most recent discussion of the Roman name of Chichester, see Rivet 1970, 50; Jackson 1970, 78–9. Both reject the interpretation given here of the epithet attached to Noviomagus (which is given as 'Regentium' in the *Ravenna Cosmography*), explaining it as the name of a British tribe.

26 *RIB* 91 + add.

27 Cunliffe 1971, 13–14.

28 Frere 1978, 85–6.

29 Tac. *Ann.* 11.19.

30 Frere 1978, 235.

31 Frere 1978, 235.

32 Wright 1956.

33 Tacitus (*Ann.* 14.33) says that it was a *municipium*, a town whose inhabitants had Latin Rights, at the time of the Boudiccan revolt in 60/1.

34 *RIB* 288.

35 It should be noted that in some areas, notably south-eastern Britain, *oppida* with massive continuous defences ('hillforts') had never been common, and in other areas, where they did exist, had ceased to be occupied by AD 43. I am grateful to Professor Cunliffe for drawing my attention to this point.

36 Wacher 1975, 260.

37 Atkinson 1942, 345–62.

38 Goodchild 1946.

39 Cunliffe 1976, 202–5.

40 Richmond 1968, 19–25.

41 Cunliffe 1978, 320–3.

42 Lewis 1966, 1–55.

43 MacMullen 1963, 32 ff.

44 Boon 1974, 62.

45 cf. Richmond 1968, fig. 3.

46 Richmond 1968.

47 Collingwood and Myres 1937, 187–8.

48 *ILS* 6092.

49 Wheeler 1943, 241. The samian pottery from Bagendon (probably the chief tribal centre of the Dobunni) appears not to start until AD 20–30 and then ends abruptly around 43: Dannell 1977. But only a minute portion of this vast site has been excavated and it would be rash to argue that all occupation must have ceased at this date.

50 Webster 1966.

51 Rivet 1977b.

52 Rivet 1977b.

53 Jobey 1976, esp. figs 10.1–2.

54 Goodburn 1978, 416–18.

55 *RIB* 2132; *Britannia* 8 (1977), 433, no. 3. The inscriptions describe Sabinianus as procurator *Aug* rather than *Augg*, which should mean that he served in Britain during the reign of a single emperor rather than the joint rule of two emperors – that is to say, he was not at Inveresk when Scotland was temporarily reoccupied in the early third century under Severus and Caracalla.

13

THE *TABULARIUM* IN PROVINCIAL CITIES

Originally published:
'The Tabularium in Provincial Cities', in P. Wilson (ed.), *The Archaeology of Roman Towns: Studies in Honour of John S. Wacher*, 2003, Oxford, 105–10

HAVING EXCAVATED WITH John Wacher at Cirencester 40 years ago, it seemed appropriate that this tribute should either be devoted to some aspect of Roman urbanisation or to Romano-British corn-drying ovens and their use for malting floors and the production of beer. Of these subjects, both dear to John's heart, malting floors have been adequately dealt with,[1] and so I shall turn to urbanisation. But what stone has John, the *doyen* of Roman urban archaeologists in this country, left unturned? Something epigraphic, perhaps, and not specifically British? The subject that I have chosen is the *tabularia*, or record offices, in provincial cities and the sort of documents, *tabellae* or *tabulae* (literally 'tablets'), that they might have once been expected to have contained. These must once have existed in Roman Britain, but as far as I know there is only one direct hint – from Wroxeter. Yet by looking at the evidence from other urban sites in the Latin west, it should be possible to see the sort of range of documents that will once have been kept in the record offices of the *coloniae*, *municipia*, and *civitas* capitals of Britannia also. What I will have to say will mostly be concerned with *coloniae*, of which, until the elevation of the *canabae* of York to the status of 'colony' early in the third century, Britain possessed three – Colchester, Lincoln and Gloucester – since the evidence from and for the *coloniae*, the most Roman of all the new city foundations in the west, is richer than from other types of city. But to a greater or lesser extent what can be said about the *coloniae* will have applied to other types of city foundation also.

Before looking at the evidence for *tabularia* and their contents outside Britain, brief mention should be made of that from Wroxeter. In 1927, Donald Atkinson excavated the forum and basilica in the *civitas* capital of the Cornovii.² This complex was erected under Hadrian, as we know from an elegant if fragmentary dedication to that emperor erected by the *Civitas Cornoviorum*.³ It was originally set up over the entrance to the forum, and some of the bases of the columns of the colonnade that once surrounded the forum *piazza* can still be seen *in situ*. Closing off the forum at the opposite end was the town hall or basilica, a great aisled structure with no doubt tribunals or speakers' platforms at one or both ends from which the magistrates of the Cornovii will have dispensed justice and perhaps those of Viroconium itself also – for no doubt, like Petuaria (Brough-on-Humber), the capital of the Parisi, it had its own magistrates in addition.⁴ What these were is not known but they will have reflected the city's status, not only as capital of the *civitas* but also as an urban community in its own right, whether, like Brough, a *vicus* (village or urban community) within the *civitas*, or, like Verulamium, a *municipium* but also the *civitas* capital of the Catuvellauni. On the side of the basilica furthest from the forum was a range of rooms. The central one may have served as a the shrine for the *tutela* or protecting goddess of the city or the *civitas*, if not Rome's own Jupiter, as may have been the case at Calleva Atrebatum, Silchester.⁵ The term for this centrally placed shrine may have been *aedes* or *capitolium*, on the analogy of the shrine of the standards in the headquarters buildings of Roman forts, to whose plan the majority of Romano-British forum and basilica complexes bear a striking resemblance (compare the *aedes principiorum* at Reculver;⁶ also the *capitolium* at Aalen (Germany) in Raetia⁷). There is also just a hint that a small room in the north-west corner of the building may have been the *tabularium*, for here Atkinson found a bronze diploma or certificate of citizenship issued by Hadrian to one Mansuetus, a time-expired veteran who had served in the *Cohors II Dalmatarum*.⁸ Such documents normally remained in the possession of the beneficiary, but in the present case it seems that Mansuetus who, though he came originally from Trier or its vicinity, had chosen to retire to Viroconium or somewhere nearby, put his on deposit at the *tabularium* for safe keeping in the *civitas* capital of the Cornovii.

If the existence of *tabularia* in Britain is thus only hinted at, their existence elsewhere is better attested. *Tabularii*, presumably the functionaries in charge, are attested at two cities in southern Gaul,

Vaison-la-Romaine (Vasio, a Roman city though of uncertain status)[9] and Vienne (Vienna, a Roman *colonia*).[10] An inscription from Aix-en-Provence (Aquae Sextiae, a Roman *colonia*),[11] besides giving a variant term for the man in charge of the *tabularium*, indicates something of the status of the holder of such an office, for a man described as *tabularii publici curator*, Keeper of the Public Record Office, later held the post of *quaestor*, a magistrate in charge of the city treasury, which virtually proves that he was of free birth since freedmen were normally debarred from holding such an office. A third term, *scriba tab(ularii)*, is found at Sarmizegethusa, *Colonia Ulpia Traiana*, in Dacia.[12] *Tabularius*, *curator*, or *scriba*, such then was the style or title by which the keeper of the city record office was known. It remains to examine the sort of documents that remained in his charge. Of these many may have been archives written on perishable material, such as wax tablets or papyrus rolls, but copies of some, including the most important were, like the military diploma referred to above, *aere incisa*, inscribed on bronze, or alternatively on marble for public display. We shall look in turn at seven classes of document, starting with the most important, that which confirmed the status of the city and laid down the laws by which it was to be governed.

1. THE *LEGES DATAE* – CITY CONSTITUTIONS

a) Coloniae

Pride of place in the documents in the *tabularium* of *coloniae* like Colchester, Gloucester or Lincoln will have gone to the city's constitution, often rather loosely referred to in English as its 'charter'. The technical name for this was a *lex data*, literally a 'given law', a term that refers to the manner in which *coloniae* were founded under the republic. After the expulsion of the kings, the people at Rome were in theory sovereign and it required a law (*lex*) passed by the popular assembly (*comitium*) before a colony could be established. Such a law was known as a *lex rogata*, an 'asked-for law', because a magistrate, often on the advice of the Senate, came before the *comitium* and literally asked the people to pass the necessary legislation. The *lex* would then be known by the name of the proposer (i.e. the *Lex Antonia* cited below) and will have appointed an official *deductor*, perhaps a provincial governor as in the case of Munatius Plancus at Raurica (Augst) and Lyons,[13] to 'lead forth' (*deducere*) the colonists. The *deductor* will have been empowered by the original *lex* to issue or 'give' a law or *lex coloniae* to the new citizens that will have laid down the actual constitution of the place – the respective roles of magistrates, people and council – and the 'bylaws' by which it will have been administered. The *deductor* and any executive officer who remained on the spot to supervise the actual setting up of the colony henceforth became hereditary 'patrons'.

A precious survival from the last days of the republic is part of the *lex data* of Urso (*Colonia Julia Genetiva Ursonensis*) in the Spanish province of Baetica.[14] The new colony was grafted onto a pre-existing town that had supported Pompey during the Civil War; its foundation was probably one of the unfinished bits of business that Mark Antony undertook in the name of Caesar after the dictator's death – at any rate the *lex rogata* under which the colony was founded was known as the *Lex Antonia*. Though the *Lex Coloniae Juliae Genetivae* relates specifically to Urso, it is exceedingly likely that it will have been virtually identical to the *leges datae* of *all* colonies. We think this partly because of similarities in the law to other pieces of general legislation (e.g. the *Lex Julia Agraria*[15]), and partly because of the almost exact correspondence between one section of the Urso Law[16] and the fragment of the *lex* of the *colonia* at Lauriacum in Austria dated 212/17.[17] The passage in question states that in an emergency, the two chief magistrates (*duoviri*) have the power, on a simple majority vote of the council, with no quorum necessary, to arm citizens, *incolae* (resident aliens), and *contributi* – the original inhabitants of the area who supported the *colonia* through taxation and so on, but did not have citizen rights, such as the Salassi at Aosta or the Trinovantes at Colchester (but the Carni and Catali attributed to the colony at Trieste enjoyed far more favourable conditions and could even stand for office[18]). Such alarms and excursions were real possibilities as is shown by the assault on Colchester during the Boudiccan revolt of AD 60/1 or that on Cologne during the Batavian revolt of 69. At Lauriacum, the appointment of a *praefectus* as a stand-in is also envisaged in the absence of the *duoviri* on a military expedition.

For anyone seriously interested in the administration of a Roman colony – any Roman colony – the *Lex Coloniae Juliae Genetivae*, even in its mutilated form, is clearly of the utmost interest. Though a clear statement as to the actual constitution of the place is among the missing sections, it can be inferred from the body of the document, while the respective roles can be deduced of: 1. the citizen body; 2. the magistrates, two judicial magistrates, *duoviri iure dicundo*, and two *aediles*, who oversaw public works; and, above all, 3. the council, whose members were known as *curiales* or *decuriones*, or collectively as *senatus* or *ordo decurionum*. This was the real power at Urso, whose decrees were flouted by citizen or even magistrates at their peril or at any rate at the risk of the enormous fine of 10,000 *sesterces*.[19] What survives deals with such matters as: the mechanics of the election of magistrates by the people, organised here into 'tribes';[20] the paid staff of the magistrates – 36 in all, ranging from heralds to soothsayers;[21] the games in honour of the Capitoline Triad and Venus Genetrix, which magistrates were required to stage, and details of expenditure involved;[22] the obligation of individual citizens to contribute time and resources to public works;[23] much on regulations concerning the role of the *duoviri* in administering criminal justice;[24] and the function of the *duoviri quinquennales* appointed every *four* years (the Romans reckoned inclusively!) in maintaining an up-to-date register (*album* – see below) of the members of the council. At least in some *coloniae*, the *quinquennales* were appointed in addition to the *duoviri iure dicundo*, when the group as a whole were known as *quattuorviri*.[25] There will also have been a periodic census of the whole citizen body. In the case of the *colonia* at Colchester, an inscription records an outside *censitor*, Munatius Bassus, seconded from the command of an auxiliary regiment for the purpose.[26] Among other things covered by the *Lex Coloniae Juliae Genetivae* are: municipal priests – there were three pontiffs and three *augures*;[27] regulations on tile-works belonging to the *colonia* of Urso,[28] such as we know were operated by the *colonia* at Gloucester;[29] the provision whereby decurions had to own a house within a mile of the city[30] – a similar provision existed at Tarentum where the house had to be within the town or its territory, and its size is specified as equivalent to '1,500 tiles',[31] probably *c.* 40 x 40 ft; the prohibition on cemeteries within the town;[32] regulations concerning the surplus water from aqueducts after the primary needs of the *colonia* have been supplied, and the requisition of land, provided it did not impinge on a pre-existing building, for the construction of new aqueducts;[33] and reserved seating in the amphitheatre and theatre for decurions, magistrates, priests and visiting Roman dignitaries.[34]

Under the empire, there was no need for an enabling *lex rogata* to be passed before a *colonia* was founded, for the emperor had the constitutional right to issue laws (*dare leges*) direct, a right that was since the time of Vespasian at any rate presumably defined in his *lex de imperio*.[35] It was by virtue of this right, for example, that the emperor could draft *constitutiones* conferring citizenship on large groups of time-expired veterans from the provinces – or issue the *leges coloniarum* to new foundations. In this he was acting technically in the role of *deductor*, although the actual direction of affairs will have been left in the hands of the governor, *legatus Augusti pro praetore*, serving as the emperor's deputy.

b) Municipia
Just as a colony was a 'detached' part of Rome and its immediate surroundings, so a *municipium* can be thought of as a detached part of Latium, whose citizens enjoyed the *ius Latii* ('the right of Latium', or simply *Latium*) which gave them limited reciprocal rights in their relations with the greatest of all the cities of Latium – Rome. By the imperial period at least, such status was awarded to certain favoured pre-existing communities in the provinces. The most dramatic example of the granting of the *ius Latii* or *Latium* is under Vespasian in Spain where, according to Pliny,[36] *universa Hispania* received the grant – estimated at up to 400 communities – while a further 100 or more were already *coloniae* of Roman Citizens or *municipia* with Latin Rights. The actual grant was followed up by the issue of *leges datae* inscribed on bronze, a lengthy process that carried on into the reign of Domitian. Major portions of three examples have been found, the last as recently as 1981 when six out of an original ten tablets were discovered south-east of Seville, which preserve over half of the *lex data* of the *municipium* of Irni, the so-called *Lex Irnitana*.[37] Each of the tablets was 3 ft wide by 2 ft high, so that when set up on the wall of a public building the *lex data* would have covered a strip some 30 ft long. Each tablet contained 3 columns of 50 lines each, and as there will have originally have been 30 columns, the total document will have consisted of 1,500 lines, perhaps about 15,000 words – or 30 typed pages of A4. The evidence of the *Lex Irnitana* is partly duplicated, partly supplemented by the surviving portions of two other *leges datae* from two other *municipia* in Baetica, Malaca[38] and Salpensa.[39] Curiously, the texts relating to these two places are complementary, for some of the provisions missing in one document are preserved in the other and vice versa. They were found together in 1850 and had been carefully hidden – but in what circumstances who can say?

In addition to the *leges* of Irni, Malaca and Salpensa, there are portions of two further *leges municipiorum*, Seville[40] and Cortegana

(Huelva),[41] so that though a complete composite text cannot yet be reconstructed, we are extraordinarily well informed about the organisation of the *municipia* of Baetica, and, by analogy, elsewhere.[42] Space does not permit a proper treatment of this material, which deals with everything from municipal elections[43] to manumissions and the appointment of guardians to orphans.[44] From the documents, we know, for example, that the popular assembly at Malaca was divided into *curiae*, an archaic division of the Roman people. Mention should be made too of the section in the *Lex Salpensa*[45] on the granting of Roman citizenship to ex-magistrates and their families – but no more new citizens to be created than the number of magistrates 'proper to be elected', i.e. probably six – a pair each of *duoviri*, *quaestores* and *aediles*. That is to say Salpensa, and by extension the other new *municipia*, enjoyed the so-called Lesser Latin Right, *Latium minus*, in contrast to the Greater Latin Right, *Latium maius*, where all members of the council were awarded this status. (This is made clear in a passage in the *Institutiones*[46] of the second-century AD Roman jurist, Gaius). An example of the latter was Thisiduum in the Bagradas Valley in Tunisia, as we know from an inscription referring to the *municipes et decuriones C(ives) R(omani)*.[47] Finally, there is a lot of information about drawing up legal agreements between the *municipia* and contractors, *mancipes*, for the collection of dues and the like, the furnishing of sureties, *praedes*, whose property had to be scrutinised by inspectors, *cognitores*, with the final contract posted by the *duoviri* during the year in which the contract had to run 'so that it may be read on level ground in whatever place the decurions or *conscripti* ('the enrolled', or 'enlisted', an alternative for councillors) may determine'. Just such notices, the so-called *merides* documents, survive for the Colony at Arausio (Orange), discussed below (under section 7, 'Contracts'). Copies of past contracts will surely have been kept in the municipal *tabularium*.

c) Civitates peregrinae

A *civitas peregrina* was a tribal or city state in the provinces which lacked either Roman Citizenship or Latin Rights. The *Civitas Cornoviorum* was a *civitas peregrina*. Was there a *Lex Cornoviana* in the *tabularium* at Wroxeter, or, if not a *lex*, some legal instrument which served as such, or did the constitution of the Cornovii remain unwritten, like the constitution of Great Britain? As far as I am aware there is no evidence on the point, though under the republic the internal organisation of nominally self-governing provincial communities was regulated to some extent by a *lex provinciae* (drawn up after the province was organised), so it would not be totally inconceivable that the implications of the *lex* were spelled out in some form of document issued to individual communities. However, it is not certain whether such 'provincial laws' continued to be issued when new provinces were established during the imperial period, although a case of sorts has been made for Roman Britain.[48]

2. *FASTI* – ANNUAL ROLLS OF MAGISTRATES

The Latin words *fastus* and *nefastus* are adjectives applied respectively to days of good omen and days of ill omen, days on which judgements literally *could* or *could not be spoken*. From such a specific meaning the plural *fasti* came to mean the calendar on which such days were marked, and then, more specifically, the lists, kept year by year, of the annual magistrates whether at Rome or in the provinces with sometimes, additionally, a brief record of major happenings in the relevant community or in the world outside. Municipal *fasti* were published by Hermann Dessau from four different places,[49] and a fifth is known from Cupra Maritima south of Ancona on the Adriatic coast of Italy[50] – it records the death of Gaius Caesar in AD 3/4. The earliest comes from Venusia on the Via Appia as it crosses over the Appenines into Apulia and covers the years 34–28 BC, and mentions important campaigns such as the *bellum Actii* or the fact that Octavian and Agrippa held a *lustrum* or purge of the Senate in 28 BC. The latest comes from Ostia and covers the years AD 83–92. The format is in all cases the same: first come the consuls, and in some cases the suffect consuls, followed by the *duoviri* (or *duoviri quinquennales*) of the local city, followed by the *aediles* (magistrates concerned with public works) and, if the city has them, *quaestores* (treasurers).

3. *ALBA* – ROLLS OF MEMBERS OF THE COUNCIL

The Latin adjective *albus* means 'white', and in the neuter form, *album*, refers either to a wooden tablet covered in light or white wax or possibly to a white-painted board. There survive two *alba* from the later empire listing the decurions or *curiales* in order of precedence. The earlier is the album of Canusium[51] in central-southern Italy near Venusia, a community that was granted colonial status under Marcus Aurelius. It begins:

> In the consulship of Lucius Marius Maximus for the second time and Lucius
> Roscius Aelianus [AD 223], the *IIviri quinquennales* saw to it that the names
> of the decurions be inscribed on bronze.

The album starts with the names of 31 senators of Rome who are patrons
followed by 8 equestrian patrons, some of whom are also decurions
of the colony itself. There follows the *ordo* of the decurions proper: 7
decurions who are ex-*quinquennales*, 4 who had been co-opted among the
quinquennales – the number 11 of these senior councillors is suspiciously
close to that of the 10 *decemviri* (or *decemprimi* or, in the Greek east,
dekaprotoi), presidents of the 10 *decuriae* into which the *curia* (senate or
council) was divided. These are in turn followed by 29 ex-*duoviri* (some
have been *duoviri* twice), 19 ex-*aediles*, 9 ex-*quaestores* (i.e. about half
the number of *aediles*, which suggests that there was only 1 *quaestor* at
Canusium), and 32 *pedani*, people at the *pes* (foot) of the list who had not
held office, for a grand total of 100. The *pedani* are, however, followed by
25 *praetextati*, young men who wore the *toga praetexta*, and who could be
enrolled as places fell vacant.

The second album[52] comes from Timgad in Algeria, Trajan's colony
of Thamugadi. The album can be dated on internal evidence to the mid-
fourth century. Space does not allow a full analysis, but it starts, as in the
album of Canusium, with the names of 14 patrons; next comes the *curator
civitatis*, originally an official appointed by the emperor on an *ad hoc* basis
to supervise the internal running of cities that had got into administrative
difficulties but by now a permanent official. The list of the *ordo* proper
begins with current magistrates, two *duoviri*, two *aediles* and one *quaestor*,
and holders of priestly offices – an interesting survival in the nominally
Christian empire of the fourth century. There would then have followed
the list of the council proper, but only the names of 12 ex-*duoviri* survive
before the text breaks off. A number of men have the letters EXCT after
their names, an abbreviation which has been expanded to *exactor*, 'tax
collector',[53] but is more probably short for *excusatus*, 'exempt'.[54] Either
would be appropriate in a fourth-century context when the collection of
taxes for the central authority became the responsibility of the *curiales*,
and both this and the stratagems whereby people sought to avoid paying
taxes became the subject of much legislation.

4. *ACTA* – THE MINUTES OF MEETINGS OF THE COUNCIL

None survive as such but large sections of what must have been the official record of the deliberations of the council were sometimes incorporated in the published versions of decrees of that body, e.g. in the standard formula (or variants), *quid de ea re fieri placeret, ita censuerunt*, 'what was pleasing to be done in this matter, so they decided', occasionally written out in full, but usually abbreviated to the initial letters.[55] Thus an inscription from Trieste[56] concludes a long introductory section with the letters QFPDER for *quid fieri placeret de ea re ita censuerunt*, 'what was pleasing to be done in this matter, so they decided', and continues 'with Calpurnius Certus first giving his opinion' (*primo censente Calpurnio Certo*). The motion proposed by Certus then follows, and the text concludes with 'they decided' (*censuerunt*).

5. *DECRETA* – DECREES OF THE COUNCIL

An inscription on the base of a statue from Caerwent[57] records the fact that it was set up by the *Res Publica Civitatis Silurum*, the 'republic' or 'commonwealth' of the *civitas* of the Silures, *ex decreto ordinis*, 'as a result of the decree of the council'. In this case, as in the very common abbreviation found on the bases of numerous honorific statues, LDDD – *loco dato decreto decurionum*, 'the place (for the statue) having been granted by decree of the decurions' – the original decree of the council is merely alluded to. The full wording of decrees themselves, along with the deliberations of the council (see above), will have been preserved in the *tabularium*, and in fact the wording of 65 examples are given by Sherk[58] in his collection of municipal decrees of the Roman west. Decrees will have ranged from the honorific, like the Trieste and Caerwent inscriptions, to decrees appointing patrons or, in the case of *civitates peregrinae*, delegates to the provincial council.

6. *FORMAE* – MAPS OF CENTURIATED LAND

In the *tabularium* will have been kept a copy of any survey of the city's territory that may have been made. Such surveys will have been produced where land had been allocated to the legionary veterans settled in military colonies. Under the republic, the agricultural territory of the colony, whether originally purchased, confiscated, or taken from a defeated enemy and so land belonging to the Roman State, *ager publicus*, was often if not always divided up by grids of roads and field tracks, *limites* and *decumani*, and boundary ditches, *fossae limitales*,[59] into great blocks of land called *centuriae* because they contained 100 *heredia* or two *iugera* plots (a *iugerum* was 240 x 120 Roman feet or about two-thirds of an acre). A complete *centuria*, in Roman terms, normally measured 20 x 20 *actus* (the *actus* being 120 Roman feet) or 700 x 700 metres. 'Centuriation', as the practice is called, became increasingly rare under the empire and there is no absolutely certain example of centuriation in Britain, although it would not be surprising to discover that it had once existed in the vicinity of the three primary colonies of Colchester, Gloucester and Lincoln.

Three actual cadastral surveys or parts of them inscribed on marble survive from Orange in the Rhone valley.[60] A detailed treatment of these fascinating documents is beyond the scope of this article, and it is enough to make three observations: 1. the centuriated grid is imposed on the schematic outline of topographical features – roads and rivers; 2. each square was designated by a unique grid reference related to the two main axial roads, the *kardo* and the *decumanus*, and is labelled as being so-many squares DD or SD, *dextra* or *sinistra decumanum*, right or left of the decumanus, and so-many squares VK or CK, *ultra kardinem* or *cis kardinem*, beyond or on this side of the kardo; 3. the earliest survey at Orange lists the status of the land in each *centuria*, how much land has been handed over to the colonists exempt from land tax (*tributum soli*) in accordance with the privileged status of the veterans, and how much belonged to the colony as a whole. In the latter case, the names of the lease-holders were given and how much they paid. Finally, the amount of each *centuria* that remained the property of the Roman state is also given.

The Orange documents were set up on the walls of a public building near the theatre, with master copies of the original surveys preserved in the *tabularium*. These will regularly have been inscribed on bronze, and the fragment of an actual example has recently come to light in Spain.[61]

7. CONTRACTS AND LEASES

As mentioned above (under section 1b), the *leges datae* of *municipia*, and no doubt *coloniae* too, give detailed regulations of how agreements between the civic authorities and contractors, *mancipes*, are to be drawn up. Among other provisions was the requirement that details of contracts be posted, and we can be sure that the actual originals of contracts, for past as well as current years, would be carefully preserved in the *tabularium*. Examples if not of the originals but of the permanent copies engraved, like the cadastral surveys, on marble also survive from

Orange. These are the so-called *merides* documents.[62] That they were inscribed on something as durable as marble can be explained by the fact that the agreements were permanent, being made *in perpet(uum)*, as is stated in the texts themselves. They appear to be leasing agreements for 'portions' (the Greek word *merides*, singular *meris*, is used) perhaps of a colonnade, presumably to shopkeepers or possibly middlemen who subcontracted. The formulae used are in each case identical. The texts give: 1. the length of the *meris* concerned; 2. the annual rate per foot; 3. the total amount payable; 4. the name of the contractor (*manceps*); and 5. the name of the surety, *fideiussor*. Somewhat similar is a third class of document which deals with the leasing of urban plots, *areae*, belonging to the colony which had been occupied illegally, to the people who were 'squatting' on them.

We began and so we shall finish with Wroxeter. Sometime in the second century, the civic centre went up in flames, and in the conflagration the goods that were for sale in the forum colonnade slid from their counters and fell into the gutter – here stacks of samian cups or mortaria, there bundles of whetstones. The men whose livelihoods had been so dramatically ruined could have been, and probably were, tribesmen of the Cornovii themselves, but here, in Viroconium, their own local market town, as the world over, nothing came free. We can be sure that, like their counterparts at Orange, they paid for their pitch; just as those who benefited from the surplus water provided by Wroxeter's ingenious water distribution system also paid (at Venafrum in central Italy detailed regulations survive for the management of the city's water supply by the council, including the charging for supplying private consumers during 'off-peak' hours[63]). We can be certain, too, that all was carefully documented by the *tabularius*, *curator*, *scriba* or whatever title was employed by the official in charge of the record office, in the little room off the basilica at Wroxeter. If Roman Britain lacks the wealth of epigraphic evidence that survives for some other provinces and Italy itself, the similarity of institutions across the western empire should allow us to fill in the gaps, at least to some extent, by analogy.

1   Reynolds and Langley 1979.
2   Atkinson 1942. See also Wacher 1995, 366.
3   *RIB* 291.
4   *RIB* 707.
5   Boon 1974, 59, 113–14.
6   *JRS* 51 (1961), 191–2, no. 1.

7   *AE* 1986, 528.
8   *RIB* II.1, 2401.8.
9   *CIL* XII, 1283.
10 *AE* 1952, 73.
11 *CIL* XII, 525.
12 *IDR* III.2, 386 = *CIL* III, 7975.
13 *ILS* 886.
14 *ARS* 114.
15 *ARS* 91.
16 *Lex Col. Jul. Gen.* ch. 103.
17 *ARS* 278.
18 *ILS* 6680, col. 2.
19 *Lex Col. Jul. Gen.* ch. 129.
20 *Lex Col. Jul. Gen.* ch. 101.
21 *Lex Col. Jul. Gen.* ch. 62.
22 *Lex Col. Jul. Gen.* chs 70–1.
23 *Lex Col. Jul. Gen.* ch. 98.
24 *Lex Col. Jul. Gen.* chs 61, 95–6, 102.
25 See *ARS* 63 n. 2.
26 *ILS* 2740.
27 *Lex Col. Jul. Gen.* chs 66–8.
28 *Lex Col. Jul. Gen.* ch. 76.
29 Heighway and Parker 1982; *RIB* II.5, 2486–8.
30 *Lex Col. Jul. Gen.* ch. 91.
31 *ARS* 63.
32 *Lex Col. Jul. Gen.* chs 73–4.
33 *Lex Col. Jul. Gen.* ch. 99.
34 *Lex Col. Jul. Gen.* chs 66, 125, 127.
35 *ARS* 136, though the clause granting the right to *dare leges* is in fact missing; Brunt 1977.
36 Pliny *NH* 3.30.
37 González 1986; Galsterer 1988.
38 *ARS* 191.
39 *ARS* 192.
40 *ARS* 193.
41 *ARS* 194.
42 Richardson 1996, 191–210.
43 *Lex Malacitana* chs 51–60.
44 *Lex Salpensa* chs 28–9.
45 *Lex Salpensa* ch. 21.
46 Gaius *Institutiones* 1.96.
47 *ILS* 6781.
48 Hassall 1979b, 250 n. 2.
49 *ILS* 6123–6.
50 *CIL* IX, 5290 = Degrassi 1937, 245.
51 *ILS* 6121.

52 *ILS* 6122; Leschi 1948.
53 For the expansion *exactor*, see Jones 1964, 728.
54 *Excusatus* written in full occurs on a second fragment of the album from Timgad, *ILS* 6122a, in the phrase [*a*]*edilici non excusati*, 'not exempt from the functions of *aedile*'.
55 *ILS* III, index 15, 785.
56 *ILS* 6680.
57 *RIB* 311.
58 Sherk 1970.
59 *Lex Col. Jul. Gen.* ch. 104.
60 Piganiol 1962; Salviat 1977.
61 Clavel-Lévêque 1993.
62 Piganiol 1962, 325–96.
63 *ARS* 136.

14
ALTARS, CURSES AND OTHER EPIGRAPHIC EVIDENCE FOR RELIGION IN THE PROVINCE

Originally published:
'Altars, Curses and Other Epigraphic Evidence', in W. Rodwell (ed.),
*Temples, Churches and Religion: Recent Research in Roman Britain, with
a Gazetteer of Romano-Celtic Temples in Continental Europe*, BAR British
Series 77 (1), 1980, Oxford, 79–89

ALTARS AND DEDICATIONS

ONE OF THE commonest types of inscribed object found in Britain, or for that matter any province of Rome's empire, is the religious altar. At its simplest it takes the form of a rectangular block of stone of a height greater than its width, bearing on its front face an inscription naming, firstly, the deity to whom the altar was dedicated, and, secondly, the name of the man or woman by whom the dedication was made. More sophisticated examples can be elaborately carved, often having a raised circular area with hollowed upper surface on the top – the *focus* (hearth), on which a small fire could be lit. This fire would consume food offerings: sacred cakes, pieces of meat from a victim sacrificed before the altar, or a drop of wine. On each side of the *focus* stylised bundles of firewood are sometimes represented. Just such an altar is depicted in one of the scenes which flank the famous 'building inscription' found at Bridgeness, the eastern terminal of the Antonine Wall.[1] It shows a solemn sacrifice, not of one victim, but of three: a pig (*sus*), sheep (*ovis*) and bull (*taurus*), the rite of the *suovetaurilia*. The three animals, vigorously, if crudely, portrayed, stand before an altar onto which an officiant pours a libation of wine from a sacred vessel, *patera*. Nearby an assistant plays a double pipe: Roman ritual decreed that if a man who was conducting a sacrifice heard any sound of ill omen during the performance of the rite, he was required to start the whole proceedings again from the beginning. This is why a pipe was played and why priests sometimes looped a fold of their garments over the head so as to cover the ears and prevent such unwelcome sounds from being heard. In the case of this particular sacrifice the rite is watched by a group of men whose identity is revealed by the inscription on the flag that one of them holds aloft on a pole: they are the men of Legion II Augusta.

The Bridgeness carving is almost certainly the portrayal of an actual sacrifice and as such is unique as far as Roman Britain is concerned. But if less explicit iconographically, the inscriptions from some of the altars found in Britain do provide an insight into why and how individuals, or groups like the men of Legion II, came to make sacrifices to the gods, of which these blocks of stone with their dedicatory inscriptions are the surviving testimony.

Offerings or sacrifices were made to the gods (the corollary of setting up an altar) for many reasons, which, at the risk of oversimplification but for convenience, can be divided into six classes.

a) Offerings made in fulfilment of a vow (ex voto)
Sacrifices were most commonly made as a result of a 'bargain' struck between a man or woman and a god or goddess. The former would promise or vow to set up an altar and perform a sacrifice if the deity undertook to help him in some specific way in return. Once the god had performed his part of the bargain, the mortal was bound to fulfil his vow. In Latin, the technical term for the initial 'declaration' of the promise or vow was called the *nuncupatio* – the 'payment' of the vow, the *solutio*. Those curses (*defixiones*) concerned with theft (discussed below) can include an undertaking, analogous to the *nuncupatio*, to reward the god whose aid is being sought, with a percentage of the value of the stolen goods if he should help in their recovery. Similarly, we know from the calendar of religious festivals to be kept by units of the Roman army[2] that every 3 January, Roman auxiliary regiments vowed sacrifices to various deities, foremost of whom was Jupiter, for the welfare of the emperor and the eternity of the Roman Empire during the next twelve months, at the same time fulfilling last year's vow by making the appropriate sacrifices. This practice may account for the large number of altars set up to Jupiter, probably annually, and found ritually buried near the parade ground at the auxiliary fort of Maryport;[3] compare the similar

series from Birdoswald.[4] An inscribed tablet, also from Maryport, set up by a civilian, a certain Antonianus, recording the dedication (in verse) of a shrine,[5] concludes with what is in effect a *nuncupatio*: Antonianus promised that, if he was successful in a business enterprise, he would rededicate his poem 'with golden letters', perhaps substituting the chisel-cut letters of the inscription with the gilded bronze letters which, as we shall see, could be purchased at temple sites throughout the province.

The dual concept of *nuncupatio* and *solutio*, the vow and its fulfilment, is also explicitly referred to in the extremely common formula found at the end of dedicatory inscriptions, *votum solvit laetus libens merito*, 'paid his vow joyfully, freely and deservedly'. The phrase and its variants is almost always abbreviated to its initial letters, VSLLM, though it is written out in full in one inscription[6] and almost so in another.[7] In the abbreviated form, it is in fact so common that the question arises whether it is not used sometimes simply as a synonym for *posuit*, 'set up (this altar)', or *donum dedit*, 'gave the gift (of an altar)'. We can be certain, however, that expressions such as *quod voverat*, 'the (offering) that he had vowed',[8] or *votum quod promisit,* 'the votive gift which he/she had promised', found twice,[9] really do indicate that a vow had actually been made. And the same will be true of dedications which include the phrase *ex voto*, 'in accordance with a vow',[10] while the unique phrase *ex nuntio*, 'in accordance with an announcement',[11] if it does not refer to a divine instruction (see class d, below), could refer to the *nuncupatio*.

b) Thank offerings for favours received

The gods did not limit their favours to those who had vowed to reward them, and when a man had experienced divine favour it was natural for him to express his gratitude. Thus an altar was set up by an officer at Carlisle *ob res trans vallum prospere gestas*, 'on account of success across the Wall',[12] while from Bollihope Common, Stanhope, comes the well-known dedication to unconquered Silvanus by an elated officer who had just killed a boar of exceptional size which had been hunted unsuccessfully by a number of his fellows.[13] Similarly, the equestrian commander of the garrison at the fort of Benwell on the Wall set up an altar to the local Celtic god, Anociticus, after his elevation to senatorial rank and his appointment as quaestor designate.[14]

c) Offerings made in anticipation of favour

Into this category come the numerous altars set up *pro salute*, 'for the health of' someone, be it the emperor, a master or patron, or a relative. Sometimes, of course, a vow was made to set up an altar if an ill friend, etc. recovered. Dedications of this type will fall into the first category discussed, and will conclude with the letters VSLLM.

d) Sacrifices made at divine instigation
Most altars were erected, ostensibly at any rate, *ex voto*, where the dedicator himself takes the initiative by promising a sacrificial gift in return for divine aid (class a, above). However, the initiative could come from the gods. Men might set up altars as a result of a divinely-inspired vision, *ex visu*,[15] or be warned to set them up by a dream, *somnio praemonitus*.[16] Divine instigation is also indicated by the phrases *ex iussu (dei)*,[17] *ex imperio*,[18] and *monitu*,[19] where the exact nature of the 'orders', 'commands', and 'warnings' is not clear. An inscription[20] from Halton Chesters on Hadrian's Wall, on the other hand, leaves us in no doubt as to the nature of the portent. It reads simply *fulgur divom*, 'lightning of the gods'. This will have come from the wall of a precinct or enclosure built around the precise spot where a bolt of lightning had fallen. Such a shrine was known as a *bidental* (from the Latin *bidens*, 'with two teeth'), either an allusion to the forked lightning itself or to the sheep which traditionally had to be sacrificed on the spot. Within the precinct, which was open to the sky, the blackened fragments of whatever had been struck were ritually buried, which explains the phrase *fulgur conditum* found inscribed on the walls of other *bidentalia* elsewhere in the empire. The *bidental* was sacred ground and none were allowed to enter.[21]

e) Sacrifices made as a result of divine consultation
When the lightning bolt fell at Halton Chesters, there was a recognised procedure which had to be carried out. Sometimes, however, it was felt necessary to consult experts to ascertain what it was that the gods required of one. Two altars from the province were set up after consultation of oracles. One from Ribchester[22] was erected *ex responsu dei*, 'in accordance with the answer of the god', presumably after he had been posed a question through a priestly intermediary. Another, from Housesteads,[23] was set up by the First Cohort of Tungrians, *Diis Deabusque*, 'to the gods and goddesses', *secundum interpretationem oraculi Clari Apollinis*, 'in accordance with explanation of the oracle of Apollo of Claros'. This is one of six similar dedications found at different places in the empire. Their erection is explained by Professor E. Birley

as the result of an order of Caracalla who, at a time of ill-health, had consulted this particular oracle.[24] The word *interpretatio* in a religious sense recalls the use of the word *interp(r)etiante*, acting as an *interpres*, to describe one of the two dedicators of a mosaic floor at the shrine of Nodens at Lydney,[25] a dedication made *ex stipibus*, 'from offerings'. If *interpres* means 'interpreter of dreams' (or oracles), then the abbreviated words used to describe the second man concerned may be *prae(positus) rel(igionum)*, 'superintendent of rites'. Be that as it may, the province has produced one undoubted expert in divination, Marcius Memor, who was attached to the temple of Sulis Minerva at Bath.[26] He was an *haruspex* (inspector of entrails, literally 'gut-gazer'). The 'science' of haruspicy had been taken over by the Romans from the Etruscans, who believed that the gods made their will known by causing blemishes to occur on the liver of sacrificial victims, as well as by sending thunder-bolts. Both the heavens and the liver were divided by the Etruscans into zones, each sacred to a specific deity or group of deities. To aid him in his work, the *haruspex* might own a model liver of bronze marked out and labelled like a phrenologist's china head, as we know from the famous find of an actual example from Piacenza. The interpreter of lightning (*fulgurator*) incidentally had similar aids, and we possess the text of a 'thunder calendar' translated into Greek in Byzantine times from a Latin translation of an Etruscan original. This calendar purports to give the outcome to be expected if it thunders on any particular day in the Rome area. The Halton Chesters inscription cited above shows that even in far-off Britain the warnings given by thunder were just as likely to be taken seriously as those indicated by an inspection of the entrails apparently were at Bath.

f) Anniversary dedications

The Dura Calendar[27] lists the anniversaries to be celebrated throughout the year by the Twentieth Cohort of Palmyrenes, anniversaries which will also have been kept by all other auxiliary units throughout the empire. The New Year dedications made by the garrisons at Maryport and Birdoswald have already been mentioned in the discussion of *ex voto* offerings, and there is a limited amount of other direct evidence to show that other anniversaries were indeed remembered in the province. Thus, 21 April was the traditional anniversary of the founding of the City of Rome, and this will have been the date on which an altar was set up to *Dea Roma n(atali) eius*, 'on her birthday', at High Rochester.[28]

Another birthday, that of the Emperor Augustus on 23 September, was celebrated by Legion II stationed at Caerleon, appropriately enough in view of the title Augusta that the legion bore;[29] and a month later, on 19 and 20 October, the unit stationed at Papcastle in Cumbria is shown by two dedications bearing these dates to have celebrated the *armilustrium*, the festival in honour of Mars when weapons were ritually cleaned and purified at the end of the campaigning season.

Anniversary dedications like these will have tended to have been public occasions celebrated by Roman army units, guilds or communities. As such the body concerned will normally have paid for the dedications and any offerings made at the same time. Sometimes this is made clear by phrases such as *ex stipibus*, 'from offerings',[30] or *a(ere) col(lato) a vikanis*, 'with money collected from the villagers'.[31] Where, however, an individual pays for the cost on behalf of his fellows, this also is made clear, for example by the common phrase *d(e) s(uo) p(osuit)*, 'set this up at his own expense'. Compare the phrase *sine stipibus aut collationibus*, 'without offerings or collections (having been made)', found on three dedications from Silchester.[32]

Before turning to other types of epigraphic evidence, something should be said briefly about the deities addressed on altars and dedicatory inscriptions. These can be Classical, native Celtic, or imported from the Rhineland or the eastern provinces, and it would be impossible, even briefly, to do justice to this large and cosmopolitan pantheon. However, a few general observations can be made, particularly as to the choice of deity honoured. Sometimes this is obvious: the homesick officer serving out his time in North Britain sets up an altar to a whole group of deities including *Fortuna Redux*, Fortune the Home-bringer;[33] Greek doctors worship the saviour gods, Asklepius, Hygeia and Panakeia.[34] But the Roman soldier or official was anxious, too, to placate the local gods, even if he was ignorant of their names, and might set up an altar simply to the *genius loci*, 'spirit of the place'. It is thus not really so surprising to find the newly-created senator, Tineius Longus (mentioned above), setting up an altar to the Celtic Anociticus.[35] The other side of the picture was that native Britons, like the Caledonian Lossio Veda could, on a single dedication,[36] associate a native Celtic god with the Victory of the Emperor Alexander Severus. Indeed, it was common for both Celt and Roman to regard each others' gods merely as versions of their own familiar ones. The process of identifying a native god with a Roman equivalent is called by Tacitus[37] the *interpretatio Romana*. For Britain, the classic example of this phenomenon is that of Sulis, the goddess of the thermal springs and health resort at Bath, who was equated with the Roman Minerva, goddess of wisdom and healing. But of all the Roman deities it was Mars, himself equated with the Greek god of war Ares but in origin an Italian god of fertility and vegetation, who was most frequently 'identified' on inscriptions from Britain with local Celtic equivalents. There are some twenty dedications to Mars either coupled with a Celtic deity, as Mars Cocidius,[38] or with a Celtic epithet attached, as Mars Rigonemetos, 'King of the Grove'.[39] Mercury was also extremely popular with the Celts, and dedications to him are also common, but he is hardly ever equated with a native equivalent, probably because he was regarded as a Celtic deity in his own right.

The inscriptions dealt with so far are mostly, though not exclusively, found on altars, but a number of other classes of object carrying inscriptions are of equal importance in assessing the nature of religious beliefs and practices in Roman Britain. They can be divided into three groups: votive gifts, charms and amulets, and curses.

VOTIVE GIFTS

Gifts to the gods could range from the substantial, such as the arches, perhaps over the entrances to the sacred enclosures, presented to the Celtic god Viridios at Ancaster[40] or the hybrid Mars Rigonemetos at Nettleham, Lincs.,[41] to quite small gifts. Some of these might still be costly, for example the silver vessel dedicated to the Numina Augustorum and perhaps Mars found at Hastings,[42] or to the Matres from the Backworth hoard.[43] On one of the Uley curses a gold ring is promised to Mercury[44] – an actual example of a silver ring, dedicated to the Celtic Sucellus (named in the dative), comes from York,[45] and of a gold one, dedicated to the Matres, from the Backworth hoard.[46] Cheaper than silver or gold would be vessels of pewter,[47] and cheapest of all simple earthenware pots, no doubt often originally containing food, with the name of the deity to whom the offering was being made scratched on the outside. The eastern god Dolichenus and the Celtic Toutatis were both honoured in this way,[48] while Mercury received such gifts no less than three times.[49]

Such simple and inexpensive gifts could be made by anyone, but for those with sufficient money who wished to present something more elaborate, a range of specially-made articles was available for purchase at 'gift shops' attached to the more important shrines and temples. Six classes of gift seem to have been commonly available. Most of them are treated by Martin Henig elsewhere,[50] but since many carry inscriptions it is appropriate that they should be mentioned here, though not discussed in detail.

a) Stone reliefs

It is worth noting here that in some cases a place had been specially prepared for an inscription that was never in fact cut; for example below the relief of the four mother goddesses re-used in the late Roman riverside wall at London,[51] and below a fragmentary relief from Chilgrove.[52] This suggests that the works concerned were made for purchase (when the purchaser's name would have been inscribed on them) rather than specially commissioned.

b) Bronze figurines[53]

Small figurines could have been bought at temple sites, either as votive gifts or to take away to be housed in a domestic shrine. They do not normally carry inscriptions, but some do,[54] including the famous Foss Dyke Mars,[55] whose inscription is discussed below.

c) Repoussé plaques

Silver plaques from Bewcastle (Fanum Cocidi) bear a representation of the god Cocidius with dedicatory inscriptions,[56] while an example from the temple of Nodens at Lydney has the figure of a dog who appears to have been associated with the god in some way.[57]

d) Votive leaves or feathers

These are triangular in shape and examples from Britain have been found made from sheet bronze, silver and even gold (from Stonea).[58] They are often pierced by a small hole at the base, either for attaching the object with a nail to a board or wall, or for suspension with a thread. They are decorated with a herring-bone pattern produced in repoussé over the greater part of their surface in imitation of the veining of leaves or the barbs of feathers. In the simpler examples this is all, but others carry representations of gods also in repoussé and, or, inscriptions.[59] There are three particularly important groups of finds from the province: one leaf found (with other ritual objects) at Stony Stratford was dedicated to Jupiter and Vulcan;[60] seven from Barkway, of which three[61] were dedicated to Mars Alator, Mars Toutatis and Vulcan; nineteen leaves from Water Newton, where six[62] carry Christian Chi-Rho symbols flanked, with one exception, by the Greek letters alpha and omega, and one[63] has an additional longer inscription, to which reference shall again be made at the end of this article.

e) Ansate plaques (i.e. having triangular handles on each side)
These carry dedicatory inscriptions which could quickly be produced to order with a punch.[64]

f) Bronze letters with nail holes
These could presumably be purchased individually and attached to a large wooden plaque, thus producing an imposing dedicatory inscription quickly and relatively cheaply. Sometimes the bronze is gilded (recalling the 'golden letters' of the Maryport inscription,[65] cited above), which would make the effect even more impressive.[66]

Charms and amulets

It has been noted above that it would have been possible to buy bronze figurines at temple sites not simply as votive gifts but to take away, and the same was probably true of other objects. R.P. Wright[67] has suggested that three octagonal rings, found at Owslebury, Hants. (two examples) and Yatton, Somerset (one example), all carrying variants of the same garbled inscription, may have been bought by visitors to the same temple site. A further example can now be added from a site in eastern Britain, Caistor St Edmund,[68] which gives what may be the most accurate version of the text so far recovered, IXSAOSC, although its meaning remains obscure. The same explanation can be advanced for the series of rings carrying the letters TOT found in Yorkshire and Lincolnshire.[69] Here the Celtic god To(u)tates may be intended. Other deities whose names occur on rings are Venus,[70] Mer(curius),[71] and, as above, the mother goddesses, Matres. We have already seen how rings *could* be presented as votive gifts (an explanation that is certain when the name of the deity is written in full and given in the dative), but most rings will have been made with the intention of being sold to pious people for personal use, the wearer no doubt considering that he or she was under the special protection of the deity concerned. Amulets of other kinds might be carried with the idea of providing similar protection. There are three examples from Britain, all carrying magical texts in Greek letters inscribed on gold sheet, from Caernarvon,[72] York,[73] and a temple site (Woodeaton).[74] Magical symbols could be cut on other material too, on haematite,[75] on a lapis lazuli intaglio,[76] and a bloodstone.[77]

Finally, for completeness, mention may be made of phallic charms.[78] The phallus was a common apotropaic symbol. In the form of a pendant, for example, it was often attached to the harness of Roman cavalry horses. It could also be carved on walls or paving stones, when it is sometimes accompanied by an inscription.[79]

CURSES (*DEFIXIONES*)

The charms and amulets described in the last section were valued because they were held to protect their possessor from the malice of his enemies. But if someone had already suffered at hostile hands it was still possible to seek redress or vengeance, and in the Classical world there was a recognised procedure for invoking divine aid against enemies or rivals, whether known or unknown. The invocation was normally written on a thin sheet of lead with a sharp instrument such as a stylus. Sometimes the text[80] or individual words[81] would be written backwards, or with alternate lines inverted as on an unpublished curse from Eccles in Kent. Once the text had been written, the sheet would be folded or rolled up, after which it might be secreted in a hiding place, just as his enemies were said to have secreted curse tablets in the walls and under the floor of the house in which Germanicus was staying;[82] alternatively the tablet might be fixed to a tree or doorpost by driving an iron nail through the soft metal. A leaden plaque from Clothall (Herts.) has as many as five large holes in it for iron nails, of which four of the latter survive.[83] This ritual act will have been regarded as 'fixing' the curse firmly on its intended victim. The Latin verb *defigo*, 'pin down', used of the operation comes to mean 'curse', and actually occurs on a number of British curse texts.[84] The noun derived from it, *defixio*, is the normal Latin word for a curse tablet.

The gods of the underworld, or the deities who presided over particular shrines or temples, might be invoked for a variety of reasons, such as theft (the most usual reason in British curses) or unrequited love.[85] In North Africa, the partisans of particular chariot factions regularly cursed the horses of rival teams, and one British curse[86] has been thought (incorrectly, in the present writer's opinion) to fall into this category. Enemies could be cursed in very specific detail. Between them, the writers of two curses from the province[87] attack their victims' heart, liver, lungs, intestines, veins and marrow, as well as, in more abstract terms, their life, mind, memory, words and thoughts. On other *defixiones* the gods are asked to strike their victims dumb and dissolve them like water,[88] not to allow them to speak,[89] or drink, sleep, walk, etc.[90] Yet others simply and comprehensively ask the gods to withhold health, *sanitas*.[91] Three British curses include phrases in which the words *sanguine suo*, 'with his [i.e. the victim's] life blood', occur.[92]

One aspect of some curse texts already referred to in discussing the announcement (*nuncupatio*) of a vow is the way in which the deity invoked can be offered a reward if he furnishes the required aid. Three curses from Britain, all directed against thieves, promise a proportion of the value of the goods stolen if they are recovered. In one case it is a tenth,[93] in another a half,[94] and in the last, two-thirds, a third to Mercury and a third to Silvanus.[95]

This 'conceptual' aspect of some curse texts is reflected in the legalistic jargon of many of them, which strongly suggests that they were written by professional scribes, who knew how to impress credulous clients. Thus the abbreviated phrases, *ssdictus* and *sstus*, for *supradictus*, 'afore-mentioned', and *suprascriptus*, 'afore-written', occur together four times on one of the Uley curses,[96] and the latter was also used by the writer of another British curse.[97] Three British curses directed against unknown enemies include a comprehensive clause, *si mulier si mascel*, 'whether female or male',[98] or *si vir si femina*, 'whether man or woman',[99] or variations.[100] The phrases on the two sides of the Uley curse[101] are also followed by the additional clause *si servus si liber*, 'whether slave or free'.

CONCLUSIONS

The professional scribes who wrote out curses to order at temple sites like Uley (where something of the order of 200 *defixiones* have been found) were not the only people to make a living out of the pilgrims who visited the shrines and temples of Roman Britain. First and foremost will have been the priests and priestesses, like Calpurnius Receptus at Bath[102] and Diodora at Corbridge,[103] together with other members of the temple staff, such as the *haruspex* at Bath, Marcius Memor, mentioned above. But in addition there will have been a large number of supernumeraries, including the craftsmen who produced the various altars and votive gifts or souvenirs available for sale – men like Civilis and Iuventinus, who signed small votive reliefs found at rural sites in the south-west;[104] Glaucus, who signed the base of a bronze statuette found at Martlesham, Suffolk;[105] Cintusmus the *aerarius*, coppersmith, who, perhaps in gratitude to the custom brought by the god, made a dedication to Silvanus Callirius at Colchester;[106] or Celatus, another *aerarius*, who made the Foss Dyke Mars at a cost of 100 *sesterces* for clients, inclusive of 3 *denarii* (12 *sesterces*) worth of bronze.[107] Such men, like Demetrius the silversmith whose workshop turned out model shrines of Diana of the Ephesians,[108] made a respectable living from the sale of votive gifts and keepsakes. But whereas at Ephesus in the first century AD, Demetrius saw Paul and the Christian doctrine that he preached as a threat to his very livelihood and roused the mob against him, the silversmiths of Britain in the fourth century did not overreact in the same way, regarding their Christian neighbours simply as a new source of patronage. The votive silver leaves in the Christian treasure from Water Newton must have been made by men who had learnt their trade at pagan shrines, and even the language of the inscription on one on them[109] echoes that on one of the pagan plaques from Lydney.[110] The religious 'gift shop' did not die with the end of paganism, and indeed is still with us.

Addendum: Since this article was written, the second volume (in fascicules) of *The Roman Inscriptions of Britain*, encompassing personal belongings and similar, bearing inscriptions, has been published.[111] Inscriptions in that volume, equivalent to those published in the original article, are referred to in the notes below.

1   *RIB* 2139.
2   Fink 1971, 422, no. 177.
3   *RIB* 815–34; Wenham 1939; Jarrett 1966.
4   *RIB* 1874–96.
5   *RIB* 2059.
6   *Britannia* 5 (1974), 462–3, no. 9.
7   *RIB* 1594.
8   *RIB* 2066.
9   *RIB* 307; *Britannia* 7 (1976), 386, no. 35; cf. *RIB* 215, the payment of six *denarii* 'which I have promised', *pro voto solute*.
10 *RIB* 458, 584, 888, 2157.
11 *Britannia* 8 (1977), 433, no. 30.
12 *RIB* 2034, cf. 946, 1142.
13 *RIB* 1041.
14 *RIB* 1329.
15 *RIB* 153, 760, 1778; *JRS* 57 (1967), 203, no. 5.
16 *RIB* 1228.

17 *RIB* 1022, 1024.
18 *RIB* 2091.
19 *RIB* 320.
20 *RIB* 1426.
21 *OCD*².
22 *RIB* 587.
23 *RIB* 1579.
24 Birley 1974; Euzennat 1976.
25 *RIB* II.4, 2448.3.
26 *JRS* 56 (1966), 217, no. 1.
27 Fink 1971, 422, no. 117.
28 *RIB* 1270.
29 *RIB* 327–8.
30 *RIB* II.4, 2448.3.
31 *RIB* 899.
32 *RIB* 69–71.
33 *RIB* 812.
34 *RIB* 461; *JRS* 59 (1969), 235, no. 3.
35 *RIB* 1329.
36 *RIB* 191.
37 Tac. *Germ.* 43.3.
38 *RIB* 993.
39 *JRS* 52 (1962), 192, no. 8.
40 *JRS* 52 (1962), 192, no. 7.
41 *JRS* 52 (1962), 192, no. 8.
42 *RIB* II.2, 2414.37.
43 *RIB* II.2, 2414.36.
44 *Britannia* 10 (1979), 343–5, no. 4.
45 *RIB* II.3, 2422.21.
46 *RIB* II.3, 2422.9.
47 *RIB* II.2, 2417.1–44.
48 *JRS* 47 (1957), 234, no. 41; *Britannia* 9 (1978), 478, no. 41.
49 *JRS* 45 (1955), 149, no. 31; *JRS* 51 (1961), 197, no. 42; *JRS* 53 (1963), 167, no. 55.
50 Henig 1980.
51 Merrifield 1977, 383 ff., pl. 17.IIIa.
52 *JRS* 55 (1965), 219–20, pl. XVII.1.
53 Green 1976.
54 e.g. *RIB* 213, 582.
55 *RIB* 274.
56 *RIB* 986–7.
57 *RIB* 307.
58 *Britannia* 11 (1980), 403–4, no. 2.
59 Toynbee 1978.
60 *RIB* 215, cf. 216–17.
61 *RIB* 218–20.

[62] *Britannia* 7 (1976), 386, no. 34.
[63] *Britannia* 7 (1976), 386, no. 35; *Britannia* 8 (1977), 448, item e.
[64] *RIB* 187, 191, 194–5 (all from Colchester), 305, 662–8, 1077 (gold); *Britannia* 5 (1974), 461, no. 2; *Britannia* 8 (1977), 427, no. 7.
[65] *RIB* 2059.
[66] *RIB* 53, 86, 198, 238–9, 242, 997, 1071, 2218; *JRS* 57 (1967), 203, nos 2–3; *Britannia* 2 (1971), 289, nos 1, 4.
[67] Wright 1970.
[68] *Britannia* 2 (1971), 300, no. 64.
[69] e.g. *RIB* II.3, 2422.37, and other examples that have been discovered since the original article was written.
[70] *RIB* II.3, 2422.14.
[71] *Britannia* 3 (1972), 360, no. 47.
[72] *RIB* 436.
[73] *RIB* 706.
[74] *Britannia* 1 (1970), 305, no. 1.
[75] *JRS* 54 (1964), 180–1, no. 18.
[76] *Britannia* 3 (1972), 356, no. 22.
[77] *RIB* II.3, 2423.16; illustrated in Boon 1974, 163, 171–2, fig. 24.1.
[78] Turnbull 1978.
[79] *RIB* 631, 872, 983, 2157; *Britannia* 6 (1975), 285, no. 3; *Britannia* 9 (1978), 474, no. 10.
[80] As on *RIB* 221.
[81] As on *RIB* 154.
[82] Tac. *Ann.* 2.69.
[83] *RIB* 221.
[84] *RIB* 6–7, 221.
[85] *RIB* 154.
[86] *RIB* 323.
[87] *RIB* 7; Turner 1963, 123.
[88] *RIB* 154.
[89] *RIB* 7.
[90] *Britannia* 3 (1972), 363–7, appendix.
[91] *RIB* 306a; *Britannia* 10 (1979), 340–2, no. 2; perhaps *RIB* 7.
[92] *RIB* 323 (accepting R.G. Collingwood's interpretation rather than that of R.P. Wright); *JRS* 48 (1958), 150, no. 3; *Britannia* 4 (1973), 325, no. 3.
[93] Turner 1963, 123.
[94] *RIB* 306a.
[95] *Britannia* 10 (1979), 343–4, no. 3, side b.
[96] *Britannia* 10 (1979), 343–4, no. 3.
[97] Turner 1963, 123.
[98] *JRS* 48 (1958), 150, no. 3.
[99] *Britannia* 10 (1979), 343–4, no. 3, side b.
[100] Turner 1963, 123; *Britannia* 10 (1979), 343–4, no. 3, side a.
[101] *Britannia* 10 (1979), 343–4, no. 3.
[102] *RIB* 155.

103 *RIB* 1129.
104 *RIB* 99, 132.
105 *RIB* 213.
106 *RIB* 194.
107 *RIB* 274.
108 *Acts* 19.23.
109 *Britannia* 7 (1976), 386, no. 35.
110 *RIB* 307.
111 *RIB* II.

15
LONDON: BRITAIN'S FIRST 'UNIVERSITY'? EDUCATION IN ROMAN BRITAIN

Originally published:
'London: Britain's first 'university'? Education in Roman Britain', in J. Clark, J. Cotton, J. Hall, R. Sherris and H. Swain (eds), *Londinium and Beyond: Essays on Roman London and its Hinterland for Harvey Sheldon*, CBA Research Report 156, 2008, York, 117–20

INTRODUCTION

I TAKE AS my starting point an imperial rescript of the Emperor Gratian issued in the year 376[1] to the Prefect of the Gauls saying that *rhetores* (literally rhetoricians or orators) and *grammatici* (grammarians) of the Attic and Roman learning should be established in each metropolis, that is the capital of each of the provinces in his prefecture – a vast administrative fief which included the diocese of Britain. London was not only the metropolis of the province of Maxima Caesariensis, it was also the capital of the diocese of Britain,[2] and it would be good to put 'London University' in the same league as, say, Trier, which besides being an imperial capital was the metropolis of Belgica Prima and had two *grammatici* (one Latin and one Greek, though the latter post was not always filled) and two or three *rhetores*,[3] or Bordeaux, the metropolis of Aquitania Secunda with its six *grammatici* and four *rhetores* so pithily described by the poet Ausonius in the *Professores*. And what applies to London should also apply to the other capitals of the constituent provinces of the British diocese, York and Lincoln, as well as Cirencester and, perhaps, Carlisle.[4]

So much for the claims of the so-called 'older universities', such as the *parvenu* Oxford with its spurious claims to a foundation by King

Alfred or, even more ridiculous, the apocryphal King Mempric![5] But intention is one thing and compliance is another. Were the terms of the rescript ever enforced? Nor does the rescript of 376 necessarily imply that there were not *grammatici* and *rhetores* operating from centres like London at a period before that date. It is time to look at the evidence, such as it is, for 'university education' in Roman Britain – or indeed the evidence for education of any kind in Britain during the Roman period.

<h2>THE BACKGROUND</h2>

Over 80 years ago, Theodore Haarhoff of the University of Cape Town produced a study of pagan and Christian education in Gaul in the last century of the western empire.[6] Haarhoff distinguished three levels of education. First is the teaching of the basic skill of reading. The teacher of such skills was known as a *litterator*, that is the one who taught the child his *litterae*, letters. Secondly, there was the teacher of the literary classics of Greece and Rome, foremost among which were the works of Virgil. The teaching of the classics was entrusted to a *grammaticus* – or, as one might call him, a grammar school teacher. Thirdly, there was a *rhetor*, the teacher of rhetoric, the nearest equivalent to a university professor. Educational establishments like those at Bordeaux, the famous Maeniana at Autun, or the imperial capital at Trier, had on their establishments both *grammatici* and *rhetores*.

<h2>PRIMARY EDUCATION – THE ROLE OF THE *LITTERATOR*</h2>

There is both indirect and, surprisingly, direct evidence for the activities of the *litterator* in Roman Britain. The former consists of the widespread evidence for literacy in the province in the scratching of the names of owners on pottery vessels and other graffiti. Direct evidence for the work of the *litterator* and their pupils comes at both ends of the social scale. At the lower end are the graffiti on tiles scrawled by workers before the clay had become too hard.[7] Some at least of these appear to have been informal writing exercises performed by the 'students' of unofficial *litteratores* 'during the lunch break'. They include alphabets, in some cases copied out a couple of times.[8] Another probable example is the personal name Bellicanus four times repeated on a tile found at Caerwent.[9]

A tile from Silchester[10] is inscribed with four (or five) personal names followed by the words *conticuere omnes*. These words are part of the line, *Conticuere omnes intentique ora tenebant...* 'They all fell silent and steadfast held their gaze...', found at the beginning of the second book of the *Aeneid*,[11] and describe Dido and her court, when Aeneas begins to tell the tale of his escape from Troy. This Virgilian tag is echoed by another from a later book of the epic poem, also used as a writing exercise, but from a very different social milieu. It was found at Vindolanda, where the medium employed for writing was ink used with pens on wooden tablets, and here the *litterator* was no workman but a member of the household of Flavius Cerealis, the equestrian commander of the *Cohors IX Batavorum* at Vindolanda, and the pupil, the tribune's young son. The child has copied out the beginning of a line, *Interea pavidam volitans pinnata (per) u(r)bem...* 'Meanwhile winged (rumour) fluttering through the trembling city...',[12] in capitals on a wooden tablet[13] and the *litterator* has written *segn(iter)*, 'sloppy', against it.

SECONDARY EDUCATION – THE ROLE OF THE *GRAMMATICUS*

The purpose of secondary education was to acquaint the student with a knowledge of the literary classics, especially the works of Virgil, the foremost of Latin poets. If direct evidence for *grammatici* themselves in Roman Britain is problematical (see below), the fruits of their labours are well attested, especially among the wealthy villa-owning class of the fourth-century diocese of Britain.[14] As young men in their teens, the 'landed gentry' acquired a lasting love of the classics. Proof of this comes from the decoration of the walls and floors of the villas, which were adorned with scenes drawn from classical mythology and literary epic. In fact, of course, the evidence from the walls has almost entirely disappeared, and it is only through meticulous excavation and restoration that the frescoes which once adorned the walls of such establishments are now coming to light.[15] However, the words *Bina manu l...* 'With two [*or* both] hands...' (referring to a warrior grasping a spear) painted on a wall at the Roman villa at Otford, Kent, shows what might have been, for these are the first two words (and part of a third) of a line, *Bina manu lato crispans hastilia ferro*, 'Brandishing in his hands two spears of broad head', which occurs twice in the *Aeneid*, once describing Achates[16] and the other the Italian King Turnus.[17] Appropriately enough, nearby were found fragments of painted plaster depicting a figure holding a spear, as well as other fragments of letters and human figures. As Sheppard Frere and Roger Tomlin reasonably conclude, 'it seems probable that a corridor was decorated with scenes from the *Aeneid* with appropriate quotations as captions'.[18]

The sort of scenes that would have been depicted are shown on the famous mosaics from villas at Low Ham in Somerset[19] and Frampton in Dorset.[20] The former shows in strip cartoon fashion the arrival of Aeneas at Carthage and his reception by Queen Dido, as recounted in *Aeneid* book 1; the latter, Aeneas plucking the golden bough before his descent to the Underworld, as described in *Aeneid* book 6.[21] It has been suggested[22] that the illustrations in the Low Ham and Frampton pavements derive from illuminated manuscripts of the *Aeneid* like the two examples in the Vatican Library[23] – manuscripts that were perhaps even produced in Britain. Even if this last were not correct, the mere existence of such pavements shows the high level of literary appreciation in Britain in the late Roman period, an aspect of the sort of literary culture fostered by the *grammatici*. A mosaic from a third villa, Lullingstone in Kent, has a scene showing the rape of Europa as described by, among others, Ovid,[24] but where there is an accompanying couplet which alludes to the *Aeneid*.[25] This passage is discussed in the following section.

TERTIARY EDUCATION – THE *RHETORES*

The first point to make is that while primary education was very much an *ad hoc* affair and stood on its own, secondary and tertiary education went together. Where *rhetores* were to be found, there also one found *grammatici*. The second point is that just as it is possible to suggest the existence of *grammatici* in Britain by pointing to the influence that they had on the villa culture of fourth-century Britain, so it may be possible to point to the influence of *rhetores* by a similar line of reasoning. What, however, was the role of the *rhetor*? His primary function was, as his name implies, to teach dialectic.[26] The student of rhetoric was set various tasks by his professor that appear to the modern mind academic, artificial and sterile. Thus the young Augustine was given the task (*negotium*) of paraphrasing the words of Juno[27] in her anger and grief at not being able to turn Aeneas aside from Italy.[28] Or the student might be required to invent an entire speech, such as the words of Dido when she saw the departure of Aeneas.[29] More elaborate exercises might be undertaken such as those described by the Greek rhetorician Aphthonius of Antioch in the later fourth century.

Aphthonius was the author of the *Progymnasmata* ('Preparatory Exercises'), in which chapter 3 is devoted to Refutation (ἀνασκευῆ). Its opening section is summarised by Haarhoff,[30] thus: 'The *first* step is to attack your opponent, the *next* to give a statement of his case, the *third* to refute this statement under the following heads: 1. *Obscurity*, 2. *Incredibility*, 3. *Impossibility*, 4. *Illogicality*, 5. *Impropriety*, 6. *Inexpediency'*. There follows an example – the story of Apollo and Daphne – a story incidentally probably shown on one of the mosaics from Brading on the Isle of Wight[31] and the recently-discovered mosaic at Dinnington in Somerset.[32] This myth is subjected to minute analysis under the heads listed, and the irrefutable conclusion is given in the closing *peroration*, 'All poets are fools – avoid them!'. It might be suggested that the story of Juno going to Aeolus to request him to raise a storm and thus prevent Aeneas and the Trojan fleet from reaching Carthage[33] could have been the object of a similar *negotium*, and that this is the origin of the couplet attached to the depiction of Europa and the Bull on the Lullingstone mosaic. Juno's request to Aeolus was certainly *inappropriate* (head 5, above), and she would have had greater justification in seeking the wind god's aid if she had been trying to prevent the rape of Europa from Crete by the Bull – the disguise adopted by her unfaithful husband Jupiter. *Invida si tauri vidisset Iuno natatus | Iustius Aeolias isset adusque domos...* 'If jealous Juno had thus seen the swimming of the bull, with greater justice would she have gone to the halls of Aeolus...'.[34] On the other hand, A.A. Barrett[35] argues convincingly that the couplet can be best explained as an Ovidian pastiche – not only in its language and metre, but in its general form, since the poet often says that 'if a certain figure of myth or legend had acted in a certain way, a certain result would have ensued'.[36] There can, however, be little doubt that in general terms the composition of the couplet was the product of the rather precious literary milieu of the rhetorical school.

Did such dry and academic exercises have any relevance to the real world? Was this the training of those who were set on a career in the law? Surprisingly – or perhaps not surprisingly – no. The budding advocate went on to Rome as Pelagius – the first attested alumnus of a British 'university' – went from Britain in the late fourth or early fifth century. And yet on occasion there was scope for the rhetorician. Some of the foremost exponents of this genre of literary writing were the orators from Gaul, such as Eumenius of Augustodunum (Autun), and the products of their *oeuvre* are preserved in a collection known as the *Panegyrici Latini Veteres*. Several of the panegyrics were addressed to the Caesar Constantius, both as patron of the Maeniana at Autun, but also as the tetrarch entrusted to wrest Britain back from the control of the usurpers Carausius and Allectus at the end of the third century. *Panegyric*

8(5) addressed to Constantius described the joy of the citizens of London when the Caesar entered London in triumph: 'at last they were free, at last Romans, at last restored afresh by the true light of the empire' (*tandem liberi, tandem Romani, tandemque vera imperii luce recreati*).[37] The language is echoed by the commemorative golden medallion found at Arras,[38] which shows the emperor on horseback welcomed by a female figure, the personification of London, kneeling before him at the gates of the city. Around the rim of the medallion flanking the emperor is the legend *Redditor Lucis Aeternae* – 'Restorer of the Eternal Light'.

But Carausius, the great rival of Constantius in Britain, had not been averse himself to using the brief messages cut on the dies used to produce coinage in his name for propaganda purposes. Remarkably two coins of the British usurper refer to the works of Virgil and imply familiarity with the works of the poet on the part of those who designed the coins:[39] *Expectate veni*, 'Come, O long expected one' – i.e. Carausius.[40] This is a quotation from the *Aeneid*,[41] which reads in full:

> *Quae tantae tenuere morae? Quibus Hector ab oris*
> *Expectate venis? ut te post multa tuorum*
> *Funera, post varios hominumque urbisque labores*
> *Defessi adspicimus!*

> ('What delays detain you? From what shores do you come, Hector, O long expected one? So that we may look upon you, depleted after the deaths of so many of your friends and worn out after the manifold labours of your people and of your city!').

Another legend on coins of Carausius, including many of those cited above, is the letters RSR found in the exergue, while the letters INPCDA are also found in the exergue of a unique medallion of this emperor.[42] These two legends have been brilliantly interpreted by Guy de la Bédoyère[43] as *R(edeunt) S(aturnia) R(egna)* and *I(am) N(ova) P(rogenies) C(aelo) D(emittitur) A(lto)*. Taken together, these two tags mean 'The golden age is back! Now a new generation is let down from heaven above', and are a quotation from Virgil's *Eclogues*:[44]

> *Iam redit et virgo, redeunt saturnia regna,*
> *Iam nova progenies coelo demittitur alto.*

('Now the virgin returns, the golden age is back! Now a new generation is sent down from heaven above').

We shall never know the precise circumstances under which the dies for producing these coins were designed. What we can say is that the designers were familiar with the works of Virgil, and that it is a familiarity that will have come from their school days when they sat at the feet of *grammatici*. One could perhaps go further and suggest that the Virgilian echoes were transmitted not directly but through the works of some rhetorician, a London-based orator who wrote panegyrics on Carausius, just as the anonymous Gallic writer – but he *could* have been British too! – wrote a panegyric on Carausius' rival, the Caesar Constantius,[45] whose language found an echo in the legend on the Arras medallion.

CONCLUSION

It is time now to turn to the direct evidence, such as it is, for 'grammarians' and 'rhetoricians' in Britain. Here not only the most important reference but also the earliest one is found in the pages of the *Life* written by Tacitus of his father-in-law, Agricola. Agricola, as Tacitus tells us,[46] was born at Forum Julii (Fréjus) in Gallia Narbonensis, and, as a young boy (*parvulus*), had had as the *alma mater* of his studies (literally *sedes ac magistram studiorum*, 'seat and mistress of his studies') Massilia (Marseilles). The Greek city of Massilia was the oldest and at the time the most prestigious centre of education in Gaul. It was here that Tacitus recalls his father-in-law told him that he would have 'imbibed the study of philosophy more deeply' than was appropriate for a Roman and a senator had not his mother prudently steered him towards a career in public service. Nevertheless, given his early enthusiasm for the life of an academic, it is not surprising that in AD 79, two years after his arrival in Britain as governor, Agricola set about introducing the Britons to the fruits of civilisation as he understood it, not only encouraging the Britons to build 'temples, market places and town houses' (*templa, fora, domos*) but also 'educating the sons of the chieftains in the liberal arts' (*principum filios liberalibus artibus erudire*).[47] In this context, Tacitus recalls that he 'rated the natural talents of the Britons above the trained skills of the Gauls' (*et ingenia Britannorum studiis Gallorum anteferre*).[48] Is this simply a literary *topos*? Is Tacitus merely attributing to Agricola the sort of actions that the conscientious governor would take? Or are we justified in taking the implication of Tacitus' words literally? In the case of the *fora* we know that it was indeed literally true, for as a famous inscription tells us, the dedication of the forum-basilica complex at Verulamium took place in *precisely* this year – AD 79.[49] But what of the 'schools for the sons of chiefs'?

The case for the establishment of a centre for higher education in Britain could be said to be proved if we could accept the statement of A.R. Burn[50] that 'Plutarch in his essay On the Cessation of Oracles (*De defectu oraculorum* 410 A) mentions how he had met at Delphi in AD 83 a Greek teacher of rhetoric (recte *grammatikos*) named Demetrius who had just come back from lecturing in Britain'. In fact, extremely interesting though the Plutarch passage is, there is no mention of Demetrius having fulfilled the function of *grammatikos* – let alone *rhetor* – while in Britain. On his own account,[51] he would appear to have been acting on imperial orders as a 'scientific observer' attached to the Classis Britannica operating off the west coast of Scotland, having been seconded from Agricola's staff.[52] Yet the establishment of some sort of school at this period to provide young British aristocrats with a grounding in Latin (if not Greek) literature, rhetoric and allied disciplines, is not unlikely, and there is a hint that this may indeed have been so. Martial, writing about AD 96, reports[53] that 'it is said that Britain declaims our verses' (*dicitur et nostros cantare Britannia*). On the other hand, for what it is worth, it was not until the reign of Hadrian that the satirist Juvenal[54] says that 'Eloquent Gaul has been teaching British lawyers. Thule now talks of hiring a rhetorician'. As it happens, the first really direct evidence for a teacher of any kind comes from the third century and then relates probably to a humble *litterator*, rather than a *grammaticus* or *rhetor*, for we read in the biography of Bonosus, a usurper under the Emperor Probus, that he was the son of a British schoolmaster (*paedagogus litterarius*).[55] Though the historical reality of Bonosus has been doubted,[56] intriguingly the name Bonosus occurs as a maker's stamp appropriately enough on an iron stylus found in London.[57]

This, then, is the sum of the evidence. And yet, I seem to recall years ago seeing a potsherd in the stores of the Museum of London with the word *rhetor* scored as a graffito. It is time to start excavating the Museum's London Archaeological Archive and Research Centre (LAARC) at Mortimer Wheeler House.

ACKNOWLEDGEMENTS
Harvey Sheldon has devoted his working life to the study of Roman London, partly as the *doyen* of practical excavators and more recently in the academic field, as a lecturer in the archaeology of London based at Birkbeck. It is appropriate therefore that the subject of this tribute should deal with some aspect of Roman London and some aspect too of education.

[1] *CTh.* 13.3.11; Pharr et al. 1952, 389.
[2] Hassall 1996.
[3] *CTh.* 13.3.11; Pharr et al. 1952, 389.
[4] Hassall 1976.
[5] Morris 1978, 7; Hearne 1745, 21.
[6] Haarhoff 1920.
[7] Tomlin 1979; *RIB* II.5, 2491.1–229.
[8] *RIB* II.5, 2491.135, 2491.142.
[9] *RIB* II.5, 2491.80.
[10] *RIB* II.5, 2491.148.
[11] *Aeneid* 2.1 = Loeb edn, vol. 1.
[12] *Aeneid* 9.473 = Loeb edn, vol. 2.
[13] Bowman and Thomas 1994, no. 118.
[14] Barrett 1978.
[15] Davey and Ling 1982.
[16] *Aeneid* 1.313.
[17] *Aeneid* 12.165.
[18] *RIB* II.4, 2447.9.
[19] e.g. Henig 1995, pls 9–10.
[20] e.g. Henig 1995, pl. 11.
[21] Barrett 1978.
[22] Henig 1995, 126.
[23] Toynbee 1962, pls 260–1.
[24] *Metamorphoses* 2.839 = Loeb edn, vol. 1.
[25] *Aeneid* 1.50–2.
[26] Haarhoff 1920, 68–93.
[27] *Aeneid* 1.37–49.
[28] Augustine *Confessiones* 1.17 = Loeb edn, vol. 1.
[29] Ennodius *Dictiones* 28 = Vogel 1885/1961.
[30] Haarhoff 1920, 74–5.
[31] e.g. Witts 2005, 37, pl. 16.
[32] Cosh and Neal 2005.
[33] *Aeneid* 1.50–2.
[34] *RIB* II.4, 2448.6.
[35] Barrett 1978.
[36] Barrett 1978, 312, with four examples.

37   *Pan. Lat.* 8(5).19.2.
38   Sutherland 1967, 167, no. Trier 34.
39   de la Bédoyère 1998.
40   Webb 1933, 439–40, 510, nos 554–8.
41   *Aeneid* 2.282–5.
42   de la Bédoyère 1998, 81.
43   de la Bédoyère 1998.
44   *Eclogues* 4.6–7.
45   *Pan. Lat.* 8(5).
46   Tac. *Agr.* 4.
47   Tac. *Agr.* 21.
48   Tac. *Agr.* 21.
49   *JRS* 46 (1956), 146–7, no. 3.
50   Burn 1969, 48.
51   Plutarch *De Defectu Oraculorum* 419e.
52   cf. *RIB* 662–3, two bronze plaques found in York, one of which is dedicated to the 'deities of the governor's headquarters' by a certain Demetrius.
53   *Epigrams* 11.3.5 = Loeb edn, vol. 3.
54   *Satires* 15.112–13.
55   *SHA, Bonosus* 14.1.
56   Birley 2005, 367.
57   *RIB* II.3, 2428.9.

16
BRITAIN AND THE RHINE PROVINCES: EPIGRAPHIC EVIDENCE FOR ROMAN TRADE

Originally published:
'Britain and the Rhine provinces: epigraphic evidence for Roman trade', in J. du Plat Taylor and H. Cleere (eds), *Roman shipping and trade: Britain and the Rhine provinces*, CBA Research Report 24, 1978, London, 41–8

NON-TRADING CONTACTS

THE SCOPE OF this article is limited to the epigraphic evidence for trade. It is, however, worth surveying briefly first the evidence for non-trading contacts between Britain and the Rhineland. Like Britain, the Rhineland, consisting from the time of Domitian of the twin provinces of Germania Inferior and Germania Superior, was a frontier zone – the nearest section of the imperial frontier to Britain – and it is hardly surprising that the military histories of the two areas should, from the beginning, be intimately connected. Of the four conquest legions of Britain, no less than three were drafted from the Rhine garrison: Legions II from Strasbourg, XIV from Mainz and XX from Neuss. The evidence for this is largely epigraphic and has been surveyed by E. Ritterling[1] for each of the legions concerned. Auxiliary regiments were also raised in, or withdrawn from, the Rhine frontier for the invasion. These included eight cohorts of Batavians raised in Lower Germany,[2] numbering some 4,000 men in all, if quingenary, as is usually assumed (or just possibly as many as 6,000–8,000 if milliary in size). Our information is fragmentary but we know that among other auxiliary units were the *Ala Indiana*,[3] raised twenty years earlier from among the Treviri, and an *ala* of Thracians which, despite

169

	Name	Business	Origin	Reference
1	L. Secundius Similis	negotiator allecarius		Stuart and Bogaers 1971, no. 5 = AE 1973, 365
2	T. Carinius Gratus	negotiator allecarius		Stuart and Bogaers 1971, no. 5 = AE 1973, 365
3	C. Gatullinius Seggo	negotiator allecarius	cives Trever	Stuart and Bogaers 1971, no. 22 = AE 1973, 375
4	Arisenius Marius (lib.)	negotiator Britannicianus		Bogaers 1971, 35
5	Placidus Viduci fil.	negotiator Britannicianus = Table 2, no. 9 + Appendix	cives Veliocassinius	Stuart and Bogaers 1971, no. 45
6	M. Secund(inius?) Silvanus	negotiator cretarius Britannicianus		Stuart and Bogaers 1971, no. 11 = AE 1973, 370
7	M. Secund(inius?) Silvanus	negotiator cretarius Britannicianus		Hondius-Crone 1955, no. 25 = ILS 4751
8	[...]M[...]	[negotiator?] Gallicanus*		Stuart and Bogaers 1971, no. 20 = AE 1973, 374
9	M. Exgingius Agricola	negotiator salarius	cives Trever	Stuart and Bogaers 1971, no. 1 = AE 1973, 362
10	C. Jul(ius) Florentinus	negotiator salarius	Agripp(inensis)	Stuart and Bogaers 1971, no. 4 = AE 1973, 364
11	C. Jul(ius) Januarius	negotiator salarius	Agripp(inensis)	Bogaers 1971, 37
12	Q. Cornelius Superstis	negotiator salarius		Stuart and Bogaers 1971, no. 25 = AE 1973, 378
13	Commodus Ufemi(?)tis filius	(negotiator vinarius)		Stuart and Bogaers 1971, no. 44
14	Bosiconius	actor navis Flori Severi		Bogaers 1971, 39
15	Vegisonius Martinus	nauta	cives Secuanus	Stuart and Bogaers 1971, no. 13 = AE 1973, 372

Table 1 Traders and shippers at Colijnsplaat and Domburg

* For negotiatores Gallicani, cf. CIL X, 7612; CIL XI, 5068 = ILS 7524. Alternatively, Gallicanus may be the cognomen of the dedicant

	Name	Business	Origin	Reference
1	L. Solimarius Secundinus	neg(otiator) Britannicianus	civis Trever	Bordeaux: CIL XIII, 639
2	C. Aurelius C. l. Verus	negotiator Britannicianus, moritex		Cologne: CIL XIII, 8164a
3	Asprius A[...]	reversus [e]x Britannia		Bonn: BRGK 27 (1937), 99, no. 167
4	Fufidius	[negoti]ator [vesti?]arius ex [Provinc]ia Br[itannia]		Kastell: CIL XIII, 7300
5	Maxsimi[nus]	[negotiator] vestia[rius ex Germania {or just possibly ex Britannia}] superio[e]		Marsal, Gallia Belgica: CIL XIII, 4564
6	L. Priminius Ingenuus	negotiator vestiarius importator		Xanten: CIL XIII, 8568
7	M. Verecundius Diogenes	sevir Augustalis, York, moritex*	cives Biturix Cubus	York: RIB 678; Birley 1966, 228
8	M. Aurelius Lunaris	sevir Augustalis, York and Lincoln, AD 237		Bordeaux: Courteault 1921 = AE 1922, no. 116
9	L. Viducius Placidus	negotiator [...], AD 221 = Table 1, no. 5 + Appendix	domo [civitate] Veliocas[s]ium	York: Britannia 8 (1977), 430-1, no. 18

Table 2 Other traders and shippers

* For moritex, cf. no. 2. An alternative interpretation, however, is preferred by J.E. Bogaers, who has suggested (pers. comm.) that the reading is III III vir Aug. Col. Ebor. itemq(ue) Mori(norum), rather than idemq(ue) morit(ex). Tervanna (Therouanne in the Pas-de-Calais), chief town of the Morini, is called Colon(ia) Morinorum on an inscription from Nijmegen: CIL XII, 8727. For a man who held the post of sevir in two colonies, cf. no. 8

the reservations of G. Alföldy,[4] had probably seen service in Lower Germany before crossing over to Britain.[5]

This close contact between the two areas, evident at the time of the initial invasion of Britain, was subsequently maintained. Legionary detachments were sent as reinforcements from the Rhineland to Britain or vice versa as need arose.[6] Vexillations from all four British legions fought in southern Germany under Domitian,[7] while others, amounting to 3,000 men drawn from Upper Germany and Spain, came to strengthen the army of Britain under Hadrian.[8] Under his successor, Antoninus Pius, detachments from both Germanies came to Britain to strengthen the three British legions in c. AD 155[9] and again in the early third century.[10] With one or other of these groups will have come the unfortunate Junius Dubitatus of Legion VIII who dropped his shield in the River Tyne.[11] Some of these soldiers lost more than their shields. An inscription from Caerleon[12] was set up as a memorial to a soldier, presumably in Legion II Augusta, defun(c)tus expeditione Germanica. Sometimes complete legions were moved, as when Legion VI came to Britain from Lower Germany early in Hadrian's reign, probably sailing directly from the Low Countries to Newcastle, where it dedicated twin altars to Neptune and Oceanus.[13] Similarly, Legion IX which left Britain sometime after 107/8,[14] initially for Nijmegen.[15] Auxiliary regiments, or parts of them, will have taken part in these movements between the two theatres: for example, the Ala Vocontiorum, part of the British garrison, which is attested in the Low Countries.[16]

Quite apart from such sporadic contacts, a very large proportion of the auxiliary forces stationed in Britain, especially the infantry, were of Germanic origin.[17] The evidence for the immediate conquest period has been reviewed above. For the later first century we have the evidence of Tacitus, who specifically mentions four cohorts of Batavians and two of Tungrians who served under his father-in-law, Agricola,[18] and the newly-enrolled Cohors Usiporum per Germanias conscripta, which mutinied in AD 83.[19] These seven units, all 'German', are in fact the only auxiliary regiments mentioned by the historian apart from certain British levies. For the second century, the military diplomas[20] provide us with many more names, while second- and third-century inscriptions, and the Notitia Dignitatum, give us not only some further names but allow us to assign garrison sites to units. From these sources we know that, in addition to the solitary Ala Tungrorum known to be in the province by 98[21] and later attested at Mumrills on the Antonine Wall,[22] there were no less than 16 cohorts or part-mounted cohorts, out of a total of perhaps about 40, which were raised in the two Germanies or Gallia Belgica.

In the third century, new units, *cunei* and *vexillationes* of cavalry and *numeri* of infantry, were raised. We know of three distinct *cunei* of Frisii serving in the area of Hadrian's Wall, each bearing an epithet derived from the forts where they were stationed. There were also vexillations of Germans at Old Penrith and of Suebi at Lanchester at least as early as the 230s. There was a *Numerus Hnaudifridi* at Housesteads ('Notfried's Irregulars'), and in the south the *Numerus Turnacensium* at Lympne, *Numerus Abulcorum* at Pevensey,[23] and *Milites Tungrecanorum* at Dover.[24] In other words, with rare exceptions, such as the Canninefates, every ethnic group west of the lower Rhine provided troops for the army of Britain, some, like the Nervii and Batavi in thousands, while even groups like the Frisii and Suebi east of the Rhine contributed too.

These units were not only raised in the Germanies or Gallia Belgica, but also preserved, at any rate for a period, their ethnic character once they had been sent to Britain, though how far this was through new drafts from their countries of origin it would be hard to prove. This ethnic character is shown by the numerous distinctive names of German origin belonging to the men who served in them, as shown by the inscriptions they set up, or which, as gravestones, were set up to them. Even when a soldier bears the *tria nomina* of a Roman citizen, a German origin is sometimes specified, or the *cognomen* may be the Latinised form of a 'German' name. Sometimes whole groups within a particular unit preserved, at any rate at first, a separate corporate identity, as the *Cives Tuihanti* from Twenthe, a group within the *Cuneus Frisiorum* at Housesteads,[25] or the *Texandri* and *Suve(vae?)*, part of a detachment of *Cohors II Nerviorum* at Carrawburgh,[26] or the men all from the same village (*pagus*) mentioned on another, damaged, inscription of the same unit from Wallsend.[27] *Cohors II Tungrorum* was recruited, on the other hand, from at least two *pagi*, the *Pagus Vellaus* and *Pagus Condrustis*.[28]

The names of the gods and goddesses, whether west German or east Celtic, worshipped by the Rhinelanders and their neighbours once in Britain tell the same story.[29] There were male gods who might be identified with Roman equivalents, like Mars Thincsus[30] and Hercules Magusanus.[31] There were also goddesses who were worshipped singly such as Viradecthis,[32] Garmangabis,[33] and Harimella;[34] or in pairs like the Alaisiagae,[35] variously named Baudihillia and Friagabis[36] or Beda and Fimilena;[37] or in trios like the Matres, who were distinguished by epithets such as *Alatervae*,[38] *Germanae*,[39] or the double epithet *Ollototae sive transmarinae*,[40] both of which terms occur singly.[41] The continental centre of the worship of the Matres was the middle Rhineland.[42] Of the male gods only the enigmatic Huiteres were worshipped collectively.[43] A dedication from Old Carlisle to the *T[erra] Batavorum*,[44] if the reading is correct,[45] though more Romanised in concept, is equally significant in the present context.

If there were many German auxiliaries serving in Britain, there were, as might be expected, far fewer legionaries, though we know of two brothers from Xanten (*Colonia Ulpia Traiana*) who served in Legion II Augusta at Caerleon,[46] and one man from the same place who died at Chester and had presumably served in Legion XX V.V.[47] These correspond to the few men from Britannia who served in the Rhine legions[48] or the *Classis Germanica*.[49] But in contrast to the large total of auxiliaries from the two Germanies and Gallia Belgica serving in Britain, only one regular cohort raised in Britain served in Germany. This was *Cohors II Brit[tonum]* (or possibly *Brit[annorum]*) *milliaria equitata Civium Romanorum*, a Flavian foundation which served for a short period in the Rhineland, where it has left tile-stamps at Xanten and Vechten.[50] There were, however, a dozen or so *Numeri Brittonum* serving on the Upper German frontier. Their first appearance there is thought by Baatz[51] to be contemporary with the earliest period of occupation of the fortlet of Hesselbach on the Odenwald Limes, that is, between AD 95 and 105.[52]

If an auxiliary soldier from Germany was sent to Britain, he would normally remain there until discharge, unless his unit as a whole was withdrawn from the province. Postings for officers were more flexible, whether for the long-service centurions who might, on an initial appointment or subsequent promotion, move from province to province, or for the short-term spells of service of equestrian and senatorial officers and officials. Both sorts of transfer will have been common between the Rhine frontier and the British frontier. Thus, to cite one example only, Titus Domitius Vindex, who made a dedication to Mars Halamard(us?) at Horn near Roermond in Limburg, on which he described himself as centurion in Legion XX V.V.,[53] was in fact probably, as Professor Bogaers suggests,[54] a *beneficiarius consularis* in Legion XXX V.V., who set up his altar on hearing of his promotion to a centurionate in Britain. At a higher level, of the procurators who served in Britain, Julius Classicianus, had Rhenish connections and was either a tribesman of the Treviri or Helvetii;[55] and in the second century a number of governors of the provinces took up their appointments immediately after the governorship of Lower Germany, as, for example, A. Platorius Nepos, the builder of Hadrian's Wall, and Lollius Urbicus, the builder of the Antonine Wall. (Alternatively the governorship of Moesia Superior was commonly held before proceeding to Britain[56]).

To summarise, it has been shown that whatever else did or did not travel from the Rhineland to Britain, personnel certainly did. Sometimes the troops and officials would travel by road westward to Boulogne, but sometimes they may have made the crossing direct from the Low Countries. Yet if the movement of important officials and military personnel between the two areas was regular, that of civilians was negligible. We know of two visitors at Bath from the Moselle area,[57] and that is virtually all. There are two dedications made to east Celtic deities like Mars Lenus[58] from Caerwent, where one is to be definitely explained by the town's proximity to the nearby legionary fortress at Caerleon,[59] and the other probably so.[60] The reading of a dedication to Mars Lenus at Chedworth[61] is not as secure as one would wish, but it may be that the two dedications found in this country made *in honorem domus divinae*[62] were made by people with a 'Rhenish connection' since the formula is commonly found in the Rhineland. Conversely, we know of two men from Chester who travelled to the Rhineland[63] and the Moselle.[64]

TRADING CONTACTS

If the epigraphic evidence for the movement of the army and officials to and from the Rhineland is very full, that for traders is more meagre. From Britain itself there is indeed very little evidence for traders of any kind: an inscription from Bowness-on-Solway[65] was set up by a man about to embark on a trading mission, but one in north-western waters rather than across the North Sea. More to the point is a sarcophagus from York (Table 2, no. 7) of a tribesman of the central Gaulish Bituriges Cubi, a *sevir Augustalis* of the colony and, if the interpretation put forward by J.C. Mann[66] is correct, a *moritex*, a Celtic word apparently meaning 'shipper' (Table 2, no. 7, with note). Another *sevir Augustalis* – of both York and Lincoln – Marcus Aurelius Lunaris, is known from an altar from Bordeaux that he set up in AD 237 (Table 2, no. 8). He is usually thought of as being concerned with the Bordeaux wine trade, but it is possible that, since he operated from the east coast of Britain, he may have had dealings with the Rhineland too. Evidence of a different kind is provided by a wooden writing tablet from London which refers to the construction of a ship – a tantalising glimpse into the business archives of a shipper based in the provincial capital.[67] Finally, in 1976 part of a dedication slab was found at York. It was set up in AD 221 by the trader L. Viducius Placidus, a tribesman of the Veliocasses of the Rouen area of northern Gaul (Table 2, no. 9). The dedicator is to be identified with the *negotiator Britannicianus*, Placidus son of Viducus, *cives Veliocassinius*, attested on an inscription from the shrine of Nehalennia near Colijnsplaat in Holland (Table 1, no. 5, and Appendix).

The clearest epigraphic evidence for trade between Britain and the Rhineland comes indeed not from Britain but from the continent, and in particular the site near Colijnsplaat and the sister site of Domburg some 25 km (15½ miles) to the west, off the north coasts of Noord-Beveland and Walcheren respectively. For Roman times, however, to describe the location of the two sites in this way would be meaningless. Then the estuary of the Scheldt lay further north than at present and neither Walcheren nor Noord-Beveland existed.[68] For Viducius and his contemporaries the site at Domburg lay south of the estuary mouth, while that near Colijnsplaat was further inland and north of the estuary. Both were shrines to the goddess Nehalennia near what were presumably important harbours: these harbours served ships trading between the Rhineland (via the Waal) and Gallia Belgica (via the Scheldt) on the one hand, and the coastal regions of Gaul and the east coast ports of Britain on the other, as the Viducius inscriptions have so graphically shown. Before leaving the sheltered waters of the estuary, it was not uncommon for traders to seek the protection of the goddess, whose name Nehalennia, or, probably more correctly, Neihalennia,[69] means 'guardian' or 'guiding' goddess, by vowing to erect an altar to her on their safe return. On many of these altars the goddess herself is represented in flowing garments, either sitting with a dog beside her and a basket of fruits on her lap or sometimes standing with one foot on the prow of a vessel. The shallow depression or hearth (*focus*) often carved on the top of Roman altars was usually replaced by an 'offering table' on which were set either fruits or loaves. Domburg, where coastal erosion exposed the remains of her temple in the seventeenth century, has produced some 27 dedications to Nehalennia, and 5 altars to Jupiter and Neptune.[70] The site near Colijnsplaat, very probably the ancient Ganuenta, or perhaps Ganuentum,[71] was located by the chance discovery of two altars brought up by trawling nets in 1970. Within the next twelve months a further

122 altars were recovered in a planned campaign of trawling and diving, many now illegible, but all probably dedicated to Nehalennia.[72] These dedications, more than 150 of them from the two sites, sometimes with the reason for their erection clearly stated by the formula *ob merces recte conservatas* or its variants, will mostly have been set up after successful landfall had been made either at the end of a one-way passage by sea or, more commonly, after the completion of a round trip.

What do these journeys – between 150 and 300 of them – mean in terms of the total volume of trade? To estimate this we would have to know: 1. for how long the ports associated with the sanctuaries at Domburg and near Colijnsplaat were used; 2. whether a trader would set up an altar on average once a trip, once a year, or once a lifetime; and 3. what proportion of the altars originally dedicated have been recovered. Unfortunately, we know the answers to none of these questions. As regards the first question, we have the evidence of the coin series from Domburg.[73] This suggests that there were two periods of activity at the site: AD 69–238 and 260–73. The latter is linked by J.S. Boersma[74] with defence measures taken against sea raiders, the former with trading activity. It is unlikely, however, that altars were set up at Domburg throughout the whole of the first period, and it is tempting to link the dedication of most of them specifically to AD 180–218 when the coin series peaks. What is true of Domburg should be broadly true of the site near Colijnsplaat since the style of the altars from both places is similar and one man, Marcus Secund(inius?) Silvanus (Table 1, nos 6–7), makes dedications at both. However, two inscriptions from Colijnsplaat have consular dates of 223[75] and 227,[76] while Placidus son of Viducus, who also makes a dedication there (Table 1, no. 5) is now attested at York on an inscription which carries the consular date 221 (Table 2, no. 9). These dates (all within the decade 220–30) could be explained by supposing that Colijnsplaat remained of importance somewhat longer than Domburg. Alternatively, they may simply reflect a contemporary epigraphic fashion for recording consular dates.

On the second question, only one man is certainly known to have made two dedications, the trader Marcus Secund(inius?) Silvanus mentioned above, although, it should be noted, the two altars were set up at different shrines. A second possible case is that of Hilarus, a decurion of Nijmegen, the *Municipium Batavorum*, who made the dedication in 227 at the shrine near Colijnsplaat. A fragment of an altar from the same shrine was set up by a trader whose name ends in -arus, and who was also a decurion of the *municipium*, but the actual identity of the two men is uncertain and is regarded by Bogaers as unlikely.[77] Whether or not identity is assumed, on present evidence it seems possible that individual traders normally set up not more than one altar at each of the Nehalennia shrines. That they set up altars on the completion of every round trip is completely out of the question and less expensive expressions of thanks to the goddess must have been offered instead. Though, therefore, it is impossible to quantify the volume of trade that passed through the two ports implied by the shrines, the evidence does at the very least show that both were flourishing, especially in the last quarter of the second century and the first half of the third century AD.

Bogaers has discussed the origins of the dedicants at the two sites.[78] Attested are men from the Rouen and Besançon areas, Nijmegen, Trier and Cologne; and Cologne (or strictly speaking Deutz) is the only place apart from the two Dutch sites to have produced dedications to Nehalennia.[79] These origins largely confirm that the East Scheldt estuary acted as the outlet for goods to and from the Rhineland.

Much of the trade carried on by *negotiatores* mentioned on other inscriptions from sites in the Rhineland proper[80] will have been of a very local nature, but the mere presence of a trader at the Nehalennia shrines implies that he was concerned with trade further afield – either by river (the Scheldt) inland, or by sea, even if this was only coasting trade with Gaul. But since any particular trader at the two Dutch sites (with one possible exception: Table 1, no. 8, with note) may have been concerned in trade with Britain, I shall consider all those cases where the trades of the dedicators are specified, in discussing the sort of goods that were carried between the two areas. My debt here, as ever, to Professor Bogaers is very great.[81]

a) Negotiatores allecarii *(Table 1, nos 1–3)*
Dealers in a type of fish: *al(l)ec, al(l)ex,* or *ha(l)lec*[82] was used as a relish on several of the dishes described by Apicius,[83] the Roman writer on cookery. *Allecarii* are attested definitely only at Colijnsplaat.[84] It may have been produced in Holland, and Bogaers[85] illustrates the sherd of a *dolium* found at Aardenburg with the inscription ALIIC XI S(emis) – eleven-and-a-half amphorae or quadrantals of *allec* (about 300 litres) – incised below the rim before firing. It could equally have been produced in Britain.

b) Negotiatores Britanniciani *(Table 1, nos 4–5)*
Presumably traders concerned with the transport of the various goods
and commodities, known from archaeology, which travelled to and
from Britain, including contents of the bottle stamped CCA found at
Silchester.[86] These bottles, even if the letters do not stand for *Colonia
Claudia Agrippinensis* (Cologne), were probably made in the Rhineland.[87]
Negotiatores Britanniciani are also known from inscriptions found
at Bordeaux and Cologne (Table 2, nos 1–2, cf. no. 3). The man from
Bordeaux was, significantly, a Treveran, while the Cologne trader is,
interestingly, described also as a *moritex*.

c) Negotiatores cretarii Britanniciani *(Table 1, nos 6–7)*
The word *cretarius* is derived from *creta*, chalk or pipe-clay,[88] and
negotiatores cretarii or *artis cretariae* are usually explained as traders in
fine pottery or pottery figurines. Inscriptions mentioning them, though
lacking the epithet *Britannicianus*, are found in the Rhineland, eastern
Gaul and southern Germany – at Wiesbaden, Mainz, Metz, Lorch,
Sumelocenna and Cologne,[89] as well as Bonn and Trier.[90] They will have
traded in east Gaulish sigillata and Rhenish wares, including the famous
motto beakers as well as clay figurines, both of which were exported
from the Rhineland to Britain.[91] Among the figurines found in this
country (which include many pieces from the Allier region of central
Gaul) is one which has, interestingly, been identified as Nehalennia,[92]
although the identification has not been universally accepted. Other
figurines made and stamped by Servandus of Cologne have also been
found in Britain.[93]

d) [Negotiatores?] Gallicani *(Table 1, no. 8, with note)*
The text of the single relevant inscription is damaged. If the word
negotiator is correctly restored, the sole trader so described will have
been engaged in general trading with Gaul.

e) Negotiatores salarii *(Table 1, nos 9–12)*
Four inscriptions from Colijnsplaat were set up by traders in salt, three
of whom were domiciled at Cologne. Bogaers[94] has suggested that
this may be significant: he points out that the trade was an imperial
monopoly and that concessions to deal in salt may have been made
to men living at Cologne, the provincial capital of Germania Inferior,
where they could be kept under close supervision. We know that in the

Flavian period the production of government salt was carried out along the coast of Gallia Belgica: two inscriptions from Rimini[95] were set up by the *salinatores civitatis Menapiorum* and *Morinorum* respectively to C. Lepidius L. f. Proculus, a centurion who had seen service in several legions including VI Victrix, then based at Neuss, from where he may have been sent to supervise the extraction. But Bogaers also raises the possibility that the salt was produced in Britain, and there is widespread and growing evidence for salt working in Roman times along the south and especially the east coasts of Britain as well as at inland sites.[96]

f) Negotiatores vinarii (Table 1, no. 13)
Bogaers[97] has identified one dedicant at Colijnsplaat as a wine merchant on the basis of the reliefs on the altar dedicated by him to Nehalennia: on its side are vine scrolls and beneath the inscription is the representation of a barge laden with barrels. A *negotiator vinarius* is attested at Bonn,[98] and the evidence for the production of wine in the Moselle and Rhineland in the Roman period is extensive,[99] so that Commodus, who set up the altar at Colijnsplaat, was probably an exporter of wine from these two centres. Finds of barrels in Britain, Germany and Belgium, when analysed, have turned out to be of silver fir and larch. The former is native to the Alpine and Pyrenean foothills, while the latter is found only in the Alps, so although the wine contained in the barrels was not necessarily produced in precisely these regions, the barrels must have been and the presumption is that the vineyards cannot have been too distant. The evidence of the barrels, then, is that some wine was being imported to the Rhineland.[100]

To summarise, the inscriptions from the two Nehalennia shrines show that pottery, and perhaps wine, were being exported to Britain, and salt and fish sauce were possibly imported from Britain in return. To these imports should be added woollen clothes.[101] The men listed in Table 2 (nos 4–6) could all have been importers of clothes from Britain, such as the famous *birrus Britannicus* known from Diocletian's *Price Edict*,[102] though in two cases crucial pieces of the inscriptions are restored and in the third there is no absolute proof that clothes were being imported from Britain, although this is quite likely. Some traders may have been exporters of some commodities, such as pottery, and importers of others, such as clothes.[103] Corn may also have been exported to the Rhineland, as it certainly was in the fourth century,[104] but we have no means of knowing whether the *negotiatores frumentarii* known from Aquae (Aachen)[105] and Nijmegen[106] dealt with grain that was imported or grown locally.

Finally, something should be said about the evidence of epigraphy for the organisation of trade. Here we may think of *corpora* – associations – whether guilds (*collegia*), whose members had a common interest, or business partnerships (*societates*). Organisations of both types could have existed for both the traders (*negotiatores*) and the shippers (*navicularii, nautae*).

We know that at Wiesbaden the *negotiatores civitatis Mattiacorum* were banded together into a guild (either *collegium* or *corpus*) which had its own *schola* or clubhouse.[107] Similar guilds, either general or for a particular trade or craft, almost certainly existed in all the major Rhineland towns, as well as towns like London, and the *coloniae* of Colchester, York and Lincoln. *Negotiatores* from other towns who had or shared *stationes* (offices), like those in the Piazza delle Corporazioni at Ostia,[108] away from home, may have banded together to form a *collegium peregrinorum*. Such *collegia* were not, as has been thought, groups of non-Roman citizens living in a city that had Roman rights, since they are attested after the *constitutio Antoniniana* of AD 212 when all free-born men in the empire received citizenship, and members of some *collegia* are known who possessed the *tria nomina* of Roman citizens.[109] *Collegia peregrinorum* existed at Silchester[110] and in Holland at Voorburg-Arentsburg.[111] The individual *negotiatores Britanniciani, cretarii Britanniciani*, etc., may have formed themselves into guilds in view of their common interests, just as it can be assumed that the lessees of the fishing rights (*conductores piscatus*) among the Frisii did.[112] The shippers based at the different ports probably belonged to *collegia*, too. One such is indicated at Fectio (Vechten) by an inscription which was set up by the *cives Tungri et nautae qui Fectione consistunt*.[113]

There is a temptation to think of the *negotiatores Britanniciani* or *negotiatores cretarii Britanniciani* as not merely guilds but actual companies on the model of those that are presumed to have operated the *stationes* around the Piazza delle Corporazioni at Ostia. Even at Ostia, however, the *stationes* may simply have been offices shared by groups of traders or shippers from the same town, rather than run by actual companies as such. Business associations are more likely to have been very small affairs. L. Secundius Similis and T. Carinius Gratus (Table 1, nos 1–2), who made a joint dedication at the shrine near Colijnsplaat, will certainly have been business partners. Sometimes a business will have been a family affair, and there is evidence for three generations of the same family all making dedications at Colijnsplaat.[114] Some business associations may have consisted of both active and sleeping partners who put up capital. Shipping, too, will have been in the hands of both individual *nautae* and small *societates*. The smaller shipowners or the active members of partnerships will have operated their own vessels (Table 1, no. 15), but the larger owners will have employed *actores navium*, agents to represent them on board ship. One such was Bosiconius, the *actor navis* of Florius Severus (Table 1, no. 14). *Actores* may also have been employed by the larger companies of *negotiatores*, although it is likely that most of the dedications at the two Dutch sites were made by merchants or shippers rather than their agents.

In conclusion, though the epigraphic evidence for trade between Britain and the Rhineland is sparse, the finds from the two Nehalennia shrines give us indications both of the extent of the trade in the late second and early third century and how that trade was organised. Evidence from Britain is at present largely lacking, but the recent discoveries of the Viducius dedication at York, and of altars built into the riverside wall of Roman London,[115] show that this is due only to the accident of survival, and we are fortunate indeed that the two Dutch sites have given us so much.

APPENDIX: THE INSCRIPTION OF LUCIUS VIDUCIUS PLACIDUS FROM YORK (TABLE 2, NO. 9; CF. TABLE 1, NO. 5)

1 [NEPTVNO] ▼ ET GENIO LOCI
[ET ▲ NVMINIB ▼ AV]GG ▲ L ▲ VIDVCIVS
[VIDVCI ▼ F ▼ PLA]CIDVS DOMO
[CIVITATE ▼]VELIOCAS[S]IVM
5 [PROV ▲ LVGD ▲ N]EGOTIATOR
[BRITANN ▼ AR]CVM ET IANVAM
[PRO SE ET SVIS DE]D[IT] GRATO ET
[SELEVCO ▼ COS]

[Neptuno] et Genio Loci | [et Numinib(us) Au]g(ustorum) L(ucius) Viducius | [Viduci f(ilius) Pla]cidus domo | [civitate] Veliocas[s]ium | [prov(inciae) Lugd(unensis) n]egotiator | [Britann(icanus) ar]cum et ianuam | [pro se et suis de]d[it] Grato et | [Seleuco co(n)s(ulibus)]

'To Neptune and the Genius of the place and the Deities of the Emperors, Lucius Viducius Placidus, the son of Viducus, from the canton of the Veliocasses in the province of Lugdunensis, trader with Britain, presented the arch and gate in the consulship of Gratus and Seleucus' (AD 221).

The left-hand part of the dedication is missing, and, with the exception of the beginnings of lines 2 and 3, the restoration offered here (Fig. 1)[116] differs from that of Roger Tomlin who first published the inscription.[117] Notes on the present restoration follow, by line number:

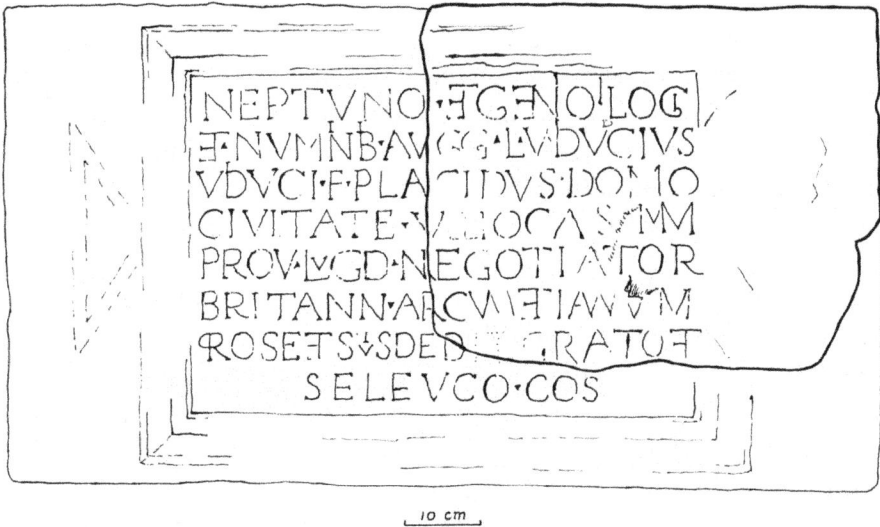

1 Suggested reconstruction of the inscription of L. Viducius Placidus from York

1 *Neptuno*: compare the dedication to Neptune from Domburg.[118] Tomlin suggests *I(ovi) O(ptimo) M(aximo) D(olicheno)*, which is too short if the restoration given here of line 3 is correct.

3 Placidus' filiation in this form occurs on his dedication to Nehalennia from the shrine near Colijnsplaat, and should be the only possible one since Viducus, the father, lacked a *praenomen*, or rather the full *tria nomina* of a Roman citizen.

5 For the inclusion of the province, compare the description of M. Aurelius Lunaris (Table 2, no. 8) as *sevir col. Ebor. et Lind. Prov. Brit. Inf.*

6 Restored on the basis of Placidus' dedication to Nehalennia, where he

is described as *negotiator Britannicianus*. A possible objection to the use of the epithet *Britannicianus* here would be that, since the dedication was found at York, there would be no need to describe Placidus as a trader *with* Britain. However, if the *negotiatores Britanniciani* formed a guild of traders, as has been suggested above, this objection loses its force. The reading IANVAM seems epigraphically preferable to FANVM.[119]

7 The phrase *pro se* or *pro se et suis* occurs on seven of the altars erected to Nehalennia at her shrine near Colijnsplaat.[120]

The main point of interest lies in the fact that Placidus is the first *negotiator* of all those who made dedications to Nehalennia to be attested on this side of the Channel. It is also interesting to note that on his Nehalennia dedications he has a single name, Placidus, appropriate to a man who lacked Roman citizenship (*peregrinus*),[121] whereas on the York stone he has the *tria nomina*, Lucius Viducius Placidus, of a Roman citizen. It is quite possible that Placidus gained citizenship as a result of the *constitutio Antoniniana* in 212, when all free-born *peregrini* living within the empire were granted this status. He will have formed a *nomen* from the single peregrine name of his father. If this is correct, his Nehalennia dedication should date to before the year 212, and it could be argued that this is also true of other dedications to the goddess where the dedicator has a single peregrine name but the language is otherwise full and formal. On the basis of this argument, six of the dedications from the shrine near Colijnsplaat should have been erected before this date.

ACKNOWLEDGEMENTS

I am most grateful to Professor J.E. Bogaers, on whose published writings this article leans so heavily, for making extensive corrections to a draft version of it. He does not, of course, necessarily subscribe to all ideas expressed, nor can he be held responsible for errors that it may contain.

Illustration note: This article was originally published with a halftone illustration of the inscription of Lucius Viducius Placidus from York, not included in the present collection, but referred to in the notes below.

Addendum: Since this article was written, the second volume (in fascicules) and third volume of *The Roman Inscriptions of Britain*, encompassing personal belongings and similar, bearing inscriptions, and inscriptions on stone, have been published.[122] Inscriptions in these volumes, equivalent to those published in the original article, are referred to in the notes below.

1   Ritterling 1924; 1925.
2   Hassall 1970.
3   RIB 108; Stein 1932, 141; Alföldy 1968, 19.
4   Alföldy 1968, 36.
5   RIB 109.
6   Saxer 1967.
7   ILS 9200, cf. 1025.
8   ILS 2726.
9   RIB 1322.
10 JRS 57 (1967), 205, no. 16; Birley 1967.
11 CIL VII, 495.
12 RIB 369.
13 RIB 1319–20.
14 RIB 665.
15 Bogaers 1965, 15–18, 21–3; Nesselhauf and von Petrikovits 1967.
16 ILS 2536; Bogaers 1965, 20–1.
17 Bang 1906.
18 Tac. Agr. 36.
19 Tac. Agr. 28.
20 CIL XVI.
21 CIL XVI, 43.
22 RIB 2140.
23 Not. Dig. Occ. 58.15, 58.20.
24 Not. Dig. Occ. 58.14.
25 RIB 1593–4.
26 RIB 1538.
27 RIB 1303.
28 RIB 2107–8, Birrens.
29 For some of the Germanic deities, see the indexes of de Vries 1956; 1957.
30 RIB 1593.
31 RIB 2140; Horn 1970.
32 RIB 2108.
33 RIB 1074.
34 RIB 2096.
35 RIB 1594.
36 RIB 1576.
37 RIB 1593.
38 RIB 2135.
39 RIB 1989.
40 RIB 1030.
41 RIB 574, 1031–2, 919.
42 de Vries 1957, 289 with distribution map.
43 Haverfield 1918; Heichelheim 1961; Frere 1978, 367; Birley 1953c, 26–37, pl.

II.6.

44 *RIB* 902.
45 Davies 1977a.
46 *RIB* 357.
47 *RIB* 506.
48 *CIL* XIII, 6679, from Lincoln, in Legion XXII Primigenia at Mainz.
49 *BRGK* 40 (1959), 200 f., no. 216.
50 *CIL* XIII, 12424 f.; Alföldy 1968, 49–50; Bogaers 1969a, 34.
51 Baatz 1973, 71.
52 cf. Wild 1975, 147.
53 *CIL* XIII, 8707.
54 Bogaers 1969b.
55 *PIR²* I, 145.
56 Birley 1958, 10; Fitz 1961, 196.
57 *RIB* 140, 163.
58 Gose 1955.
59 *RIB* 310.
60 *RIB* 309.
61 *RIB* 126.
62 *RIB* 89, Chichester; *Britannia* 7 (1976), 378–9, no. 2.
63 *CIL* XIII, 6221, Worms.
64 *BRGK* 17 (1927), 6, no. 20, Trier.
65 *RIB* 2059.
66 Birley 1966, 228.
67 *JRS* 21 (1931), 247, no. 2c.
68 Bogaers 1967b, 6, 102, fig 4.
69 Bogaers and Gysseling 1972a.
70 Hondius-Crone 1955.
71 Stuart and Bogaers 1971, no. 27; Bogaers and Gysseling 1972b.
72 Bogaers 1971; Stuart and Bogaers 1971.
73 Boersma 1967, 68–70.
74 Boersma 1967, 70.
75 Stuart and Bogaers 1971, no. 46.
76 Stuart and Bogaers 1971, no. 32; Bogaers 1972.
77 Bogaers 1972.
78 Bogaers 1971, 37–8; with corrections to Stuart and Bogaers 1971, nos 27, 32 in Bogaers and Gysseling 1972b, and Bogaers 1972.
79 *CIL* XIII, 8498–9.
80 *CIL* XIII, index 13.
81 Bogaers 1971, 40 ff.
82 Pliny *NH* 31.44.95.
83 *Artis Magiricae Libri X.*
84 But note *CIL* XIII, 8513, tentatively restored by Bogaers as *neg(otiator) a[llecarius]*.
85 Bogaers 1971, 40, pl. 53.
86 Boon 1974, 263.

[87] cf. *CIL* XIII, 10025.III, reading CCAA for *C(olonia) C(laudia) A(ra) A(grippinensium)*, i.e. Cologne.

[88] *OLD*.

[89] *CIL* XIII, index 13.

[90] *BRGK* 27 (1937), 104, no. 188; *BRGK* 40 (1950), 124, no. 3.

[91] Toynbee 1964, 420–2.

[92] Jenkins 1956.

[93] *JRS* 59 (1969), 244, no. 61; *Britannia* 5 (1974), 464, no. 15 = *RIB* II.4, 2456.7.

[94] Bogaers 1971, 41.

[95] *CIL* XI, 390–1.

[96] de Brisay and Evans 1975.

[97] Bogaers 1971, 42.

[98] *CIL* XIII, 8105.

[99] e.g. Wightman 1970, 189–92.

[100] See Bogaers 1971, 42; Boon 1974, 263–6; 1975, 52–67; Wightman 1970, 191, with discussion and further references on this complex question.

[101] Wild 1967, 648–9.

[102] *Price Edict* 19.48.

[103] cf. Messius Fortunatus, *negotiator artis cretariae, neg(otiator) paenul(larius)* – a dealer in pottery and cloaks (*CIL* XIII, 6366) but located at Sumelocenna in Raetia and, therefore, perhaps unlikely to have been concerned with trade with Britain.

[104] Frere 1978, 390, 402 n. 32.

[105] *CIL* XIII, 7836.

[106] *CIL* XIII, 8725.

[107] *CIL* XIII, 7587.

[108] Meiggs 1973, 283–8; Calza 1915.

[109] Bogaers 1960/1, 306 n. 232.

[110] *RIB* 69–71; Boon 1974, 58.

[111] Bogaers 1960/1, 306 n. 232.

[112] cf. *CIL* XIII, 8830 = *ILS* 1461: a joint dedication made by the lessees to the goddess Hludana.

[113] *CIL* XIII, 8815 = *ILS* 4757.

[114] Bogaers 1971, 32.

[115] *Britannia* 7 (1976), 378, nos 1–2.

[116] See also Hassall 1978, fig. 43a.

[117] *Britannia* 8 (1977), 430–1, no. 18. Subsequently published in *Britannia* 9 (1978), 484, item c = *RIB* III, 3195. The restoration of missing portions given above differs in places from *RIB* III, the latest publication of the inscription, but has been retained here.

[118] Hondius-Crone 1955, no. 36.

[119] *Britannia* 8 (1977), 430, no. 18.

[120] Bogaers 1971, 39.

[121] It is very unlikely that Placidus simply omitted his *praenomen* and *nomen*, since he included both filiation and tribal origin.

[122] *RIB* II; *RIB* III.

Part IV

Later Military History: the Fourth Century

17
BRITAIN IN THE *NOTITIA*
DIGNITATUM

Originally published:
'Britain in the Notitia', in R. Goodburn and P. Bartholomew (eds),
*Aspects of the Notitia Dignitatum: Papers presented to the conference in
Oxford, December 13 to 15, 1974*, BAR Supplementary Series 15, 1976,
Oxford, 103–17

A DETAILED EXAMINATION of a single diocese of the Gallic prefecture as
it appears in the pages of the *Notitia Dignitatum* might seem to be
of relatively local interest. However, the British diocese can be regarded
in some ways as typical of a frontier area of the empire, and to appreciate
its place in the late imperial bureaucracy is to know something about
the workings of the late imperial bureaucratic machine as a whole. At
the local level the survey needs no justification, for the *Notitia* is a prime
source for Roman Britain in the fourth and early fifth centuries. It is,
however, a source that has, in the present writer's opinion, sometimes
been misused. This has stemmed from general misconceptions about
the nature of the document, and a second function of this study will be
to re-examine one or two basic assumptions that have been made about
it. Finally, the attempt at the end of this article to take another look at
two of the units under the command of the Duke of the Britains, along
with some of the identifications of the garrison forts in his chapter of
the *Notitia*, will be of use if only as a reminder that we know little about
any specialist functions that his troops may have had and that the Latin
place-names on the Ordnance Survey *Map of Roman Britain* do not have
the authority of 'received truth' that they are sometimes accorded. It is
to the general questions concerning the nature of the *Notitia* that I shall
turn first.

THE FUNCTION OF THE *NOTITIA*

Work by students of Roman Britain on the *Notitia* places great emphasis on the notion of 'returns' made by local army commanders to the *Primicerii Notariorum*. An extreme example of this is the recent study by John Ward.[1] The doctrine implicit behind that article is that the *Notitia* troop lists were constantly being revised by the *primicerii* in the light of fresh status reports sent in by local army commanders – even during the fluid conditions of a single campaign – and that the anomalies in the troop lists can be explained by this method of procedure for compiling the *Notitia* lists. Of course, there is good evidence for actual status reports, both daily records of individual units, monthly summaries, and the perhaps-yearly *pridiana*.[2] Arthur S. Hunt's *pridianum*, moreover, is probably a composite document based on the *pridiana* of several units.[3] It is just this sort of document that could have been compiled by the legate at provincial headquarters and forwarded by him to his imperial superior. But how frequently were such reports sent? Did the practice continue rigorously into the early fifth century? How often would the *primicerius* have revised his lists? And, above all, how often would this information have been incorporated into the *Notitia*? The answer to all these questions is that we do not know; and we still would not know even if we were justified in assuming with Ward that there ought to be no 'glaring example of incompetence or sloth on the part of the Roman Chancery'.[4] This assumption is reminiscent of the plea of Professor E. Birley who, when arguing for the *Notitia* as an unofficial compilation, claimed that this theory would at least 'allow us to suppose that there were rational men in the Roman Record Offices'.[5] In fact, it would be rash to adopt such optimistic attitudes towards Roman chancery procedure as the case of Flavius Abinnaeus shows:

> Their imperial majesties (Constantius and Constans) had appointed Abinnaeus to the command of the *ala* at Dionysias. But when he arrived at Alexandria and handed in the imperial letter of appointment, he was met with the information that other gentlemen had also arrived with similar letters of appointment to the same command... a situation which, while it smacks of comic opera, was perhaps not uncommon in these times.[6]

Yet if Abinnaeus' difficulties reveal the chancery in an unfavourable light, we need not necessarily explain the anomalies and inconsistencies in the *Notitia* by mere incompetence. After all, what was the document for? Was it really intended as an up-to-date status report on the condition and resources of the empire? It certainly was part of the duties of the *primicerius* to have at his fingertips the relevant information for such a report, and the poet Claudian is explicit on this: *regnorum tractat numeros, constringit in unum | sparsas imperii vires cuneosque recenset | dispositos.*[7] But he had another function also, *cunctorum tabulas adsignat honorum:*[8] that is to say he issued the codicils of appointment to imperial appointees to office. These codicils were presumably illuminated with the insignia that accompany the relevant sections of the *Notitia*, copied directly from the examplars provided in that document. If a post remained unfilled, its section in the *Notitia*, including the master copy of the insignia, naturally remained 'on file'. It is misleading to say that, at the date when the western *Notitia* was compiled, certainly after AD 410, the inclusion of the British sections was anachronistic, for they were only 'out of date' once the British diocese was officially renounced and this probably never actually happened. If Britain had been recovered and new appointments made, the lists of troops under the relevant commanders would, of course, have had to have been revised. While the diocese remained lost to Rome this could not be done, but it might still be useful to know what the old establishment had been for each command, while it is even possible that some of the old units, especially those under the command of the *dux*, actually remained on the island.

THE MILITARY AND CIVIL ORGANISATION OF THE BRITISH DIOCESE
The individual sections of the *Notitia* devoted to each of the high civilian officials or military commanders consist of three elements: the insignia of office (discussed above); a 'statement' of the sphere of competence of the official concerned (often taking the form of, or including a list of, his hierarchical subordinates), introduced by the phrase *sub dispositione* followed by the title of the officer in the genitive; and finally a listing of some of the members of the immediate office staff attached to the post. The total of such minor officials has been estimated[9] for the British diocese as approximately 1,000. The listing of the hierarchical subordinates renders the construction of a simple administrative chart of the British diocese a straightforward matter (Fig. 1). The chart shows in diagrammatic form the hierarchical relationship which those civil (financial and administrative) and military officers and officials who were actually stationed in the diocese bore to the centralised bureaucracy; this

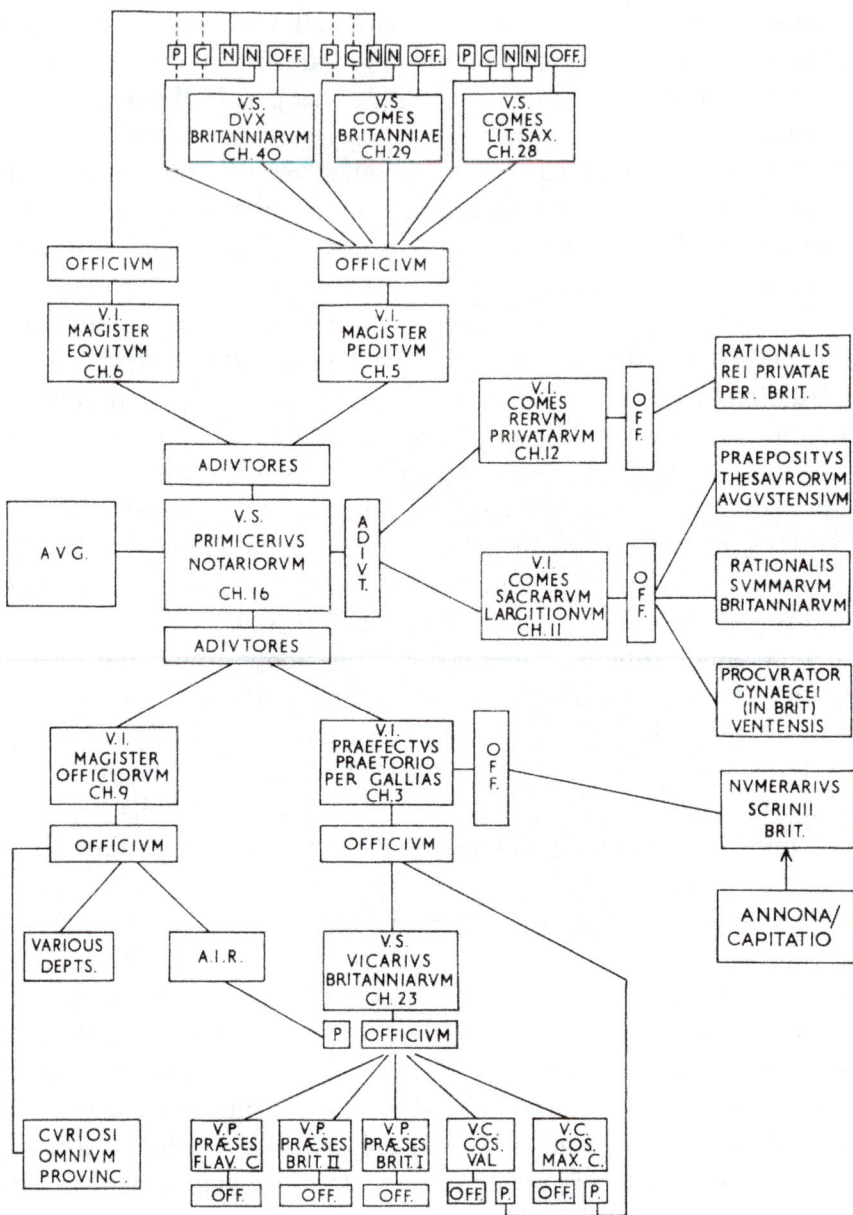

Top row boxes: P | C | N | N | OFF.   P | C | N | N | OFF.   P | C | N | N | OFF.

V.S. DVX BRITANNIARVM CH.40   V.S. COMES BRITANNIAE CH.29   V.S. COMES LIT. SAX. CH.28

OFFICIVM   OFFICIVM

V.I. MAGISTER EQVITVM CH.6   V.I. MAGISTER PEDITVM CH.5

RATIONALIS REI PRIVATAE PER. BRIT.

ADIVTORES

V.I. COMES RERVM PRIVATARVM CH.12 — OFF.

PRAEPOSITVS THESAVRORVM AVGVSTENSIVM

AVG. — V.S. PRIMICERIVS NOTARIORVM CH.16 — ADIVT.

V.I. COMES SACRARVM LARGITIONVM CH.11 — OFF.

RATIONALIS SVMMARVM BRITANNIARVM

ADIVTORES

PROCVRATOR GYNAECEI (IN BRIT) VENTENSIS

V.I. MAGISTER OFFICIORVM CH.9

V.I. PRAEFECTVS PRAETORIO PER GALLIAS CH.3 — OFF.

NVMERARIVS SCRINII BRIT.

OFFICIVM   OFFICIVM

VARIOUS DEPTS.   A.I.R.   V.S. VICARIVS BRITANNIARVM CH.23

ANNONA/ CAPITATIO

P | OFFICIVM

CVRIOSI OMNIVM PROVINC.

V.P. PRAESES FLAV. C — OFF.
V.P. PRAESES BRIT.II — OFF.
V.P. PRAESES BRIT.I — OFF.
V.C. COS. VAL — OFF | P
V.C. COS. MAX. C. — OFF | P

1 Administrative hierarchy of the British diocese. The princeps *and*
commentariensis *in the* officia *of* dux *and* comes *were appointed alternately*
each year from the officia *of the two* magistri militum. *P =* princeps; *C =*
commentariensis; *N =* numerarius; *A.I.R. =* agentes in rebus; *V.I. =* vir
illustris; *V.S. =* vir spectabilis; *V.C. =* vir clarissimus; *V.P. =* vir perfectissimus;
COS = consularis

bureaucracy being personified by the two western financial *comites*, the two western *magistri militum*, and the Praetorian Prefect of the Gauls.

To take financial officials first, the representative of the Count of the *Res Privata*, the *rationalis*, was primarily responsible for imperial property throughout the diocese. Such property will have accrued to the emperor partly through legacies and partly by confiscations. For the former category we have the direct statement of Tacitus that Prasutagus, king of the Iceni, left the Emperor Nero co-heir in his will together with his own daughters.[10] For the latter we can assume that confiscations were made of property belonging to the adherents of the British usurpers from Clodius Albinus at the end of the second century to Magnentius and Magnus Maximus in the fourth. The supporters of Magnentius particularly seem to have suffered badly at the hands of the notary Paulus.[11] The estates themselves, whether they came by way of legacy or confiscation, will in some cases have been administered directly by procurators[12] or other imperial agents, while in others they will have been leased out to tenants.

Parallel to the department of the *Res Privata* was that of the *Sacrae Largitiones*. Subject to the count of this department were three officials stationed in the diocese: the *procurator* of the *gynaeceum* at Venta, variously located at Winchester or Caistor-by-Norwich,[13] the nature of whose operations is the subject of a paper by John Wild;[14] the *praepositus* of the diocesan treasury at the diocesan capital Augusta, London;[15] and the *rationalis summarum Britanniarum* who, operating at local level through tax collectors (some, but not all, of whom were drawn from the curial classes of the individual *civitates*), collected taxes and levies. It would be out of place to go into detail about these, but they included levies for clothing and recruits, both eventually commuted to payment in gold; a land tax; a surtax (*collatio glebalis*) on the property of senators, some of whom may actually have held estates in Britain;[16] levies of gold, made on the accession of emperors and on each quinquennial anniversary, which were imposed on senators (*aurum oblacticium*) and the *civitates* (*aurum coronarium*); and a similar levy imposed on merchants and traders (*collatio lustralis*). To be connected with the levies of bullion by the Count of the Sacred Largess, or rather with the distribution made to favoured officials and soldiers on imperial accessions and at quinquennial celebrations, are the finds of silver ingots of fourth-century date studied recently by Kenneth Painter:[17] no less than 24 of these have been found at various sites in the British Isles, one from the Tower of London even

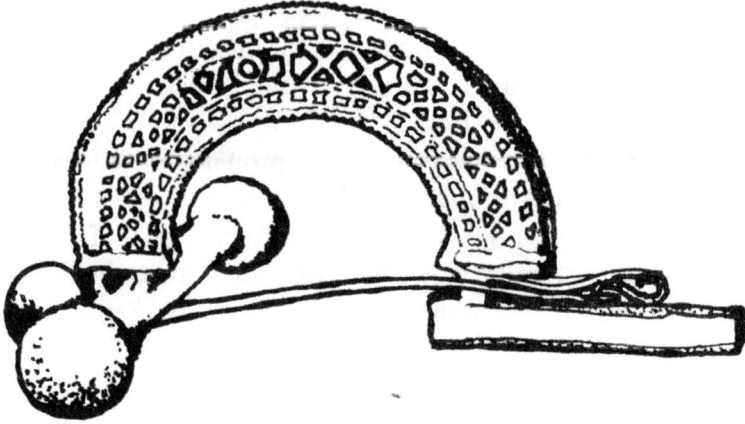

2 Gold cross-bow brooch found near Moffat, Dumfriesshire (arms, terminals and pin restored)

recalling the presence of the diocesan treasury in the city. The broken open-work gold cross-bow brooch from near Moffat, Dumfriesshire (Fig. 2), with its inscription commemorating the twentieth anniversary of the accession of Diocletian on 20 November 303, no doubt also emanated as an official gift from this department, or the *Res Summa* as it was then called, perhaps being lost by an officer during Constantius Chlorus' campaigns against the Picts two years later.[18] Other gold cross-bow brooches have been found at Caernarvon,[19] Odiham, Hants.,[20] and, in fragmentary condition, at an unrecorded site in Montgomeryshire.[21]

    More important in the financial sphere than the Count of either the *Res Privata* or the *Sacrae Largitiones* was the Praetorian Prefect of the Gauls, whose function as a financial official is not apparent from the *Notitia*, which lists only the provinces and dioceses under his command and his personal *officium*. It does not, for example, mention the *scrinia*, which dealt with the finances of each diocese under their own *numerarii*, or the *tractatores*, who dealt with the accounts of individual provinces.[22] Finance came into the sphere of the prefect's duties because he was concerned with the supplying of the army and the civil service, and was minister for (certain) public works and transport. For the upkeep of both of these latter, *ad hoc* levies in kind were made and compulsory labour exacted (*munera sordida*). To provide the army and quasi-military civil service with ration and fodder allowances (*annonae* and *capita*, from the Greek χαπητόν, 'fodder'), the provincials had long been subject to requisitions of corn (the *annona militaris*). By the third century, this had become a regular tax based on the amount of land and property held, including numbers of cattle and agricultural workers. This accounts for the fourth-century name of the tax, *capitatio* (a poll-tax – from the Latin *caput*). In the course of the century, the supply of foodstuffs was commuted to money payments. The details of the system are described by A.H.M. Jones,[23] to whom this survey, especially the financial section, owes so much. It is enough to say that the officials who made the collections were *curiales*. A rescript issued to Pacatianus, Vicar of Britain in 319, by Constantine,[24] shows that at that date at any rate, the land-owning curial classes in Britain were responsible for the tax obligations of their own estates and those of their tenants, but did not underwrite the total amount to be collected from their own *civitas*.

The Praetorian Prefect of the Gauls was the hierarchical superior of the *Vicarius* of Britain, who acted *vice* or as deputy to his chief. His subordinates, in turn, were the governors of the five provinces that formed his diocese: the *consulares* of Maxima Caesariensis and Valentia, and the *praesides* of Flavia Caesariensis, Britannia Prima and Britannia Secunda. Valentia was the creation of Count Theodosius after the troubles of 367. Its precise location and capital have long been matters of dispute; but it can hardly have been anywhere but in the north of the diocese, where Theodosius' reorganisation is most clearly attested, in particular by the newly-built signal stations on the north-east coast of Yorkshire. Its capital, as befitted the status of its governor, a *consularis*, must have been at York, the old York province Flavia Caesariensis becoming a rump perhaps centred on Carlisle. It is possible that the governor of Flavia had previously been a *consularis* but became a *praeses* after this administrative change.

The arguments of John Mann[25] for the location of the other provinces and their capitals seem to me to be conclusive, and there is no need to repeat them in detail here. In accordance with the principles of the Diocletianic system, each of the two Severan provinces was in turn subdivided. Britannia Inferior, the Severan northern province, is known from an inscription from Bordeaux[26] to have included the two *coloniae* of York and Lincoln, and these naturally became the capitals of the new Flavia Caesariensis (as originally constituted) and Britannia Secunda respectively. Britannia Superior, the Severan southern province, was split to form Maxima Caesariensis (which, with its relatively high-ranking governor, a *consularis*, must have been based on London) and Britannia Prima, which is shown by an inscription from Cirencester[27] to have had its capital in that city, after London the largest in the diocese.

The fourth-century date of this inscription, which records a dedication
by the *praeses* of Britannia Prima, Lucius Septimius, to Jupiter Optimus
Maximus on the restoration of a monument erected 'by the old religion'
(*prisca religione*), has been doubted by A.R. Birley on the basis of the
inclusion of a *praenomen* for the dedicator.[28] The objection, however, is
hardly conclusive,[29] and the natural inference, as Haverfield, cited by
The Roman Inscriptions of Britain,[30] long ago pointed out, is that the
restoration took place during the reign of Julian. In this connection,
it may be worth noting that Alypius, the *Vicarius* of Britain on Julian's
accession, was later an enthusiastic ally of the emperor in the attempt to
restore paganism.[31]

Turning now to the military organisation of the diocese, we find
three subordinates of the western *Magister Peditum* stationed in Britain:
the Duke of the Britains commanding the troops of Hadrian's Wall and
its hinterland; the Count of the Saxon Shore, whose command I have
discussed at length elsewhere;[32] and the Count of Britain, with his small
field army. The latter's troops, as *comitatenses*, are given not in the short
section devoted to him in the *Notitia* but in the chapters of the western
magistri militum, while the designs on their shields appear with the
shields of the other comitatensian units as the insignia of office of the
two commanders. These two chapters do not, of course, actually attribute
the units to the Count of Britain, for all the units are listed in them in
order of seniority and not according to geographical location. But the
so-called *Distributio Numerorum* does give a geographical breakdown
of the two *magistri* lists, and the count's six cavalry and three infantry
regiments are duly specified there as belonging to his command. The
date of the creation of the count's command is controversial. As is well
known, Gratian, the father of Valens and Valentinian, had held the office
of *comes* in Britain,[33] but this was probably an *ad hoc* appointment, like
that of Count Theodosius in the late 360s, and the position only became
institutionalised at the end of the fourth century. Some of the units under
the count have been thought by many to be identical to similarly-named
units under the command of the Count of the Saxon Shore and the Duke
of the Britains, but only in one case is the name actually identical – the
Equites Stablesiani, who appear on the Saxon Shore – and even this may
not be significant as there were many regiments of *Stablesiani* in the
field armies of the late empire.

Before dealing with problems of the command of the duke in
greater detail, we should call attention to one aspect of the chart (Fig.

1) not yet commented upon: the appointment of *principes* and, in some cases, other officials, such as *commentarienses* and *numerarii*, to the *officia* of the administrative and military officials in Britain from the *officium* of a hierarchical superior, or sometimes from a body such as the corps of the *agentes in rebus* which had no obvious connection at all. Jones points out that such appointments would have carried perquisites, since many of the documents countersigned by higher members of the various *officia* would have carried a fee.[34] He also points to the 'security' aspects of the system,[35] and the chart reveals this particularly clearly: the *Magister Officiorum* would have had a contact in the *officium* of the *Vicarius* who could report back directly to him, while the Praetorian Prefect of the Gauls had his own sources of information in the *officia* of the two *consulares*. Again, the hierarchical superior of the *Dux Britanniarum* and *Comes Britanniae*, the western *Magister Peditum*, had his own representatives in the *officia* of both these commanders – but so did the *Magister Equitum*, so that an independent check was provided. This sophisticated system of checks and counter-checks would have made collusion between any particular grouping of these civil and military officials virtually impossible. The *Magister Officiorum* also had his own official inspectors, *curiosi*, in all provinces of the diocese, whose reports need not always have been confined to the state of the *cursus publicus*, their official concern.

THE SECTION OF THE DUKE OF THE BRITAINS – SOME PROBLEMS

The text of the section on the Duke of the Britains is, if one ignores the tailpiece on his *officium*, divided into two parts: first, the units and forts of the hinterland of Hadrian's Wall (these alone are represented on his insignia); and secondly, those of the list *per lineam valli*, which includes the Cumbrian coast. The first part begins with three units of *equites* and continues with the *Barcarii Tigrisienses* and nine units of infantry, all *numeri*. Many of their fort sites are known: for example the sequence of fort names Lavatres, Verteris, Braboniaco (Bowes, Brough under Stainmore, and Kirkby Thore) occurs also in the *Antonine Itinerary* and their identification is certain. This particular sequence runs from east to west. Braboniaco is followed by two entries with fort names that cannot be so easily tied down, Maglone and Magis. One of these sites must surely be Old Carlisle, which lies west of Kirkby Thore, and from which comes an altar[36] set up to Jupiter Optimus Maximus and Vulkan for the safety of Gordian by the *Vik(ani) Mag(lonenses)* or

Mag(enses). The dedicators are usually interpreted as being Vik(anorum) Mag(istri); but against this interpretation and in favour of our own, it can be argued, first, that, normally, magistri would precede vicanorum (though vicomagistri as masters of wards are attested in the Notitia Urbis Constantinopolitanae); secondly, magistri of vici are rare in the western provinces, the officials most commonly mentioned on inscriptions being curatores (Aelius Mansuetus, who is introduced by the phrase curam agente on the dedication by the vicani from Carriden,[37] and the unknown man introduced by the similar phrase on the vicani dedication from Vindolanda,[38] were both presumably curatores); and thirdly, such semi-official dedications are normally made by the vicani themselves, and they usually qualify themselves by a geographical epithet (e.g. the Vicani Vindolandesses of the Vindolanda inscription).

The second problem treated in this section is the precise function of two of the units listed in the first part of the duke's section, the Numerus Directorum at Verteris, Brough under Stainmore, and the Numerus Supervenientium at Derventio. The word director is derived from the verb dirigere, 'to aim' or, specifically, 'to shoot'. It seems to me that it is just conceivable that the meaning intended is that of 'direct', in the sense of 'send' or 'dispatch'. Brough has produced the unique series of lead sealings studied by Professor Richmond,[39] which were, it seems, originally attached to bundles and packages routed to the south from northern forts through a forwarding depot at Brough. A possible parallel for this use of the word would be directoria, some form of dispatch dockets or address labels mentioned at one place in the Theodosian Code.[40]

The Supervenientes (Petueriensium) were linked in their function by E. Böcking[41] with the technical word superventus, 'surprise', used by Vegetius in describing the fourth-century British scouting vessels, called in army slang 'pictae':

> In addition, light scouting vessels are attached to the battle cruisers. These have a crew of about forty, twenty rowers on each side. The Britons call them Picts, and they use them for superventus. They can prevent the coming of the enemy at all times and forestall their plans by careful scouting. Both sails and rigging are painted sea blue so that the scout ships do not give themselves away. Even the wax that they use to calk their vessels is dyed. The crews wear camouflaged clothing so that when they make their sorties they escape notice by day as well as by night.[42]

The other possible meaning of *superventus* is 'reinforcements', and this is preferred by Roger Tomlin,[43] but the fact that Petuaria, the old station of the *Supervenientes* from which they derived part of their name, was a naval base, supports the claim that the word has a nautical meaning. As regards the location of Derventio, there are two possibilities, Papcastle and Malton, both of which were known by that name. The proximity of the latter to Petuaria – Brough-on-Humber – makes the equation with Malton the more likely, but the inland position of Malton on the Yorkshire Derwent all but precludes the use of boats. This fact sheds light on the way in which the strategy behind the north-east coastal defences changed during the course of the fourth century. Down perhaps to the middle of the century, fleets may well have been stationed on the Humber, and the Rivers Tees and Tyne; but silting was reducing the usefulness of Brough-on-Humber as a harbour,[44] and in 367 the defences were found wanting. Count Theodosius therefore instituted a new system, more passive but possibly more effective, which allowed raiders to land, their approach being signalled back from the series of new signal stations on the north-east Yorkshire coast, and their retreat being intercepted by troops based at Malton, Piercebridge and elsewhere.

The final problem concerns the identification of sites in the second part of the duke's section, *per lineam valli*. It has long been recognised that if one could identify a *Notitia* unit with a unit epigraphically attested at a particular fort on the Wall, it would be possible to deduce the actual name of the fort from the *Notitia* lists. Occasionally, the evidence of inscriptions can even be used to check the accuracy of the *Notitia*. Thus, the First Cohort of Astures, recorded in the *Notitia* at Aesica, is almost certainly a mistake for the Second Cohort, which is known from inscriptions to have been stationed at Great Chesters. Yet such discrepancies are small, and with the aid of inscriptions, it is possible to show that the *Notitia* is working along the line of the Wall from east to west. But after the fort of Camboglanna[45] (usually held to be Birdoswald, but see below), things get more difficult, for an inscription from Papcastle[46] which mentions a *Cuneus Frisionum Aballavensium* was thought at one time to show that that fort was the Aballaba of the *Notitia*, which, if correct, would prove that the *Notitia* list had left the line of the Wall. Fortunately, in the 1930s, a new inscription studied by Professor E. Birley[47] showed that the *Numerus Maurorum Aurelianorum*, the *Notitia* unit at Aballaba, was present at Burgh-by-Sands, thus demonstrating that the *Notitia* sequence sticks to the Wall.

Meanwhile Richmond, by studying the sequences of sites in the *Ravenna Cosmography*,[48] showed that Maio or Maia, which appears in that document but not in the *Notitia*, was probably Bowness-on-Solway. This meant that a piece of evidence that had long been neglected, the famous Rudge Cup, could be brought into play. This small enamelled vessel, with its stylised representation of the Wall and its turrets, has a list of five names round its rim:[49] it begins with the sequence *a Mais, Aballava*, and was now recognised to be a list of the Wall forts, running from west to east. In 1951, Jacques Heurgon published a similar cup from Amiens – the so-called Amiens Patera – with six Wall fort names instead of five, but otherwise confirming the names on the Rudge Cup and, like it, working along the Wall from west to east.[50] There are still difficulties, however, which are reflected in the discrepancies in Latin place-name attributions between the third edition (published in 1956) of the Ordnance Survey *Map of Roman Britain*, and the first and second editions of the *Map of Hadrian's Wall* (1964 and 1972). The problem is that Camboglanna of the *Notitia* and the Rudge Cup seems unquestionably to be placed at Birdoswald because of the presence there, attested by inscriptions, of the *Notitia* garrison, *Cohors I Aelia Dacorum*. This means that there is no room for the Banna of the Rudge Cup and Amiens Patera lists before the next fort, Great Chesters (Aesica or Esica) is reached. A second difficulty is the omission of Banna from the *Notitia* series. The solution of the compilers of the Ordnance Survey *Map of Hadrian's Wall* was to regard Banna as an alternative name for Magna (Carvoran) since this fort is not mentioned on the Cup and the Patera. This, however, is improbable because Carvoran is not physically attached to the Wall in the same way as the other Wall forts. On the other hand, Richmond and the compilers of the Ordnance Survey *Map of Roman Britain* detached the name Banna completely from the Wall series and placed it at Bewcastle, a suggestion which is even more implausible. There is yet another problem if, as is usually accepted, the Petriana of the *Notitia* was the original name for Stanwix, for Petriana does not occur in the Rudge or Amiens lists at all; yet Stanwix was the most important of all the Wall forts, garrisoned as it was by the *Ala Petriana*, the sole milliary *ala* in Britain.

One solution to all this would be to regard Banna as the name for Birdoswald, an interpretation supported by an inscription found at the site which mentions the *Venatores Banniesses*,[51] and to place Camboglanna at Castlesteads, its name perhaps connected with the first element in the name of the river, the Cambeck, that flows at the foot of the hill upon which it stands. The Uxelod(un)um of the Rudge and Amiens lists would then be the original and alternative name for Petriana – Stanwix. This means emending the text of the *Notitia*, which would now seem to contain no reference to Birdoswald. In the Oxford manuscript, the entry in the list for *Cohors I Dacorum*, which like many entries occupies two lines, is split between the last line of one column and the first of the next. If this reflects something of the layout of the archetype, then I believe that we can restore in the text of the *Notitia* an unsuspected lacuna which consists of two lines, and was caused by damage at the bottom of the folio:

> *Tribunus cohortis primae Aeliae Dacorum*
> *(Banna*
> *Tribunus cohortis secundae Tungrorum)*
> *Camboglanna*

It will be recalled that the presence of *Cohors II Tungrorum* at Castlesteads is attested epigraphically.[52]

As those familiar with the problems posed by the list of Wall names in the *Notitia* will realise, the succeeding names still do not correspond with the order of the Rudge or Amiens lists. Again, the puzzling name Congavata[53] is present in the *Notitia* but absent from the Rudge and Amiens lists, while Mais, as we have seen, occurs in the latter but not in the former (unless it is represented by Magis, which appears in the list of hinterland forts). One is thus forced to admit that until more inscriptions with the names of units are found from forts on the west end of the Wall and the western coastal forts that continue the series, it will probably be impossible to make more sense of the *Notitia*. However, until these are found, the evidence of the Rudge Cup and Amiens Patera should at least give us the names of the forts on the western end of Hadrian's Wall, even though we cannot yet place the *Notitia* units in them.

Addendum: Since this article was written, a recent study of the Rudge Cup, the Amiens Patera and notably the newly-discovered Staffordshire Moorlands Pan (Ilam Pan) has been published.[54]

[1]   Ward 1973.
[2]   Fink 1971, nos 47–57 (daily records), 58–62 (monthly summaries), 63–4 (*pridiana*).
[3]   Fink 1971, no. 63; originally published by A.S. Hunt: Fink 1958.

4   Ward 1973, 263.
5   Birley 1939, 210.
6   Bell et al. 1962, 7–8.
7   Claudian *Epithalamium of Palladius and Celerina* 86–8.
8   Claudian *Epithalamium of Palladius and Celerina* 85.
9   Professor A.H.M. Jones, in a lecture on 'Roman Britain in the fourth century' given on behalf of the Society for the Promotion of Roman Studies at Exeter in 1966.
10 Tac. *Ann.* 14.31.
11 Amm. Marc. 14.5.6.
12 *RIB* 179, from Combe Down, near Bath.
13 Wild 1967; Manning 1966.
14 Wild 1976.
15 For the name, cf. Amm. Marc. 27.8.7, 28.3.1.
16 cf. *Vita Sanctae Melaniae Junioris* 11–12, 18–21, 37 = *Analecta Bollandiana* 8 (1889), 19–63 (Latin); *Analecta Bollandiana* 22 (1903), 7–49 (Greek).
17 Painter 1972.
18 Curle 1932, 370–1; cf. Noll 1974.
19 Wheeler 1923, 130–1.
20 Brailsford 1964, 20.
21 Allen 1890, 156.
22 Jones 1964, 449–50.
23 Jones 1964, 448–62.
24 *CTh.* 11.7.2.
25 Mann 1961.
26 *AE* 1922, 116.
27 *RIB* 103.
28 Birley 1967, 85.
29 See, e.g., the late fourth-century inscription from nearby Lydney, which probably reads T. Flavius Senilis: *CIL* VII, 137.
30 *RIB* 103, with references.
31 Amm. Marc. 23.1.2–3.
32 Hassall 1977b.
33 Amm. Marc. 30.7.3.
34 Jones 1964, 580.
35 Jones 1964, 128.
36 *RIB* 899.
37 *JRS* 47 (1957), 229–30, no. 18.
38 *RIB* 1700.
39 Richmond 1936.
40 *CTh.* 14.15.3.
41 Böcking 1839/53, 879, cf. 446–7.
42 Vegetius *De Re Militari* 4.37.
43 Tomlin 1969.
44 Wacher 1969, 81.
45 The text of the *Notitia* reads Amboglanna, but Camboglanna is the generally

accepted form.

[46] *RIB* 883.

[47] Birley 1939, 191–4.

[48] Richmond 1935.

[49] The Rudge Cup list runs as follows: A MAIS ABALLAVA UXELODUM CAMBOGLANS BANNA.

[50] Heurgon 1951. The Amiens Patera list runs as follows: MAIS ABALLAVA UXELODUNUM CAMBOG[LANI]S BANNA ESICA.

[51] *RIB* 1905.

[52] *RIB* 1981–3.

[53] In uncials, Congavata, minus the first 'a', would look suspiciously like the *torquata* title of the *Ala Petriana*: cf. *ILS* 2728; *RIB* 957. Indeed, before the discovery of the Staffordshire Moorlands Pan (in 2003), I had wondered whether the place-name as given in the *Notitia* was simply a corruption of this title!

[54] Breeze 2012. See also Hassall 2010, 18.

18
THE HISTORICAL BACKGROUND AND MILITARY UNITS OF THE SAXON SHORE

Originally published:
'The historical background and military units of the Saxon Shore', in
D.E. Johnston (ed.), *The Saxon Shore*, CBA Research Report 18, 1977,
London, 7–10

THIS CONTRIBUTION MIGHT equally have been entitled 'The Saxon Shore and the *Notitia Dignitatum*' since it consists basically of a commentary on what that document has to say about the forts and units under the command of the *Comes Litoris Saxonici*. The attempt to do this requires no apology in a conference on the Shore, since *without* the *Notitia* there would be no Saxon Shore at all: at least, historians and archaeologists would have to think up a new name for it, since the term *Litus Saxonicum* is found only in the pages of the *Notitia*. Some such survey is also rendered timely by the appearance of Professor Hoffmann's *Das spätrömische Bewegungsheer und die Notitia Dignitatum.*[1] This massive work, though confined to fourth- and early fifth-century field armies, is relevant to the nominally limitanean command of the *comes*, since the relation between *comitatenses* and *limitanei* would appear to be more fluid than the rigid distinction found in the *Notitia* might suggest.

The precise character of the *Notitia* is, of course, relevant to the information that it contains, and it will be as well to say something first of the nature and purpose of the *Notitia*. There are in reality two '*Notitias*': the *Notitia dignitatum omnium tam civilium quam militarium in partibus Orientis*, and a similarly-entitled *Notitia... in partibus Occidentis*. The names reveal the function: they are handbooks or calendars of offices, both military and civil, in the eastern and western parts of the empire respectively. The *Notitia*, as the two together are often loosely called, survives in manuscript copies made at three or four removes from an early fifth-century original, and the most important of these copies are now in libraries in Munich, Paris and Oxford. The lost originals from which they were ultimately derived should have belonged to the departments of the chief secretaries of the imperial chanceries in the east and west, the *Primicerii Notariorum*. In fact, the archetypes for both the western and the eastern *Notitia* may have originated in the department of the western *primicerius*, a copy of the eastern *Notitia*, which is less up to date, being kept by him for reference purposes. One important aspect of the *Notitia* is explained by the actual function of the *primicerius*: it was his task, among other things, to issue to appointees the illuminated commissions of their appointment to office in the form of small books or codicils. These codicils were embellished with the insignia of office of the official concerned, and it may well have been one of the main functions (if not the main function) of the *Notitia* to provide a series of exemplars of all the insignia. This explains why certain sections of the *Notitia* are 'out of date', a statement which immediately begs a question. The exemplars of all insignia would remain in date and on file until a particular post was known to have been abolished for good. Thus, the inclusion of so-called 'obsolete' British material in the *Notitia*, after a date at which the British provinces had been abandoned, is interesting as a statement of official policy towards Britain: the island had not yet been written off by the Roman higher command, even if there was as yet no immediate possibility of recovering it.

Besides the insignia of office, the sections or chapters of the *Notitia* also list the hierarchical subordinates of the particular officials concerned. Thus among the lists of *comites* (counts) and *duces* (dukes) in charge of regional frontier armies subject to the *Magister Peditum* in the west, we find the Count of Britain in charge of a small field army, and the Count of the Saxon Shore and the Duke of the Britains in charge of the garrisons of Hadrian's Wall and the Wall hinterland. This aspect of the *Notitia* is a valuable one, since it allows historians to define the military and bureaucratic structure of the empire of the fourth century. Similarly, at a lower level, the individual sections devoted to the Duke of the Britains and Count of the Saxon Shore list the commanders, prefects and tribunes of the different units under their command and the names of the forts which they garrisoned.

Turning now in detail to the command of the Count of the Saxon Shore and his section in the western *Notitia*,[2] his insignia consists of a stylised 'map' of Britain with nine garrison sites represented by pictures of forts (in some manuscript versions looking more like fortified towns) dotted over the island. The forts are labelled with their names but their positions on the 'map' do not correspond to geographical reality; instead they correspond to the order of forts in the list of units and bases that follows. This list is in part defective, for the names of two of the bases (*Rutupis* and *Anderidos*) have dropped out from the manuscripts but they can be supplied from the captions of the forts on the insignia. Indeed, it is likely that the captions initially derived from the list, and so we are justified in using them in this way. This can be shown to be definitely the case elsewhere, for example the 'fort site' *Corumosismis* on the insignia of the *Dux tractus Armoricani*[3] obviously derives from the text entry *Praefectus militum Maurorum Osismiacorum Osismis*,[4] or the 'fort site' *Nuncinercisa* on the insignia of the *Dux provinciae Valeriae*[5] from the text entry *Cuneus equitum Constantianorum, Lusionio, nunc Inercisa.*[6]

With the names of the two missing fort sites restored, the list runs as follows:

> *Praepositus numeri Fortensium, Othonae*
> *Praepositus militum Tungrecanorum, Dubris*
> *Praepositus numeri Turnacensium, Lemanis*
> *Praepositus equitum Dalmatarum Branodunensium, Branoduno*
> *Praepositus equitum Stablesianorum Gariannonensium, Gariannonor*
> *Tribunus cohortis primae Baetasiorum, Regulbio*
> *Praefectus legionis secundae Augustae, Rutupis*
> *Praepositus numeri Abulcorum, Anderidos*
> *Praepositus numeri Exploratorum, Portum Adurni*

Most of the nine garrison sites can be identified with certainty, partly due to the similarity between ancient and modern names (e.g. *Branodunum* = Brancaster; *Othona* = Ythanceaster, the old name for Bradwell) and partly through ancient geographical sources such as the *Antonine Itinerary* or the *Peutinger Table*, which though defective for most of Britain does include the south-east coast. The only difficulty arises from the fact that there are only nine names whereas if one counts Walton Castle, Essex, whose site has now been eroded into the sea, there are ten sites which are strong candidates to be included in the Shore fort series. C.E. Stevens[7] explained the anomaly by eliminating Portchester (usually identified with *Portus Adurni*) from the series as listed in the *Notitia*, since on the archaeological evidence then available it did not appear to have been occupied in the second half of the fourth century. He then attached the name to the otherwise-unnamed site at Walton. We now know, however, that Portchester *did* remain in occupation, so that the formal resemblance between the first element in the name and that of *Portus Adurni* should allow one to draw the natural conclusion that the two sites should be identified.

A second reason for defending this identification can be found in a phenomenon pointed out by Stevens himself: although the fort sites of the Saxon Shore do not follow a strict geographical order in the *Notitia*, as for example is followed by the forts of Hadrian's Wall listed under the command of the Duke of the Britains,[8] they are not listed in a random fashion but appear to be paired on a geographical basis. Thus, Dover makes a pair with Lympne in Kent, Brancaster with Burgh Castle both in East Anglia, Reculver with Richborough once more in Kent, and Pevensey and Portchester on the south coast. Only Bradwell, at the beginning of the list, is not paired, yet it would form a natural twin with Walton Castle. The omission of Walton from the manuscripts could be explained by the faulty manuscript tradition. Here one can compare the omission of the two fort names in the list of units, and note the suggested position of the Walton entry at the beginning of the list: both the bottom of the folio containing the illustration or the top of the folio with the main body of the text would be particularly prone to damage. Alternatively, the Walton unit could have been transferred (perhaps sea erosion had already begun to threaten the site) and the entry deleted from the archetype. That the pairing of fort sites corresponded at least in part to an actual administrative pairing of units, a feature found elsewhere in the military organisation of the fourth century, is suggested by the recurrence of the *Abulci* and *Exploratores*, the units at Pevensey and Portchester, as a pair under the command of the *Magister Equitum per Gallias*.[9] A detailed examination of these two and the other units of the Shore system is now called for.

I. THE *NUMERUS FORTENSIUM, OTHONAE* (BRADWELL)

There are difficulties in explaining the epithet *Fortenses*. Both E. Böcking[10] and Hoffmann[11] were of the opinion that units of *Fortenses*, which are found both among troops of limitanean and comitatensian status, were in origin vexillations of the old legion of Egypt, *II Traiana Fortis*. There are problems, however, though not necessarily insuperable ones, in accepting this view. In the first place, the total number of *Fortenses* units is rather larger than one might have expected for all to have been derived from a single parent unit. Secondly, legionary detachments ought, obviously, to have given rise to infantry units, yet in the *Notitia* lists we find two cavalry units, a *Cuneus Equitum Fortensium* and a *Cuneus Equitum Dalmatarum Fortensium*. Hoffmann has explained the former as a unit formed from the legionary cavalry, like the cavalry units of *promoti* who are thought to have originated in this way. The latter, he believes, could have been accounted for by the amalgamation of a detachment of legionary cavalry with a cavalry unit of *Dalmatae*. The unit at Bradwell, he considers, should have belonged originally to the field army. Its presence with the frontier forces on the Shore could, he has held, be explained as a transfer to Britain under Valentinian as a consequence of the troubles of AD 367. It is possible, however, to envisage a much earlier context for the transfer of a detachment of *Legio II Traiana Fortis* to Britain. Victorinus complimented *II Traiana* among the legions honoured by him with special issue of *aurei* in the late 260s or early 270s. E. Ritterling[12] interpreted this to mean that he had been accompanied by a vexillation of *II Traiana* when he came from the east to quash the independent Gallic Empire, and that the detachment followed him when he went over to the rebels. After the final defeat of the Gallic Empire, it would not have been inconceivable for Aurelian to have sent the disgraced unit to help hold the expanding Shore defences in Britain rather than return it to Egypt.

2. THE *MILITES TUNGRECANI, DUBRIS* (DOVER),
AND 3. THE *NUMERUS TURNACENSIUM, LEMANIS* (LYMPNE)

Stevens has linked these two units on the basis of their names and, indeed, the *Tungrecani* from Tungri (Tongres, as Aduatuca Tungrorum became in the later empire in the same way that Lutetia Parisiorum became Parisii) and the *Turnacenses* from Turnacum (Tournai) seem at first sight to be obviously connected in some way. He has suggested that they had been sent from Tournai and Tongres after the strategic Cologne–Boulogne road had ceased to be garrisoned by regular Roman troops during the reign of Gratian (375–83). There are two objections to this. Firstly, the fortified posts along this road – e.g. at Liberchies[13] – may here have continued in occupation into the beginning of the fifth century. Secondly, the different adjectival form of the geographical epithets of the units could be significant. The *Turnacenses* may well have been limitanean, but the *Tungrecani*, as we know from the pages of Ammianus Marcellinus,[14] were a famous regiment of the field army. In fact, as Ammianus Marcellinus shows, there was a unit of *Tungrecani Iuniores* and, by implication, a corresponding unit of *Tungrecani Seniores*, created from a single parent body after the division of the imperial armies between Valentinian and Valens in 364.[15] Hoffmann has explained the presence of a detachment of the *Tungrecani* in Britain in the same way as the presence of the *Fortenses*: as a loan from the field army to the Shore, drastically weakened as a result of the crisis of 367. But, again, another possibility would be that they were the *Tungrecani Iuniores* who proclaimed the usurper Procopius at Constantinople in 365.[16] This unit, unlike the *Seniores*, is not specifically attested in the *Notitia*, and a demotion to limitanean status would be perfectly natural, though the actual arrival of the unit in Britain might well not have taken place until reinforcements were sent after the disaster of 367. If the *Tungrecani* arrived at this late date, we may be justified in thinking that they were not the first unit to be in garrison at Dover.

4. The *Equites Dalmatae Branodunenses*, *Branoduno* (Brancaster) + *Cohors Prima Aquitanorum*, and 5. the *Equites Stablesiani Gariannonenses*, *Gariannonor* (Burgh Castle)

Units of Dalmatian cavalry were, we are specifically told by the Byzantine writer Cedrenus,[17] first raised by Gallienus (260–8). They also played a distinguished part in Claudius' wars against the Goths.[18] A unit of Dalmatian cavalry could, therefore, have come to Britain at any time after the recovery of the island with the rest of the Gallic Empire on the defeat of Tetricus in 274 but not before. This might be thought to cause difficulties for those who, like the present writer, would see in Brancaster a fort that is typologically among the earliest of the Shore forts, with rounded corners, internal bank and no external bastions. This difficulty is, however, resolved by the recent find of a tile-stamp of *Cohors I Aquitanorum* just outside the Shore fort, since this unit can now be regarded as the original garrison.[19] *Cohors I Aquitanorum* has been previously attested at Carrawburgh on Hadrian's Wall under Hadrian,[20] and at Brough-on-Noe under Antoninus Pius,[21] and there is no evidence as yet that it was ever stationed at a site in the Wall hinterland with

easy access to the east coast. The point is important because it is just
conceivable that the tile came to Brancaster as ship's ballast in the same
way that a tile of *Legio VI Victrix P.F.* found at Gayton Thorpe, Norfolk,
must almost certainly have come from York.[22] Professor Toynbee[23] has
linked the Dalmatian cavalry at Brancaster with parts of two fine cavalry
helmets found in the River Wensum which she dates stylistically to the
third century, a date which receives support from the recent study by
Russell Robinson of Roman armour.[24]

Paired with the *Dalmatae* at Brancaster were the *Stablesiani* at
Burgh Castle with its fine bastions, and hints (if one could trust the
indications of air photographs) of resemblances in the planning of
buildings in the intervallum space to similarly-sited buildings at Eining
on the Rhaetian Limes. The name *Stablesiani*, which is applied to a
large number of units in the *Notitia*, has recently been studied by M.P.
Speidel.[25] His conclusion is that just as the legionary cavalry seem to
have been promoted ('*promoti*') to self-standing units under Gallienus,
so the *stratores*, grooms or equerries on the staffs of provincial governors
serving under the command of an officer, hypothetically named the
'*stablensis*', were elevated to independent status at the same time. The
explanation of the name is not entirely convincing but the date of the
creation of these units seems on general grounds reasonable, in which
case the arrival of the *Stablesiani* in Britain should have taken place,
like the *Dalmatae*, after the recovery of the island together with the rest
of the Gallic Empire by Aurelian in 274. If the British *Stablesiani* were
identical with the unit of *Stablesiani* attested by the inscription on the
famous Deurne helmet and associated coin finds in Holland under
Constantine,[26] its arrival would have to be set even later, and there might
be a temptation to link its transfer with that of the *Turnacenses* from the
same general area. There is, however, no compelling reason to identify
these two units of *Stablesiani*. It is possible, on the other hand, that the
Stablesiani at Burgh Castle are the same unit listed in *Not. Dig. Occ.* 7,
the *Distributio Numerorum*, as serving (later) under the command of the
Count of the Britains.

6. COHORS PRIMA BAETASIORUM, REGULBIO (RECULVER), AND 7. LEGIO SECUNDA AUGUSTA, RUTUPIS (RICHBOROUGH)

Both were units of the garrison of Britain in the early empire, and for
this reason an administrative pairing quite apart from the proximity of
their two garrison sites seems reasonable. But the real twin to Reculver

is Brancaster, which is typologically so close to it: at both there are the same rounded corners, internal earth banks, and lack of bastions and tile courses, all early features. The siting of these two, protecting the approaches to the Thames estuary and the Wash respectively, both particularly vulnerable avenues of attack for seaborne raiders, also suggests that the two sites were the earliest elements in the defensive system of the south-east. *Cohors I Baetasiorum*, attested at Reculver not only by the *Notitia* but also by tile-stamps,[27] would then be matched by *Cohors I Aquitanorum*, now shown by a tile-stamp to have been at Brancaster. The *Baetasii*, like the Aquitanians, can be traced by finds of inscriptions at other forts in Britain: at Maryport in the late second century,[28] and at Bar Hill on the Antonine Wall.[29] A recently-found altar from Old Kilpatrick[30] set up by the unit has been dated by Professor E. Birley to the time of Severus, but more probably indicates that the unit was stationed at the fort in the second Antonine occupation of the Wall.[31] Reculver is unique in having produced a building inscription which one day may give us a hard date for the construction (or reconstruction) of part of the *principia*.[32] Unfortunately, the governor of Britannia Superior, mentioned on the stone, probably Aradius rather than Triarius Rufinus, cannot be precisely dated. Professor A.R. Birley[33] dates his governorship very tentatively to the period 238–44.

　　Legio II Augusta, a vexillation of which formed the garrison at Richborough, has been the subject of a study by M.G. Jarrett,[34] who has pointed out that the latest epigraphic evidence for the unit at its old base at Caerleon is a building inscription[35] recording the buildings of barracks *a solo* for the Seventh Cohort of the legion under Valerian and Gallienus, which, Jarrett suggests, might imply the cohort's return to Caerleon after a prolonged absence, perhaps at Corbridge. If J.S. Johnson[36] is right and the construction of Richborough dates as early as the reign of Probus – or even his predecessor Aurelian, who took the title *Britannicus Maximus* (it occurs on one inscription and one papyrus only[37]) – the section of *Legio II Augusta* that is found there could be the first unit in garrison, whether or not a part still remained at Caerleon. Jarrett correctly points out that there is no evidence that the other half of the legion went to garrison the fourth-century fort of Saxon Shore type at Cardiff (although there is no evidence that it did not in fact do so). Finally, the view often expressed that the detachment of the legion at Richborough is identical with units of *secundani* in the *Distributio*[38] is not at all certain, for even if the parent body of the units in question were

Legio II Augusta, it need not be the part stationed at Richborough. In fact, the *Secundani Britones*[39] have an ethnic name that, under the early empire at any rate, would suggest a non-legionary origin – compare the existence of *Numeri Brittonum* in Upper Germany – while Hoffmann argues that the *Secundani Iuniores*[40] were one of a small number of new units created by Stilicho in 399 or 400.

8. *Numerus Abulcorum, Anderidos* (Pevensey),
and 9. *Numerus Exploratorum, Portum Adurni* (Portchester)

The name of the *Abulci* has puzzled commentators: it may be a tribal designation but this is not certain. Hoffmann has identified it with a homonym that took part in the Battle of Mursa in Pannonia in 351 when Magnentius was defeated by Constantius II.[41] If this is correct, it provides a *terminus post quem* for its arrival in Britain. Was it the first unit in garrison? Pevensey is a late fort typologically, or at least it is typologically different from most of the Shore fort series, while stratified coins may give a date of post-335 for its construction, although this is not quite certain,[42] but it could still be earlier than 351 or the post-367 period, if that is the context in which the arrival of the *Abulci* should be placed. In fact, as Stevens has pointed out, we have traces of the previous garrison actually in the *Notitia*, for the *Classis Anderetiana* at Paris[43] and the *Milites Anderetiani* at Mainz[44] both bear geographical epithets that show that they once formed the garrison and associated fleet detachment stationed at Anderetia/Anderida. The tile-stamps reading HON AVG ANDRIA have been shown by D.P.S. Peacock[45] to be modern forgeries, but it is just possible that the *Abulci* have left traces of their presence in the form of other stamped tiles at Chester-le-Street, where tiles read as ΛΒΟΛCΙ (conceivably for Αβολκι) have been found.[46] If this were indeed correct, then it would link the *Abulci* with the *Numerus Exploratorum* at Portchester, with which it is paired, for this almost certainly had seen earlier service with the army in North Britain: there is epigraphic evidence for two certain units of *exploratores* at the outpost forts north of Hadrian's Wall of Risingham and High Rochester, while in the *Antonine Itinerary* Netherby is called *Castra Exploratorum*, which strongly suggests that a similar unit was stationed there. A possible context for the transfer of *exploratores* from North Britain to the south coast could have been the abolition by Count Theodosius of the *Areani* (or *Arcani*) patrols north of the Wall after the troubles of 367, as recorded by Ammianus Marcellinus.[47]

THE GALLIC SAXON SHORE

The two commands in the *Notitia* that appear to have superseded an earlier 'Gallic' Saxon Shore are those of the *Dux Belgicae Secundae* and the *Dux tractus Armoricani*.[48] The former has only three units listed under his command: the *Equites Dalmatae* at *Marcis in litore Saxonico*, the *Classis Sambrica*, attested by tile-stamps from Etaples,[49] and *Milites Nervii*, regarded by Hoffmann as a loan from the field army. The *Dux tractus Armoricani*, or more fully *Dux tractus Armoricani et Nervicani*, has no less than ten units under his command. The first listed, a *Cohors Prima Nova Armoricana*, stationed at *Grannona*, again qualified as '*in litore Saxonico*', sounds like a unit of the early empire although it is not attested on inscriptions or military *diplomata*. One might compare it with the *Cohors Prima Cornoviorum* under the command of the Duke of the Britains at Newcastle,[50] also otherwise unattested: both look like attempts, in the third century perhaps, to raise units more or less locally from areas that had not previously supplied troops. Of the other units, some have geographical epithets derived from their places of garrison, which suggest that they were limitanean units of long standing: these include two infantry units of *Mauri* and one of *Dalmatae*, thought by Hoffmann to be downgraded cavalry regiments, for the *Mauri* no less than the *Dalmatae* were enrolled in Gallienus' new cavalry regiments. Others, such as the *Martenses* have names typical of field army units, and may be detachments sent to strengthen the coastal defences. The *Ursarienses*, exceptionally, are attested epigraphically in the general area of their garrison town of Rouen by a tombstone from Amiens,[51] and they, or a homonym, are also known by tile-stamps from the Rhineland. These units, under the *Dux tractus Armoricani*, appear to be listed in a fairly random geographical order, although this is not absolutely certain since many of the fort sites are not as yet securely located. However, seven of the ten units concerned are also listed in *Not. Dig. Occ. 7*, the *Distributio Numerorum*, where they are described as under the command of the *Magister Equitum Galliarum*. In that chapter they do not form a precise block, but they do seem to be listed in a rough geographical order, running from north-east to south-west. This suggests that the command might not have been broken up at the time that the *Distributio* was compiled. That the actual command of the *Dux tractus Armoricani*, as found in the *Notitia*, had in fact become subject to the *Magister Equitum Galliarum*, though nowhere stated in the *Notitia*, should be implied by its absence from the list of ten ducates subject to the western *Magister*

Peditum at the beginning of chapter 5.

CONCLUSIONS

The earliest dispositions on the British Saxon Shore, probably predating the Gallic Empire, would appear to be the old-style cohorts of Aquitanians and *Baetasii* holding the typologically early forts of Brancaster and Reculver. These units, as the Reculver inscription with its mention of the governor of Britannia Superior shows, were not as yet under a joint command that extended to both sides of the Channel, although the position of the praefect of the *Classis Britannica*, with important bases at Dover and Boulogne, already provided a precedent for such a command. If forts were built across the Channel, they too would have been under the command of the relevant provincial governor, the *Legatus Augusti propraetore provinciae Belgicae*, or possibly the governor of Germania Inferior. After the collapse of the Gallic Empire, the south-east coastal defences were strengthened, Richborough built, and part of *Legio II Augusta* transferred from Caerleon to hold it. At the same time, the new cavalry arm developed under Gallienus began to make its appearance, units of *Dalmatae* and *Stablesiani* being stationed at Brancaster and Burgh Castle in East Anglia, where the open terrain particularly favoured their deployment. The *Fortenses* could now have been 'banished' to Bradwell, and a unit (conceivably the Aquitanians from Brancaster) established at Walton Castle.

The main defect will have been the division of the overall command between the governors in Britain and the continent and the prefect of the *Classis Britannica*. But the logical solution, the creation of a single unified command of all the coastal areas threatened by Saxons, was shown by the Carausius episode to have its own inherent dangers. In the early fourth century there would thus have been two offices on each side of the Channel, but co-ordination was to some extent ensured by the fact that both were responsible to the western *Magister Peditum*. With the creation of the post of *Magister Equitum Galliarum*, virtually the whole of the *tractus Armoricanus et Nervicanus*, as the continental command was known, was transferred to him, a rump ducate of Belgica Secunda remaining subject to the *Magister Peditum*. Other changes can also be traced: the change of garrison at Pevensey from a unit of the fleet to the *Numerus Exploratorum*, and the new arrival of fresh units, sometimes in disgrace and as an act of demotion from the field army – the *Abulci* after *Mursa* in 351, and the *Tungrecani* shortly after 365 and

Procopius' abortive coup. Finally, the transfer of some units such as the *Exploratores* and *Abulci* to the continent during the early fifth century can also be detected from the *Notitia*.

Hoffmann has argued strongly[52] that transfers from the western field army to the Gallic channel defences, the Mainz Ducate, the British Ducate, and the command of the Count of the Saxon Shore took place during the reign of Valentinian during the course of a general reorganisation of frontier defences, particularly important for Britain after the barbarian inroads of 367. No doubt Valentinian and his great general Count Theodosius were responsible for fundamental changes. Perhaps for the British Saxon Shore these included the removal of the *Classis Anderetiana* and the substitution of *Exploratores* at Pevensey (compare the transfer of the naval *Supervenientes Petuarenses* from Brough-on-Humber to inland Malton, which probably took place at about the same time). But the detailed examination of the units of the British Saxon Shore given above suggests, in some cases, other and earlier reasons for the transfer of certain field army units to Britain. *Tungrecani*, *Abulci*, and *Fortenses* could all have been sent to serve with the *limitanei* in Britain as a punishment for backing the wrong side during periods of civil war. As with the large-scale changes in the way the Shore defences were organised, so the small-scale alterations, such as the redeployment of individual units, may often have been dictated by events rather than initiated by an all-prescient Roman higher command.

Addendum: Since this article was written, the second volume (in fascicules) and third volume of *The Roman Inscriptions of Britain*, encompassing personal belongings and similar, bearing inscriptions, and inscriptions on stone, have been published.[53] Inscriptions in these volumes, equivalent to those published in the original article, are referred to in the notes below.

1   Hoffmann 1969.
2   *Not. Dig. Occ.* 28.
3   *Not. Dig. Occ.* 37.
4   *Not. Dig. Occ.* 37.17.
5   *Not. Dig. Occ.* 33.
6   *Not. Dig. Occ.* 33.26.
7   Stevens 1940.
8   *Not. Dig. Occ.* 40.
9   *Not. Dig. Occ.* 7 = *Distributio Numerorum*, lines 109–10.
10   Böcking 1839/53.
11   Hoffmann 1969.

12 Ritterling 1924; 1925.
13 Mertens 1974.
14 See *Tungrecani* references in the indexes of the three Loeb volumes of Ammianus Marcellinus.
15 Tomlin 1972.
16 Amm. Marc. 26.6.12.
17 *Synopsis Historion* = Bonn edn, vol. 1, 454.
18 *SHA, Claudius* 11.19.
19 *Britannia* 6 (1975), 288, no. 25 = *RIB* II.4, 2466.
20 *RIB* 1550.
21 *RIB* 283.
22 *JRS* 47 (1957), 233, no. 27 = *RIB* II.4, 2460.90.1.
23 Toynbee 1962.
24 Robinson 1975.
25 Speidel 1974.
26 Klumbach 1973.
27 e.g. *JRS* 51 (1961), 196, no. 30 = *RIB* II.4, 2468.
28 *RIB* 830, 837–8, 842–3.
29 *RIB* 2169–70.
30 *Britannia* 1 (1970), 310–11, no. 20 = *RIB* III, 3509.
31 Breeze and Dobson 1973.
32 *JRS* 51 (1961), 191–2, nos 1–2; *JRS* 55 (1965), 220, no. 1 = *RIB* III, 3027–8.
33 Birley 1967.
34 Jarrett 1964.
35 *RIB* 334.
36 Johnson 1970.
37 *CIL* III, 12333; *Pap. Lips.* I, 119.
38 *Not. Dig. Occ.* 7.
39 *Not. Dig. Occ.* 7.84.
40 *Not. Dig. Occ.* 7.156.
41 Zosimus 2.51 f.
42 Bushe-Fox 1932, 67.
43 *Not. Dig. Occ.* 42.23.
44 *Not. Dig. Occ.* 41.17.
45 Peacock 1973.
46 *JRS* 49 (1959), 138, no. 14; *PSAN*⁴ 6 (1934), 120, no. 18 = *RIB* II.5, 2489.1.1.
47 Amm. Marc. 28.3.8.
48 *Not. Dig. Occ.* 37–8.
49 *CIL* XIII, 12560.
50 *Not. Dig. Occ.* 40.
51 *CIL* XIII, 3492.
52 Hoffmann 1969; 1974.
53 *RIB* II; *RIB* III.

19
THE DEFENCE OF BRITAIN IN THE FOURTH CENTURY

Originally published:
'The defence of Britain in the 4th century', in Y. Le Bohec and C. Wolff (eds), *L'armée Romaine de Dioclétien à Valentinien Ier: Actes du Congrès de Lyon (12–14 septembre 2002)*, Collection du Centre d'Études Romaines et Gallo-Romaines nouvelle série 26, 2004, Lyon, 179–89

THIS ARTICLE TAKES as its starting point the evidence provided by the *Notitia Dignitatum*. In that document – or more precisely that part of it devoted to the *partes Occidentis* – four chapters or sections relate to the defence of the diocese of Britain in the late Roman period. Two of these concern *comitatenses*, or field army troops, and two *limitanei*, or frontier troops. I shall first discuss briefly the units of *comitatenses* as these appear in the *Notitia*, and then look at the possible light that archaeology may throw on the role played by these troops and where they may have been based. I shall then follow the same procedure with the units of *limitanei*, first looking at the *Notitia* text and then at the evidence of archaeology. Hopefully a balanced picture of the defence of Britain in the fourth century will then emerge.

THE COMITATENSES

The Comes Britanniae

a) The Notitia
There are two relevant chapters or sections in the *Notitia*. The first, chapter 29, is devoted to the command of the *Comes Britanniae*, but it is of minimal value since it only includes that official's insignia of office and *officium*. Of much more use is chapter 7, the so-called *Distributio*

Numerorum, which follows on from the chapters devoted to the western *Magister Peditum* and *Magister Equitum* (chapters 5–6, where the units under their command are listed in hierarchical order). The *Distributio* lists the units under the command of these marshals once more, but this time not by status but broken down on a geographical basis under the command of regional *comites*, 'counts' or field army commanders. The units listed in chapters 5–6 do not precisely correspond with those listed in the *Distributio*, though in certain cases they do match and so the status of some of them can be ascertained. Thus we learn from the *Distributio* that the *Comes Britanniae* had under his command a total of nine units, three regiments of infantry and, significantly, six regiments of cavalry (Appendix 1). Cross-reference to chapter 5 shows that the first of the infantry regiments, the *Victores Iuniores Britanniciani*, was drawn from the corps of *auxilia palatina*, and I am grateful to Christophe Schmidt[1] for drawing my attention to the potential significance of this. It appears that these units were distributed on the basis of one each per comitatensian command, and it seems possible that this high-status unit was normally based at London, the diocesan capital and seat of the *Vicarius Britanniae*, the deputy of the Praetorian Prefect of the Gauls in the British diocese.

b) Archaeology
Unlike the chapters devoted to the command of the Count of the Saxon Shore, chapter 27, and the Duke of the Britains, chapter 40, no permanent locations are given for the units under the command of the Count of Britain, since they were (even the sole unit of *auxilia palatina*) – in theory at least – mobile and had no need for fixed bases. Nevertheless, it is likely that they may have remained for extended periods in permanent or semi-permanent quarters, even if these changed from time to time in response to changing strategic necessity. It is usually assumed, and in the author's view correctly so, that they were stationed in the walled towns, whether the four (later five) capitals of the sub-provinces into which the fourth-century British diocese was divided, the capitals of the *civitates*, or the lesser walled towns. It is easy to suggest likely bases on the grounds of inherent probability. London must certainly have had a unit of *comitatenses* more or less permanently in residence – perhaps the *Victores Iuniores Britanniciani*, as suggested above – and indeed one of its late Roman cemeteries has recently produced a fourth-century 'military' grave,[2] but it is possible to suggest other garrison places too. One such

is Canterbury, connected directly by road not only to London but also to no less than four of the Saxon Shore forts (Reculver, Richborough, Dover and Lympne) – and an obvious candidate for a unit of the strategic reserve. Significantly, Canterbury has produced a stamped fourth-century silver ingot (perhaps issued as a donative).[3] Tension between the civil and the military would not be surprising at such a place and is dramatically indicated by the third-century burial of two soldiers in suspicious circumstances:[4] if these are our friends, the gods preserve us from our enemies! Other places in south-eastern Britain may also have housed units or part-units of *comitatenses* in support of the defences of the Saxon Shore. One such location is the small walled town of Rochester (Durobrivae) on the direct route from Canterbury to London, a way-station at the strategically important bridge over the Medway estuary. Garrisons at Colchester and Caistor St Edmund (Venta, the *civitas* capital of the Iceni), just south of Norwich, would also be well placed to house strategic reserves.

The list could be easily extended simply on the basis of *a priori* geographical considerations, but occasionally it is archaeology that provides the clearest evidence. Thus, finds of *martiobarbuli* at Wroxeter suggest the presence of troops in Viroconium, the *civitas* capital of the Cornovii, in the Welsh Marches.[5] At Catterick, on the main road from York to the northern frontier, finds of barbed javelin heads, probably from *martiobarbuli*, also occur along with spurs in a particularly interesting context. Sometime, probably after AD 380, a section of street in the town was closed off to form a narrow courtyard between buildings. These appear to have been used as barrack accommodation, perhaps for a detachment of *comitatenses*, with access provided by an arched entrance at one end of the courtyard.[6] In size and character it is not dissimilar to the 'fort' at Pinianis (Bürgle bei Gundremmingen) on the Donau–Iller–Rhein Limes, which according to chapter 25 in the *Notitia* (the command of the *Dux Rhaetiae*) housed *Cohors V Valeria Phrygum*.[7] It is now known that a regular fort also existed at Catterick in the fourth century.[8] This, however, could have housed a permanent limitanean unit, and does not necessarily invalidate John Wacher's[9] interpretation of the buildings in *insula* VII. Strictly speaking outside this period are the two walled enclosures for detachments of Legions VI and XX in the walled town of Corbridge just south of Hadrian's Wall,[10] but they illustrate the point that 'troops in towns' were not simply a phenomenon of the late empire but had earlier antecedents going back to the third century.

THE *LIMITANEI*

The Comes Litoris Saxonici

a) The Notitia *(Appendix 1)*
Chapter 28 of the *Notitia* is devoted to the command of the Count of
the Saxon Shore. According to information provided there, the Count
commanded nine units of *limitanei*, the same number of regiments
as the Count of Britain, but whereas the Count of the Saxon Shore
commanded mostly infantry regiments, the Count of Britain had at his
disposal twice the number of cavalry units compared to infantry, and
of course all of them were the elite *comitatenses*. Until recently, there
seemed no real problem about the identification of the bases where the
units under the Count of the Saxon Shore were stationed.[11] They stretched
from Brancaster on the approaches to the Wash to Portchester near
Portsmouth harbour, with a particularly high concentration in Kent – four
out of the nine. In the *Notitia*, with the exception of the first, the *Numerus
Fortensium* at Othona (Bradwell, Essex), they appear to have been listed
topographically in pairs, thus the *Milites Tungrecani* at Dubris, Dover and
the *Numerus Turnacensium* at Lemanis, Lympne, both in Kent, followed
by the *Equites Dalmatae Branodunienses* at Branodunum and the *Equites
Stablesiani Gariannonses* at Gariannonum (Burgh Castle or Caister-on-
Sea), both in East Anglia, then the *Cohors Prima Baetasiorum* at Regulbium
(Reculver) and Legion II Augusta at Rutupiae (Richborough), both again
in Kent, and finally the *Numerus Abulcorum* at Anderida (Pevensey) and
the *Numerus Exploratorum* at Portus Adurni (Portchester), both on the
south coast. It is possible that even the first of these units, the *Numerus
Fortensium* at Bradwell, was originally paired also – with the unit based
in the third-century fort at Walton Castle near Felixstowe, Suffolk, but
that either this was omitted in error from the *Notitia* list, or else the
coastal erosion, which has now claimed what once existed of the fort,
had already commenced at the time that the list was compiled and the
site had therefore already been abandoned.

b) Archaeology
It might be supposed, in default of other evidence, that the forts of the
Saxon Shore had all been built as part of a single programme, like, for
example, the forts listed under the rubric *item per lineam valli* under
the command of the Duke of the Britains – the forts of Hadrian's

Wall. Archaeology shows, however, that typologically the forts were constructed at different periods.[12] Thus, the original fort at Dover precedes the later Saxon Shore fort by about a century, and in plan has various features typical of the early second century such as its rounded 'playing-card shaped' corners. It was constructed by and for the British Fleet, as is shown by numerous finds of tiles stamped CLBR – Cl(assis) Br(itannica).[13] It may well have been the most important fleet base on the British side of the channel, but the main base of the fleet was of course at Boulogne, which in area was similar in size to that of a legionary fortress. In the third or fourth centuries the Classis Britannica fort was levelled and a new and larger fort was built partly on the same site. The new fort had a trapezoidal plan and solid polygonal towers.

Richborough has a particularly interesting history. In AD 43, it had served as an invasion base and short-lived supply depot. Then, at the end of the first century, a triumphal arch (quadrifrons) had been erected on the site, perhaps to mark the 'final' conquest of Britain under Agricola. In the third century this structure was surrounded by multiple ditches and appears to have been used as a look-out post to warn of the approach of seaborne raiders. Signals could also have been sent from the top of the monument southwards to the fleet base at Dover or north-westwards to the fort at Reculver, typologically one of the earliest of the Saxon Shore forts proper. Reculver itself, though square in plan and probably built in the early third century, was basically constructed in a second-century tradition, its defensive walls provided with rounded comers and an internal earth bank. It has produced an important inscription referring to the rebuilding of the aedes and basilica of the principia,[14] and tile-stamps with the letters CIB,[15] clearly for the Notitia garrison C(ohors) I B(aetasiorum). Guarding the approaches to the Thames estuary, it will have been the equivalent to Brancaster on the southern approaches to the Wash. Brancaster, with its rounded comers, is typologically similar to Reculver, and has also produced a tile-stamp of an early imperial unit, Coh(ors) I Aq(uitanorum),[16] though by the time that the Notitia list was compiled it had been replaced by one of the rare cavalry regiments stationed on the Saxon Shore, the Equites Dalmatae.

Typologically later than Reculver and Brancaster are the forts at Bradwell and Burgh Castle. Their walls have rounded corners, but they also have tile-bonding courses, taken by some to be a late feature, and external towers, even if, as at Burgh Castle, they are only bonded in above foundation level. Later still are the forts of 'Diocletianic type' at Portchester and Richborough. At Portchester, the area enclosed by the Roman defences was used in Norman times as the outer bailey of a castle which itself was built into one corner of the enceinte, and there is a possibility that the earthworks surrounding this were in origin Roman and sheltered the late fourth-century garrison in a redoubt that was drastically reduced in size, a situation reminiscent of that at Eining (Abusina)[17] and elsewhere. Richborough must have been the most important of all. It housed Legion II Augusta, either greatly reduced in strength from the 5,000–6,000 men of the high empire, or possibly divided between Richborough and the fort of Saxon Shore type at Cardiff, not mentioned in the *Notitia* (see below under 'Systems not mentioned in the *Notitia*').

THE *DUX BRITANNIARUM*

a) The Notitia (Appendices 1–2)

According to chapter 40 of the *Notitia*, the Duke of the Britains had under his command 35 units, a number that could be increased to 36 if the emendation[18] suggested in Appendix 2 is accepted. They break down into three groups:

i. The first part of the Duke's list

This comprises fourteen units. Their names are typical of the late empire, though occasionally they may be identical with units attested in the third century. Thus the *Numerus Longovicanorum*[19] at Lanchester could be identical with the *Vexillatio Sueborum Lon(govicanorum) Gor(diana)* attested at Lanchester in the earlier third century.[20]

The identification of most of the forts attributed to these units presents no problems, although geographically six of them form no really coherent pattern.[21] These include Legion VI[22] at York, the old capital of Britannia Inferior and, after the restoration of Count Theodosius in 369, perhaps the capital of the province of Valentia and surely the seat of the *dux* himself. It is possible that the next entry in the *Notitia* list, the *Equites Dalmatae*,[23] described as '*in praesidio*', may have been brigaded with Legion VI in the fortress – multiple garrisons occur elsewhere in the *Notitia*. South of York were the *Equites Crispiani* at Danum,[24] that is Doncaster (unless there were two places called Danum and the one intended here is Jarrow on the River Don), and, on the road to the north of York and leading to the frontier, the Catafracts[25] at Morbium, if this represents a corruption of the known place-name Vinovium (Binchester). The other two in this sub-group are the *Numerus Longovicanorum*[26] at Longovicium (Lanchester) and the *Numerus Supervenientium Petueriensium*,[27] which I have argued elsewhere may have been transferred from Petuaria (Brough-on-Humber) to Derventio (Malton) during the Theodosian restoration of 369.[28] The attribution to Malton is not quite certain, however, since Derventio was also the name of Papcastle in Cumbria.

The remaining eight forts in the first part of the duke's list, however, do form a coherent sequence, running in an arc from east to west through the Wall hinterland. Starting with the Tigris Lightermen[29] at Arbeia (South Shields) near the eastern terminal of Hadrian's Wall, the list progresses westward, passing by way of a couple of garrisons based at forts in County Durham and thence over the Stainmore Pass across the Pennines to end with the *Numerus Pacensium Magis* (perhaps Mais, Bowness-on-Solway).

ii. The list of Wall forts

This is headed with the rubric *item per lineam valli*,[30] and comprises fifteen unit entries, or sixteen if the emendation[31] is accepted. This list of sixteen unit entries excludes Mais, the fort at the western terminal of the Wall (Bowness-on-Solway) that may have appeared already as Magis,[32] and includes Congavata (the small fort at Drumburgh between Burgh-by-Sands and Bowness).[33] Without exception, these sixteen units had their origin in the high empire. Twelve out of the total are attested in the relevant fort sites by inscriptions of third-century date, the four exceptions being the *Cohors I Cornoviorum*,[34] *Cohors I Frisiavonum*,[35] *Ala Petriana*,[36] and *Cohors II Lingonum*,[37] which we now know was certainly at Drumburgh.

iii. The forts of the Cumbrian coast and western Pennines

The location of the forts in this section is the most problematical of all. There appear to have been five units[38] based in forts that ran southward along the coast from Maryport to Lancaster, and a further three on the coastal plain and in the western Pennines.[39] The units, like the units listed along the line of the Wall, go back in origin to the period of the high empire, and four of the eight, and perhaps as many as six, are attested by inscriptions in the relevant fort sites. In plotting the location of the fort sites, the apparent gap between the western terminal of the Wall (whether at Drumburgh or Bowness) and Maryport is remarkable: at an earlier period, the fort at Beckfoot, between Bowness and Maryport, plugged this gap.

The question arises whether all three parts of the list of forts in chapter 40 are of the same date. It seems likely that this is true of the list of forts along the line of the Wall and those on the Cumbrian coast and in the western Pennines, since they were all garrisoned by earlier-style *alae* and cohorts. It may not be true of the first part of the duke's list, in which the units bear later-style names. However, there could be other possible explanations to account for the difference in the style of unit name: for example, the forts of the Pennines could have been reoccupied in the restoration of Count Theodosius following the disaster of 367 by new units which bore new-style names, while the garrisons along the line of the Wall and the Cumbrian coast did not suffer the same dislocation.

b) Archaeology

All of the three dozen forts that housed the units under the command of the *dux* were built during the period of the high empire, if not actually during the reign of Hadrian himself. However, there is one feature of those forts that have been excavated in more recent time that is worth drawing attention to: the conversion at a number of sites – e.g. the cohort fort sites at Wallsend[40] and Housesteads[41] – of regular barrack blocks to a series of separate units, the so-called 'chalets'.[42] Each chalet corresponded to a single *contubernium* in the original barrack block, that is the quarters for the smallest section of a century, i.e. eight men. If each chalet in the fourth century housed a *single* man – and his family – as has been suggested instead of the full complement of eight men, it implies that the number of men in the unit had been drastically reduced. Put another way, the milliary unit at Housesteads instead of comprising 800 men will have now numbered only 100! Reductions in unit size in the fourth century have been postulated on the evidence of pay records,[43] and this hypothesis would thus appear to receive confirmation from archaeology (see further below under 'Conclusions').

SYSTEMS NOT MENTIONED IN THE *NOTITIA*

The evidence of archaeology shows that the *Notitia* lists, even if they reflected the actual disposition of troops in Britain at the time that they were compiled, perhaps c. AD 400, cannot be regarded as showing the full picture for the *earlier* fourth century. A full review of the evidence is beyond the scope of this article, and what is required is a survey which would include all forts that can be shown to have been occupied during this period, such as the late forts Newton Kyme and Catterick, both in

North Yorkshire. However, two areas in particular should be mentioned:

Signal stations from Wallsend to the Wash
Five of these defended sites are known on the north-east coast of Yorkshire. They run from Goldsborough in the north to Flamborough Head in the south, but it is highly probable that others remain to be located or else have been destroyed by coastal erosion, and that the system originally ran from the mouth of the River Tyne to the northern shore of the Wash – thus, in a sense, linking Hadrian's Wall with the Saxon Shore system, or, specifically, the forts of Wallsend and Brancaster. The sites themselves consisted of a lofty tower surrounded by a defended enclosure furnished with turrets at the four corners, a plan corresponding neatly with the description on the sole building record to be found at one of them, as a *turris (et) castrum*.[44] The garrisons at these sites will have been too small to take offensive action against seaborne raiders and instead will have sent messages back to larger units based in defended sites to the rear. One such unit will have been the *Notitia* unit based at Malton.[45] Another will almost certainly have been stationed at the walled town of Horncastle in Lincolnshire. Neither it nor its garrison are mentioned in the *Notitia*, unless it was occupied by a comitatensian unit. It may be that the defensive system described above was initiated by Count Theodosius in 369 after the failure of a more proactive system based on fleets located on the estuaries on the Rivers Tyne and Tees, and the Humber, had failed, and that it was under Count Theodosius that the *Numerus Supervenientium Petueriensium*[46] was transferred from Petuaria (Brough-on-Humber) to Derventio (Malton).[47]

Coastal defences in Wales
Mention has already been made of Cardiff, a fort of 'Saxon Shore' type but built in South Wales to combat the raids of Scots from Ireland. Its counterpart in North Wales was Segontium (Caernarvon),[48] and there will have been other installations such as the coastal fortification at Caer Gybi in Anglesey.[49] The removal of the Welsh garrisons has been attributed to the usurper Magnus Maximus in the 380s.

CONCLUSIONS

As we have seen, the *Notitia* lists 9 units of *comitatenses* and 46 units of *limitanei*, a figure that should perhaps be raised to 48 if the two suggested omissions from the lists relating to the commands of the Saxon Shore and the Duke of the Britains are taken into account. This gives a grand total of 57 'Notitia units' in Britain. In the famous British diploma of AD 122,[50] a not dissimilar number of auxiliary units – 50 – are named. The figures might be even closer if the diploma does not give the full auxiliary establishment for the province, but even if it does, the comparison would ignore the presence of the three legions permanently stationed in the island, equivalent to a further 30 infantry cohorts. However, for any comparison to be worth making at all, one would have to assume that the picture of the military situation as reflected in the Notitia is a homogenous one: that the commands of the three officers – Count, Dux, and Count of the Saxon Shore – as we have them, all existed at the same time, and specifically that the lists in chapter 40 of the units along the line of the Wall, on the Cumbrian coast and in the western Pennines were still 'in date' at the time that the Notitia was compiled, and, along with the forts of the Wall hinterland, provide a picture that corresponded with reality. Even if they were in date, the Notitia would only give a snapshot of the situation at the very end of the Roman period of occupation, after the withdrawal of the Roman garrisons in Wales (including Legion XX from Chester), perhaps by Magnus Maximus in the 380s.

But even taking all this into account and trying to reconstruct the situation before the withdrawals by Magnus Maximus, it is likely that in numerical terms the total number of Roman troops in the island had fallen to a fraction of its former size. This is because the strengths of the individual units in the late period had been so heavily reduced. This reduction in unit strength is the implication of the 'chalet' accommodation in the Wall forts and of, for example, a crude comparison in size of the plans of the fortress of Caerleon with that of the Saxon Shore fort at Richborough, which ostensibly succeeded it as the base of Legion II Augusta. The phenomenon of reduced unit size, argued for by Richard Duncan-Jones[51] on the basis of the papyrological evidence, is borne out by limitanean forts on other imperial frontiers: some old-style forts, which in the high empire housed single units, have in the Notitia lists multiple garrisons; at others, where old-style forts were still occupied by single units, the defended area has been drastically reduced in size, as at Eining (and perhaps Portchester). Finally, others built for the first time like Pinianis, ostensibly for old-style alae or cohorts, occupy a tiny proportion of the area that they would have done in, say, the second century. The conclusion is inescapable. There had been a drastic reduction in the size of the garrison in Britain, and the wonder is not that Britain and the western empire as a whole fell in the early fifth century, but that it did not fall much sooner.

APPENDIX 1: THE DEFENCE OF BRITAIN AS REFLECTED IN THE *NOTITIA DIGNITATUM* (LINE NUMBERING AS SEECK 1876/1962)

Ch. 29 Comes Britanniae *gives insignia and* officium *only. The actual units under his command are listed in ch. 7, the* Distributio Numerorum, *as follows:*

(Infantry)
153 Intra Britannias cum viro spectabili Comite Britanniarum
154 Victores Iuniores Britanniciani (unit of *auxilia palatina*)
155 Primani Iuniores
156 Secundani Iuniores
(Cavalry)
199 Intra Britannias cum viro spectabili Comite Britanniarum
200 Equites Catafractarii Iuniores
201 Equites Scutarii Aureliaci
202 Equites Honoriani Seniores
203 Equites Stablesiani
204 Equites Syri
205 Equites Taefali

Ch. 28 Comes litoris Saxonici per Britanniam
12 Sub dispositione viri spectabilis comitis litoris Saxonici per Britanniam:
[12 (bis?) Praepositus ... ... (Walton Castle)]
13 Praepositus numeri Fortensium, Othonae (Bradwell)
14 Praepositus militum Tungrecanorum, Dubris (Dover)
15 Praepositus numeri Turnacensium, Lemanis (Lympne)
16 Praepositus equitum Dalmatarum Branodunensium, Branoduno (Brancaster)
17 Praepositus equitum Stablesianorum Gariannonensium, Gariannonor (Burgh Castle or Caister-on-Sea)
18 Tribunus cohortis primae Baetasiorum, Regulbio (Reculver)
19 Praefectus legionis secundae Augustae, [Rutupis (supplied from insignia)] (Richborough)
20 Praepositus numeri Abulcorum, [Anderidos (supplied from insignia)] (Pevensey)

21 Praepositus numeri exploratorum, Portum Adurni (Portchester)

Ch. 40 Dux Britanniarum
17 Sub dispositione viri spectabilis ducis Britanniarum:
(First part of the Duke's list)
18 Praefectus legionis sextae (York)
19 Praefectus equitum Dalmatarum, Praesidio (i.e. also in garrison at York?)
20 Praefectus equitum Crispianorum, Dano (Doncaster?)
21 Praefectus Catafractariorum, Morbio (corrupt: Seeck suggests Vinovio, i.e. Binchester)
22 Praefectus numeri Barcariorum Tigrisiensium, Arbeia (South Shields)
23 Praefectus numeri Nerviorum Dictensium, Dicti (Wearmouth or Jarrow?)
24 Praefectus numeri vigilum, Concangios (Chester-le-Street)
25 Praefectus numeri exploratorum, Lavatres (Bowes)
26 Praefectus numeri directorum, Verteris (Brough)
27 Praefectus numeri defensorum, Braboniaco (Kirkby Thore)
28 Praefectus numeri Solensium, Maglone (Old Carlisle)
29 Praefectus numeri Pacensium, Magis (Bowness-on-Solway?)
30 Praefectus numeri Longovicanorum, Longovicio (Lanchester[52])
31 Praefectus numeri Supervenientium Petueriensium, Derventione (Malton)
32 Item per lineam valli
33 Tribunus cohortis quartae Lingonum, Segeduno (Wallsend)
34 Tribunus cohortis primae Cornoviorum, Ponte Aeli (Newcastle)
35 Praefectus alae primae Asturum, Conderco (Benwell)
36 Tribunus cohortis primae Frixagorum, Vindobala (Rudchester)
37 Praefectus alae Sabinianae, Hunno (Onnum: Halton Chesters)
38 Praefectus alae secundae Asturum, Cilurno (Chesters)
39 Tribunus cohortis primae Batavorum, Procolitia (Carrawburgh)
40 Tribunus cohortis primae Tungrorum, Borcovicio (Vercovicium: Housesteads)
41 Tribunus cohortis quartae Gallorum, Vindolana (Chesterholm)
42 Tribunus cohortis primae (recte secundae) Asturum, Aesica (Great Chesters)
43 Tribunus cohortis secundae Dalmatarum, Magnis (Carvoran)
44 Tribunus cohortis primae Aeliae Dacorum, [Banna (Birdoswald)

44 (bis) Tribunus cohortis secundae Tungrorum], Camboglanna (Castlesteads)

45 Praefectus alae Petrianae, Petrianis (Stanwix)

<46 Seeck unnecessarily restores a unit at Carlisle>

47 Praefectus numeri Maurorum Aurelianorum, Aballaba (Burgh-by-Sands)

48 Tribunus cohortis secundae Lingonum, Congavata (Drumburgh)

(Forts of the Cumbrian coast)

49 Tribunus cohortis primae Hispanorum, Axeloduno (Maryport)

50 Tribunus cohortis secundae Thracum, Gabrosenti (Moresby)

51 Tribunus cohortis primae Aeliae classicae, Tunnocelo (Ravenglass)

52 Tribunus cohortis primae Morinorum, Glannibanta (unlocated)

53 Tribunus cohortis tertiae Nerviorum, Alione (Lancaster?)

54 Cuneus Sarmatarum, Bremetenraco (Ribchester)

55 Praefectus alae primae Herculeae, Olenaco (Elslack)

56 Tribunus cohortis sextae Nerviorum, Virosido (Brough-by-Bainbridge)

APPENDIX 2: NOTES ON THE *NOTITIA* ENTRIES (CH. 40 *DUX BRITANNIARUM*) AT THE WESTERN END OF HADRIAN'S WALL, THE CUMBRIAN COAST AND THE WESTERN PENNINES, IN SUPPORT OF THE FORT IDENTIFICATIONS GIVEN ABOVE (LINE NUMBERING AS SEECK 1876/1962)

44 Tribunus cohortis primae Aeliae Dacorum, [Banna *(Birdoswald)*
44 *(bis)* Tribunus cohortis secundae Tungrorum], Camboglanna *(Castlesteads)*
After writing the unit name *(Cohors Prima Aelia Dacorum)* in line 44, it seems likely that the eye of the copyist skipped to the fort site at the end of the next line, thus conflating two entries.[53] This suggestion, which reconciles the evidence of the *Notitia* with that of the place-names along the line of the Wall as listed on the Rudge Cup and Amiens Patera, has found general acceptance.[54] The unit at Castlesteads, *Cohors II Tungrorum*, is restored on the basis of inscriptions[55] found at the site.

45 Praefectus alae Petrianae, Petrianis *(Stanwix)*
On the Rudge Cup and Amiens Patera, the fort at Stanwix is called Uxelodunum, but by the time this section of the *Notitia* was compiled, it had apparently been replaced by the unit title, as is found not uncommonly elsewhere.[56]

47 Praefectus numeri Maurorum Aurelianorum, Aballaba *(Burgh-by-Sands)*

The *Cuneus Frisionum* either formed the earlier garrison at Burgh-by-Sands or shared garrison duties there with the *Numerus Maurorum Aurelianorum*. The latter unit had been transferred to Papcastle, Cumbria, by 241, where it was known as the *Cuneus Frisionum Aballavensium*.[57] The *Numerus Maurorum Aurelianorum* is independently attested at Burgh-by-Sands in the period 253–8.[58]

48 Tribunus cohortis secundae Lingonum, Congavata *(Drumburgh)*

An enamelled bowl found in Staffordshire in 2003[59] bears the names of four forts from the western end of the Wall, all attested by recognisable, if slightly different, forms from those given in the *Notitia*, Amiens Patera and Rudge Cup. On the Staffordshire Moorlands Pan (Ilam Pan), the sequence runs Mais, Congavata, Uxelodunum, Camboglanna (spellings normalised). These four must correspond to the forts of Bowness, Drumburgh, Stanwix and Castlesteads, with Burgh-by-Sands (Aballava) omitted. The evidence of the new find not only establishes the existence of Congavata beyond doubt,[60] but also fixes its location in the section of Wall between Mais (Bowness) and Stanwix (Uxelodunum), and the only unnamed Wall fort site in this sector is Drumburgh.[61]

49 Tribunus cohortis primae Hispanorum, Axeloduno *(Maryport)*

Cohors I Hispanorum equitata is attested at Maryport under the command of Maenius Agrippa, a friend of Hadrian.[62] Maenius held the rank of tribune and, unless this was by favour of the emperor,[63] the unit that he commanded should have been milliary. One other tribune of the unit is also attested at Maryport (C. Caballius Priscus[64]). This milliary unit should probably not be identical with *Cohors I Aelia Hispanorum milliaria equitata*, which was stationed at Netherby, Castra Exploratorum, one of the outpost forts beyond the western end of Hadrian's Wall, in the early third century[65] in view of the title 'Aelia' which the Maryport unit lacks. Forty years ago, Michael Jarrett[66] suggested that the milliary *Cohors I Hispanorum* at Maryport was originally quingenary, since there are inscriptions which prove the presence there of a *Cohors I Hispanorum* that was commanded by prefects.[67] This is certainly possible, however it is equally possible that the unit is not identical and that its period of occupation fell in the later second or the third century, and this is the interpretation adopted here and that it is in fact the *Notitia* unit. The fact that in that document it is commanded by a tribune rather than a prefect is not an objection, since in the course of the third century the prefects of quingenary cohorts were all 'upgraded' to tribunes, as the *Notitia* lists demonstrate.

To make matters even more complicated, two other units are also attested at Maryport, *Cohors I Delmatarum*[68] and *Cohors I Baetasiorum*.[69] However, neither of these units would appear to have been the third-century garrison. Inscriptions show that the Delmatae were probably at Chesters on Hadrian's Wall in the Antonine period,[70] while the Baetasii were certainly the garrison of the Saxon Shore fort of Reculver in third century.[71]

Uxelodunum, for which Axelodunum is a corruption, means 'High Fort', and is an appropriate name for Maryport, on a plateau overlooking the Irish Sea. Not surprisingly, it is a name that occurs elsewhere, and indeed was the original name of the fort at Stanwix on Hadrian's Wall.[72] The name Alauna has also been suggested for Maryport.[73]

50 Tribunus cohortis secundae Thracum, Gabrosenti *(Moresby)*
Cohors II Thracum is attested at Moresby by inscriptions,[74] while *Cohors II Lingonum*, the *Notitia* garrison at Congavata, was at some time also stationed there.[75]

51 Tribunus cohortis primae Aeliae classicae, Tunnocelo *(Ravenglass)*
Cohors I Aeliae Classica is probably attested at Ravenglass by the fragment of a military diploma[76] and a lead sealing bearing the unit's name found there.[77] As portable objects, neither by themselves would necessarily prove the presence of the unit at Ravenglass, but, taken together, they strongly suggest that it was. If this is correct, it would rule out the attractive suggestion that the name Tunocelum is a corruption of *Itunocelum, 'Eden Head' – i.e. a promontory where the River Eden, Ituna, flows into the Solway Firth – for Ravenglass cannot by any stretch of the imagination be so described. The name has also been linked with the unlocated Portus Trucculensis of the *Agricola*.[78]

52 Tribunus cohortis primae Morinorum, Glannibanta *(unlocated)*
Glannibanta should lie between Ravenglass and Alione (Lancaster?). The name occurs as Clanoventa in Iter X of the *Antonine Itinerary*, where it has been identified as Ravenglass,[79] and other interpretations have also been proposed, most recently by Ian G. Smith.[80]

53 Tribunus cohortis tertiae Nerviorum, Alione *(Lancaster?)*
Smith identifies Alione with Lancaster, and acutely draws attention to the
dedication to the local deity, Ialonus Contrebis, from Lancaster.[81] 'Alione'
could easily be a corruption of Ialonus or similar, perhaps the original
name of Lancaster in Roman times. Against this identification is the fact
that *Cohors III Nerviorum* is not attested at Lancaster in the third century,
whereas other units are: the *Ala Sebosiana*[82] and a *Numerus Barcariorum*.[83]
The suggestion has also been made that Alione is a corruption of Alauna,
and that this was the original name for Maryport, lying at the mouth of
the River Ellen (Alauna).[84]

54 Cuneus Sarmatarum, Bremetenraco *(Ribchester)*
A *Numerus Equitum Sarmatarum Bremetenn(acensium)* is attested at
Ribchester by an inscription,[85] and the *Ala Sarmatarum* by two others,[86]
so the identification of the fort site is therefore certain.

55 Praefectus alae primae Herculeae, Olenaco *(Elslack)*
Olenacum has been identified as the Roman fort at Elslack.[87] It lies on
the route between Ribchester and Brough-by-Bainbridge, both securely
identified as Bremetennacum and Virosidum.

56 Tribunus cohortis sextae Nerviorum, Virosido *(Brough-by-Bainbridge)*
Cohors Sexta Nerviorum is attested at Brough-by-Bainbridge by an
inscription.[88]

Illustration note: This article was originally published with an illustration of a
map, not included in the present collection, but referred to in the notes below.

Addendum: Since this article was written, the third volume of *The Roman
Inscriptions of Britain*, encompassing inscriptions on stone, has been
published.[89] Inscriptions in that volume, equivalent to those published in
the original article, are referred to in the notes below. A recent study of the
Rudge Cup, the Amiens Patera and notably the newly-discovered Staffordshire
Moorlands Pan (Ilam Pan) has also been published.[90]

1   C. Schmidt, pers. comm.
2   Barber and Bowsher 2000, 206–8 (burial 538).
3   *RIB* II.1, 2402.9.
4   Bennett et al. 1982, 44–6, fig. 10.
5   Barker 1979; cf. Sherlock 1979.
6   Wilson and Wacher 2002, 118–19.

7   Garbsch 1970, fig. 13.
8   Wilson 2002, 446–57, 461, fig. 426.
9   Wilson and Wacher 2002, 118–19.
10 Richmond 1943.
11 Hassall 1977b. However, Note the recent identification of Caister-on-Sea, just north of Burgh Castle, as a regular Shore fort: Pearson 2002, 15–16. Caister, rather than Burgh Castle, may be the *Notitia* site of Gariannonum.
12 Cunliffe 1977; Johnson 1979; Maxfield 1989; Pearson 2002.
13 *RIB* II.5, 2481, stamps of the *Classis Britannica* arranged by dies and from various sites including Dover.
14 *JRS* 51 (1961), 191, no. 1 = *RIB* III, 3027.
15 *RIB* II.4, 2468.
16 *RIB* II.4, 2466.
17 Baatz 1993, 322–3, fig. 150.
18 *Not. Dig. Occ.* 40.44–44 bis = Appendix 2, lines 44–44 bis.
19 *Not. Dig. Occ.* 40.30 = Appendix 1, line 30.
20 *RIB* 1074.
21 Hassall 2004, map.
22 *Not. Dig. Occ.* 40.18 = Appendix 1, line 18.
23 *Not. Dig. Occ.* 40.19 = Appendix 1, line 19.
24 *Not. Dig. Occ.* 40.20 = Appendix 1, line 20.
25 *Not. Dig. Occ.* 40.21 = Appendix 1, line 21.
26 *Not. Dig. Occ.* 40.30 = Appendix 1, line 30.
27 *Not. Dig. Occ.* 40.31 = Appendix 1, line 31.
28 Hassall 1976, 111–12.
29 *Not. Dig. Occ.* 40.22 = Appendix 1, line 22.
30 *Not. Dig. Occ.* 40.32 = Appendix 1, line 32.
31 *Not. Dig. Occ.* 40.44–44 bis = Appendix 2, lines 44–44 bis.
32 *Not. Dig. Occ.* 40.29 = Appendix 1, line 29.
33 For the identification of Congavata with Drumburgh, now certain, see Appendix 2, line 48.
34 *Not. Dig. Occ.* 40.34 = Appendix 1, line 34.
35 *Not. Dig. Occ.* 40.36 = Appendix 1, line 36.
36 *Not. Dig. Occ.* 40.45 = Appendix 1, line 45.
37 *Not. Dig. Occ.* 40.48 = Appendix 1, line 48.
38 *Not. Dig. Occ.* 40.49–53 = Appendix 1, lines 49–53.
39 *Not. Dig. Occ.* 40.54–6 = Appendix 1, lines 54–6.
40 *Not. Dig. Occ.* 40.33 = Appendix 1, line 33.
41 *Not. Dig. Occ.* 40.40 = Appendix 1, line 40.
42 Breeze and Dobson 2000, 225–6.
43 Duncan-Jones 1978; with revised version in Duncan-Jones 1990.
44 *RIB* 721, Ravenscar.
45 *Not. Dig. Occ.* 40.31 = Appendix 1, line 31.
46 *Not. Dig. Occ.* 40.31 = Appendix 1, line 31.
47 Hassall 1976, 111–12.
48 Casey et al. 1993.

49 Jarrett 1969, 135–7.
50 *CIL* XVI, 69.
51 Duncan-Jones 1978; with revised version in Duncan-Jones 1990.
52 cf. *RIB* 1074.
53 Hassall 1976, 113–14.
54 Rivet and Smith 1979, 221.
55 *RIB* 1981–3, 1999.
56 See n. on Appendix 2, line 49.
57 *RIB* 883.
58 *RIB* 2042 + add.
59 *Britannia* 35 (2004), 326, no. 8, 344–5, no. 24.
60 It had been doubted as a genuine place-name in Hassall 1976.
61 *Britannia* 35 (2004), 326, no. 8, 344–5, no. 24.
62 *RIB* 823–6; *ILS* 2735.
63 cf. *RIB* 1791.
64 *RIB* 817–20.
65 *RIB* 976, 978.
66 Jarrett 1966; 1976, 15–26; Davies 1977b.
67 *RIB* 816: L. Antistius Lupus Verianus; *RIB* 821: P. Cornelius Ur[...]; *RIB*
    822: Hestrius Novellus; *RIB* 827–9: L. Cammius Maximus.
68 *RIB* 810, 831–2, 850.
69 *RIB* 830, 837–8, 842–3.
70 *JRS* 47 (1957), 229, no. 14 = *RIB* III, 3300.
71 *RIB* II.4, 2468.
72 See n. on Appendix 2, line 45.
73 See n. on Appendix 2, line 53.
74 *RIB* 797, 803–4.
75 *RIB* 798, 800.
76 *Britannia* 26 (1995), 389–90, item f.
77 *RIB* II.1, 2411.94.
78 Hind 1974.
79 Rivet and Smith 1979, 367.
80 Smith 1997.
81 *RIB* 600.
82 *RIB* 605 + add.
83 *RIB* 601.
84 Rivet and Smith 1979, 244–5.
85 *RIB* 583.
86 *RIB* 594–5.
87 Rivet and Smith 1979, 431.
88 *RIB* 722.
89 *RIB* III.
90 Breeze 2012.

20

THE WRITTEN RECORD AND THE LATE ROMAN FRONTIER

Originally published:
'The written record and the late Roman frontier', in R. Collins and
L. Allason-Jones (eds), *Finds from the Frontier: Material Culture in the
4th–5th Centuries*, CBA Research Report 162, 2010, York, 17–19

INTRODUCTION

L ATE THIRD- AND early fourth-century inscriptions from the frontier
zone in general and Hadrian's Wall in particular are surprisingly
rare. The latest-dated inscriptions from sites on Hadrian's Wall are the
famous 'building' record[1] found at Birdoswald and dedicated to the period
AD 297–305 by the mention of the tetrarchs (the Emperor Diocletian
and his three colleagues), and a more-or-less contemporary inscription
from Chesters. The latter is a dedication to Jupiter Dolichenus, and can
be precisely dated to the end of the third century, in 286.[2] There is also
a late tombstone from Carlisle of Flavius Antigonus Papias, a Greek,[3]
whom, it has been argued, was Christian on the basis of a feigned(?)
lack of concern about the precise age of the deceased, who lived 'more
or less 60 years' (*vixit annos plus minus LX*). If this is correct, then it
should probably date to the fourth century, after Constantine's formal
recognition of Christianity in 313, although the mere fact that the
deceased's religious affiliations are ambiguous means that even if it is
Christian it could be earlier than that date. A second tombstone, from
Carvoran,[4] may also be Christian. It records that Aurelia Aia lived for 33
years 'without any stain' (*sine ulla macula*), and this too has been taken
to be a Christian formula.

Taking the frontier to include the system of fortlets on the
Yorkshire coast, then the honour of being the latest inscription will
probably go to another building record, from the installation at

Ravenscar.[5] The creation of this system of fortlets is usually attributed
to Count Theodosius as part of the defensive measures taken in 369,
after the Barbarian Conspiracy of 367 when Nectaridus, Count of the
Coastal District (the Saxon Shore), was killed and Fullofaudes, the Duke
in charge of the northern military district, including Hadrian's Wall,
was ambushed and captured.[6] In the passage recording the Roman
response,[7] Ammianus Marcellinus describes how Theodosius, having
recovered the military situation, protected the frontiers with watch-posts
and garrisons (*vigiliis et praetenturis*), and both the words used here and
the language of the Ravenscar inscription with its mention of a tower
and fort (*turrem et castrum*) accord with the actual plan of the fortlets
with their lofty towers set in a small, rectangular, defended enclosure
for the garrisons (*praetenturae*). The rounded corners of these latter are
furnished with token bastions whose actual military effectiveness may
be doubted since they do not project beyond the line of the adjacent
walls and would not enable archers or soldiers armed with *manuballistae*
who were stationed on them to provide enfilading fire.

MILESTONES

Apart from these four inscriptions, there is a group of over a dozen third-
or early fourth-century milestones from the Wall hinterland. One of
the most interesting is also the earliest, a milestone from Langwathby
in Cumbria dated to 222/3, so considerably earlier than the period
under discussion. It was set up by the *Civitas Carvetiorum* and names
the Emperor Severus Alexander.[8] An earlier find from Brougham,[9]
also set up by the *Civitas Carvetiorum*, in honour of the Gallic usurper
Postumus (258–68), fits better into the general chronological horizon.
These two inscriptions will be cited below in another context. A third
milestone found at Gallows Hill, a mile south of Carlisle,[10] carries three
inscriptions of which the primary text[11] names Carausius (286–93). The
remainder include mentions of Diocletian, his colleague Maximian,
and their immediate successors.[12] The suggestion has been made[13]
that these, and others of similar date from elsewhere in the province,
were not so much records of work carried out on particular stretches
of road, the ostensible reason for their erection, as instruments of
propaganda in a period of political instability, drawing the attention of
passers-by to the particular emperor or usurper named at the expense
of his rivals.

CORVÉES AND CIVITATES

Possibly the most significant group of inscriptions from the frontier region, if also the most enigmatic, is the series of building inscriptions from the Wall itself, detailing work done by *corvées* from three southern *civitates* – the Durotriges Lendinienses, the Dumnonii and the Catuvellauni – as well as three other inscriptions recording work on *pedaturae* (specific lengths measured in feet) carried out on the initiative of individuals such as Vindomorucus, attested on a building inscription found at Drumburgh.[14] In the early 1940s, C.E. Stevens suggested that these recorded work undertaken during the general reconstruction of the frontier by Count Theodosius.[15] Building work on the Wall by the southern *civitates* would, in the present writer's opinion, suit a late Roman context well, for this was the age when *civitates* throughout the empire were expected to carry out unpleasant tasks, referred to in the legal literature as *sordida munera*, which included, among other things, the repair of military roads, the manufacture of arms and the rebuilding of fortifications, as a law of AD 441 specifically indicates.[16] Compare the work on road building undertaken by the *Civitas Carvetiorum* as recorded on the inscriptions from Langwathby and Brougham mentioned above. Other milestones from the province also record work done on roads by the *civitates*, for example the *Res Publica Belgarum* in 238–44,[17] the *Res Publica Lindensis*, 253–9,[18] and the *Res Publica Civitatis Dobunnorum*, 283–4.[19] All are of a broadly similar third-century date and not earlier. However, that works of this kind, and even co-operative efforts like the work on the Wall, could be undertaken by civilian authorities at a much earlier period is shown, for example, by the construction of the bridge at Alcantara near Carceres in the province of Lusitania (Portugal), which was built in AD 106.[20] Indeed, dates earlier than the fourth century have been suggested for the *civitates* inscriptions from the Wall. In a recent survey, Michael Fulford proposed that 'all the named *civitates* [stones] are associated with the initial construction of the stone Wall and the replacement of the turf wall in stone, and that they belong to the second century, before the division of Britain into Inferior and Superior'.[21] Roger Tomlin also prefers an early date, and in discussing a very fragmentary building inscription perhaps set up by the [C(ivitas) Durot]rac(um), found in association with the north mound of the *Vallum* at Cawfields,[22] concludes that this stone and the other *civitas* building inscriptions relate to the original construction of the *Vallum* in the Hadrianic period. Formally, it would be impossible to disprove the

views of either Fulford or Tomlin; nevertheless, I can think of no other
overtly military work of second-century date from any frontier of the
empire which was undertaken by civilians. For Britain, the two third-
century milestones cited above provide some sort of parallel, showing
as they do one civilian authority, the *Civitas Carvetiorum*, engaged in
large-scale engineering works in that period, though it is of course not
impossible that the *civitates* undertook this sort of work earlier but that
their participation is simply not mentioned on the inscriptions.

PLACE-NAMES

The dramatic discovery in 2003 of an enamelled bowl, the so-called
Staffordshire Moorlands Pan (Ilam Pan),[23] bearing an inscription
which includes the names of the four westernmost Wall forts, though
itself probably not of late Roman date, has given new certainty to the
identification of the names of the forts which are listed with the units
in garrison in chapter 40 of the *Notitia Dignitatum*. In particular, the
presence of the second fort listed, COGGABATA,[24] which is missing
from the forts listed on the two analogous inscribed vessels, the Rudge
Cup and the Amiens Patera, confirms that this is a genuine place-
name, and there is no longer any doubt about the normally-proposed
identification of the place with Drumburgh. Apart from the evidence
of these inscribed vessels, the identification of the Wall forts with
those listed in the *Notitia* is aided by the occurrence at various sites
of inscriptions naming units given in that document, even though the
inscriptions themselves are of third- rather than fourth-century date. A
recent attempt to make sense of the fort names listed in the *Notitia* in
the Wall hinterland and on the Cumbrian coast has been undertaken by
the present writer.[25]

CONCLUSION

From the survey given above, it is apparent that epigraphy plays only
a small part in our understanding of the Wall, its garrison, and its
hinterland in the fourth century. Nevertheless, inscriptions of an earlier
date, notably the list of forts named on the Staffordshire Moorlands
Pan and its analogues, and the inscriptions that name the third-century
Wall garrisons, are crucial in helping to elucidate the evidence of that
vitally important fourth- or early fifth-century document, the *Notitia
Dignitatum*. One *desideratum* would be to settle once and for all the
date of the *civitas* inscriptions, for these are of great intrinsic interest

in showing civilian involvement in a major military project, something that would be unusual before the fourth century. Here Fulford[26] has rightly drawn attention to the significance of the recently-discovered Langwathby milestone attesting to work done by the *civitas* of the Carvetii on road building in AD 222/3. This really does suggest that the *civitas* inscriptions on the Wall could be of Severan date, and this is the date at which I have argued the western end of the Wall was converted from turf to stone.[27] If this were indeed the case, and they do not belong to a fourth-century context, then apart from the assistance that inscriptions provide to the identification of the place-names mentioned in the *Notitia*, the significance of epigraphy for the later phase of the frontier would be almost negligible!

Illustration note: This article was originally published with an illustration of a building inscription, and a separate colour illustration of the Staffordshire Moorlands Pan (Ilam Pan) in the same volume, not included in the present collection, but referred to in the notes below.

Addendum: Since this article was written, a recent study of the Rudge Cup, the Amiens Patera and notably the newly-discovered Staffordshire Moorlands Pan has been published.[28] Inscriptions in the third volume of *The Roman Inscriptions of Britain*,[29] encompassing inscriptions on stone, equivalent to those published in the original article, are referred to in the notes below.

1   *RIB* 1912.
2   *Britannia* 36 (2005), 480–1, no. 8 = *RIB* III, 3299.
3   *RIB* 955.
4   *RIB* 1828.
5   *RIB* 721; Hassall 2010, fig. 3.1.
6   Amm. Marc. 27.8.
7   Amm. Marc. 28.3.
8   *Britannia* 36 (2005), 482, no. 11 = *RIB* III, 3526.
9   *JRS* 55 (1965), 224, no. 11 = *RIB* III, 3525.
10 *RIB* 2290–2.
11 *RIB* 2291.
12 *RIB* 2288, 2292–3, 2297, 2301.3–4, 2302–3, 2310–11.
13 Sauer 2007.
14 *RIB* 2053.
15 Stevens 1940, 148; 1941, 359.
16 Jones 1964, 205, 452.
17 *RIB* 2222.
18 *RIB* 2240.
19 *RIB* 2250.

20   *ILS* 287–7a.
21   Fulford 2006, 68.
22   *JRS* 50 (1960), 237, no. 10 = *RIB* III, 3376, with Tomlin's note on the date.
23   *Britannia* 35 (2004), 326, no. 8, 344–5, no. 24; Collins and Allason-Jones 2010, pl. 4.
24   cf. *Not. Dig. Occ.* 40.48, CONGAVATA.
25   Hassall 2004.
26   Fulford 2006, 69–70.
27   Hassall 1984.
28   Breeze 2012.
29   *RIB* III.

BIBLIOGRAPHY

Abbott, F.F. and Johnson, A.C. 1926. *Municipal Administration in the Roman Empire*, Princeton

Alcock, J.P. 1976. *The Classical Cults in Roman Britain*, London

Alföldy, G. 1968. *Die Hilfstruppen der römischen Provinz Germania Inferior*, Epigraphische Studien 6, Düsseldorf

Allen, D. 1944. 'The Belgic Dynasties of Britain and their Coins', *Archaeologia* 90, 1–46

Allen, J.R. 1890. 'Gold Objects Found in Montgomeryshire', *Archaeologia Cambrensis* (5th series) 7 (26), 155–6

Askew, G. 1951. *The Coinage of Roman Britain*, London

Atkinson, D. 1942. *Report on Excavations at Wroxeter (the Roman City of Viroconium) in the County of Salop, 1923–1927*, Oxford

Baatz, D. 1973. *Kastell Hesselbach und andere Forschungen am Odenwaldlimes*, Limesforschungen 12, Berlin

Baatz, D. 1993. *Der römische Limes: Archäologische Ausflüge zwischen Rhein und Donau* (3rd edn), Berlin

Baatz, D. 2000. *Der römische Limes: Archäologische Ausflüge zwischen Rhein und Donau* (4th edn), Berlin

Bang, M. 1906. *Die Germanen im römischen Dienst bis zum Regierungsantritt Constantins I*, Berlin

Barber, B. and Bowsher, D. 2000. *The Eastern Cemetery of Roman London: Excavations 1983–1990*, MoLAS Monograph 4, London

Barker, P.A. 1979. 'The plumbatae from Wroxeter', in M.W.C. Hassall and R.I. Ireland (eds), *De Rebus Bellicis*, BAR International Series 63 (1), Oxford, 97–9

Barrett, A.A. 1978. 'Knowledge of the Literary Classics in Roman Britain', *Britannia* 9, 307–13

Bartoli, P.S. 1704. *Gli Antichi Sepolcri, ovvero Mausolei Romani, ed Etruschi*, Rome

Beard, M. 1980. 'A British Dedication from the City of Rome', *Britannia* 11, 313–14

Bell, H.I., Martin, V., Turner, E.G. and van Berchem, D. (eds) 1962. *The Abinnaeus Archive: Papers of a Roman Officer in the Reign of Constantius II*, Oxford

Bennett, P., Frere, S.S. and Stow, S. 1982. *The Archaeology of Canterbury. Volume I: Excavations at Canterbury Castle*, Canterbury

Bicknell, P. 1968. 'The Emperor Gaius' Military Activities in AD 40', *Historia* 17, 496–505

Bidwell, P.T. and Boon, G.C. 1976. 'An antefix type of the Second Augustan Legion from Exeter', *Britannia* 7, 278–80

Birley, A.R. 1967. 'The Roman Governors of Britain', *Epigraphische Studien* 4, Beihefte der Bonner Jahrbücher 25, 63–102

Birley, A.R. 1981. *The Fasti of Roman Britain*, Oxford

Birley, A.R. 1997. *Hadrian: the Restless Emperor*, London

Birley, A.R. 2005. *The Roman Government of Britain*, Oxford

Birley, E. 1939. 'The Beaumont Inscription, the *Notitia Dignitatum*, and the Garrison of Hadrian's Wall', *Transactions of the Cumberland and Westmorland Antiquarian and Archaeological Society* (2nd series) 39, 190–226

Birley, E. 1952. 'Britain under Nero: the Significance of Q. Veranius', *Durham University Journal* 44 (3), 88–92

Birley, E. 1953a. *Roman Britain and the Roman Army*, Kendal

Birley, E. 1953b. 'Roman garrisons in Wales', *Archaeologia Cambrensis* 102, 9–19

Birley, E. 1953c. 'The Roman fort at Netherby', *Transactions of the Cumberland and Westmorland Antiquarian and Archaeological Society* (2nd series) 53, 6–39

Birley, E. 1958. 'Beförderungen und Versetzungen im römischen Heere', *Carnuntum Jahrbuch* (1957), 3–20

Birley, E. 1961. *Research on Hadrian's Wall*, Kendal

Birley, E. 1963. 'The Fourth-century subdivision of Britain', in G. Novak (ed.), *Quintus Congressus Internationalis Limitis Romani Studiosorum, 1961*, Acta et Dissertationes Archaeologicae/Arheološki Radovi i Rasprave 3, Zagreb, 83–8

Birley, E. 1966. 'Review: R.G. Collingwood and R.P. Wright, *The Roman Inscriptions of Britain I: Inscriptions on Stone*', *JRS* 56, 226–31

Birley, E. 1967. 'Troops from the Two Germanies in Roman Britain', *Epigraphische Studien* 4, Beihefte der Bonner Jahrbücher 25, 103–7

Birley, E. 1974. 'Cohors I Tungrorum and the Oracle of the Clarian Apollo', *Chiron* 4, 511–13

Birley, E. 1986. 'The Deities of Roman Britain', in W. Haase (ed.), *Religion, Aufstieg und Niedergang der römischen Welt* 2.18.1, Berlin/New York, 3–112

Böcking, E. (ed.) 1839/53. *Notitia Dignitatum et administrationum omnium tam civilium quam militarium in partibus Orientis et Occidentis* (2 vols), Bonn

Boersma, J.S. 1967. 'The Roman coins from the province of Zeeland', *Berichten van de Rijksdienst voor het Oudheidkundig Bodemonderzoek* 17, 65–97

Boëthius, A. and Ward-Perkins, J.B. 1970. *Etruscan and Roman Architecture*, Harmondsworth

Bogaers, J.E. 1960/1. 'Civitas en stad van de Bataven en Canninefaten', *Berichten van de Rijksdienst voor het Oudheidkundig Bodemonderzoek* 10/11, 263–317

Bogaers, J.E. 1965. 'De bezettingstroepen van de Nijmeegse legioensvesting in de 2de eeuw na Chr.', *Numaga* 12, 10–37

Bogaers, J.E. 1967a. 'Die Besatzungstruppen des Legionslagers von Nijmegen im 2. Jahrhundert nach Christus', in J. Heider (ed.), *Studien zu den Militärgrenzen Roms: Vorträge des 6. Internationalen Limeskongresses in*

Süddeutschland, Beihefte der Bonner Jahrbücher 19, Cologne/Graz, 54–76

Bogaers, J.E. 1967b. 'Enige opmerkingen over het Nederlandse gedeelte van de limes van Germania Inferior (Germania Secunda)', *Berichten van de Rijksdienst voor het Oudheidkundig Bodemonderzoek* 17, 99–114

Bogaers, J.E. 1969a. 'Cohortes Breucorum', *Berichten van de Rijksdienst voor het Oudheidkundig Bodemonderzoek* 19, 27–50

Bogaers, J.E. 1969b. 'Ruraemundensia', *Archeologische Werkgemeenschap Limburg: uitgave bij gelegenheid van het eerste lustrum 1963–1968*, 13–43

Bogaers, J.E. 1971. 'Nehalennia en de epigrafische gegevens', in P. Stuart (ed.), *Deae Nehalenniae: gids bij de tentoonstelling Nehalennia de Zeeuwse godin, Zeeland in de Romeinse tijd, Romeinse monumenten uit de Oosterschelde, Stadhuis Middelburg 17/6–29/8 1971*, Middelburg/Leiden, 33–43

Bogaers, J.E. 1972. 'Romeins Nijmegen. Van Nijmegen naar Nehal(a)en(n)ia', *Numaga* 19, 7–11

Bogaers, J.E. and Gysseling, M. 1972a. 'Over de naam van de godin Nehalennia', *Naamkunde* 4 (3–4), 221–30

Bogaers, J.E. and Gysseling, M. 1972b. 'Nehalennia, Gimio en Ganuenta', *Naamkunde* 4 (3–4), 231–40

Boon, G.C. 1972. *Isca: the Roman Legionary Fortress at Caerleon, Mon.* (3rd edn), Cardiff

Boon, G.C. 1974. *Silchester: the Roman Town of Calleva* (revised edn), Newton Abbot

Boon, G.C. 1975. 'Segontium fifty years on: I. A Roman stave of larch-wood and other unpublished finds mainly of organic materials, together with a note on late barracks', *Archaeologia Cambrensis* 124, 52–67

Boon, G.C. 1984. *Laterarium Iscanum: the Antefixes, Brick and Tile Stamps of the Second Augustan Legion*, Cardiff

Bowman, A.K. and Thomas, J.D. 1983. *Vindolanda: the Latin Writing-tablets*, Britannia Monograph 4, London

Bowman, A.K. and Thomas, J.D. 1994. *The Vindolanda Writing-tablets*, Tabulae Vindolandenses II, London

Brailsford, J.W. 1958. *Guide to the Antiquities of Roman Britain* (2nd edn), London

Brailsford, J.W. 1964. *Guide to the Antiquities of Roman Britain* (3rd edn), London

Branigan, K. 1974. 'Vespasian and the South-West', *Proceedings of the Dorset Natural History and Archaeological Society* 95, 50–7

Breeze, A. 2001. 'The British-Latin place-names *Arbeia, Corstopitum, Dictim* and *Morbium*', *Durham Archaeological Journal* 16, 21–5

Breeze, A. 2004. 'The Roman place-names *Arbeia* and *Corstopitum*: a reply', *Archaeologia Aeliana* (5th series) 33, 61–4

Breeze, D.J. 1976. 'The Ownership of Arms in the Roman Army', 93–5, in D.J. Breeze, J. Close-Brookes and J.N.G. Ritchie, 'Soldiers' Burials at Camelon, Stirlingshire, 1922 and 1975', *Britannia* 7, 73–95

Breeze, D.J. (ed.) 2012. *The First Souvenirs: Enamelled Vessels from Hadrian's Wall*, Cumberland and Westmorland Antiquarian and Archaeological Society Extra Series 37, Kendal

Breeze, D.J. and Dobson, B. 1973. 'The Development of the Mural Frontier in Britain from Hadrian to Caracalla', *Proceedings of the Society of Antiquaries of Scotland* 102, 109–21

Breeze, D.J. and Dobson, B. 1978. *Hadrian's Wall* (2nd edn), Harmondsworth

Breeze, D.J. and Dobson, B. 2000. *Hadrian's Wall* (4th edn), London

Brodribb, G. 1969. 'Stamped tiles of the 'Classis Britannica'', *Sussex Archaeological Collections* 107, 102–25

Brodribb, G. 1980. 'A further survey of stamped tiles of the Classis Britannica', *Sussex Archaeological Collections* 118, 183–96

Brunt, P.A. 1960. 'Tacitus and the Batavian Revolt', *Latomus* 19 (3), 494–517

Brunt, P.A. 1977. 'Lex de Imperio Vespasiani', *JRS* 67, 95–116

Burn, A.R. 1969. *The Romans in Britain: an Anthology of Inscriptions* (2nd edn), Oxford

Bury, J.B. 1923. 'A Lost Caesarea', *Cambridge Historical Journal* 1, 1–9

Bushe-Fox, J.P. 1932. 'Some Notes on Roman Coast Defences', *JRS* 22, 60–72

Calza, G. 1915. 'Il Piazzale delle Corporazioni e la funzione commerciale di Ostia', *Bullettino della Commissione Archeologica Comunale di Roma* 42, 178–206

Casey, P.J. 1978. 'Constantine the Great in Britain – the evidence of the coinage of the London mint, AD 312–314', in J. Bird, H. Chapman and J. Clark (eds), *Collectanea Londiniensia: Studies in London Archaeology and History presented to Ralph Merrifield*, London and Middlesex Archaeological Society Special Paper 2, 180–93

Casey, P.J. and Davies, J.L. with Evans, J. 1993. *Excavations at Segontium (Caernarfon) Roman Fort, 1975–1979*, CBA Research Report 90, London

Clavel-Lévêque, M. 1993. 'Un plan cadastral à l'échelle. La forma de bronze de Lacimurga', *Estudios de la Antigüedad* 6/7, 175–82

Clay, P. 1980. 'Seven inscribed Leaden Sealings from Leicester', *Britannia* 11, 317–20

Colledge, M.A.R. 1976. *The Art of Palmyra*, London

Collingwood, R.G. 1921. 'Hadrian's Wall: a History of the Problem', *JRS* 11, 37–66

Collingwood, R.G. and Myres, J.N.L. 1937. *Roman Britain and the English Settlements* (2nd edn), The Oxford History of England 1, Oxford

Collins, R. and Allason-Jones, L. (eds) 2010. *Finds from the Frontier: Material Culture in the 4th–5th Centuries*, CBA Research Report 162, York

Cosh, S.R. and Neal, D.S. 2005. 'Daphne at Dinnington', *Mosaic* 32, 23–5

Courteault, P. 1921. 'An Inscription Recently Found at Bordeaux', *JRS* 11, 101–7

Crawford, M.H. 1974a. *Roman Republican Coinage. Volume I: Introduction and Catalogue*, Cambridge

Crawford, M.H. 1974b. *Roman Republican Coinage. Volume II: Studies, Plates and Indexes*, Cambridge

Crema, L. 1959. *L'Architettura Romana*, Enciclopedia Classica 3.12.1, Turin

Cunliffe, B.W. 1971. *Excavations at Fishbourne 1961–1969. Volume I: the Site*, Reports of the Research Committee of the Society of Antiquaries of London 26, London

Cunliffe, B.W. 1976. 'Danebury, Hampshire: second interim report on the excavations 1971–5', *Antiquaries Journal* 56 (2), 198–216

Cunliffe, B.W. 1977. 'The Saxon Shore – some problems and misconceptions', in D.E. Johnston (ed.), *The Saxon Shore*, CBA Research Report 18, London, 1–6

Cunliffe, B.W. 1978. *Iron Age Communities in Britain: an account of England, Scotland and Wales from the seventh century BC until the Roman Conquest* (2nd edn), London

Curle, J. 1932. 'An inventory of objects of Roman and provincial Roman origin found on sites in Scotland not definitely associated with Roman constructions', *Proceedings of the Society of Antiquaries of Scotland* 66, 277–397

d'Andria, F. 2003. *Hierapolis of Phrygia (Pamukkale): an Archaeological Guide*, Istanbul

Daniels, C.M. (ed.) 1978. *Handbook to the Roman Wall* (13th edn), Newcastle upon Tyne

Dannell, G.B. 1977. 'The Samian from Bagendon', in J. Dore and K. Greene (eds), *Roman Pottery Studies in Britain and Beyond: Papers presented to John Gillam, July 1977*, BAR Supplementary Series 30, Oxford, 229–34

Daremberg, C. and Saglio, E. 1912. *Dictionnaire des Antiquités Grecques et Romaines. Volume V: T–Z*, Paris

Davey, N. and Ling, R. 1982. *Wall-painting in Roman Britain*, Britannia Monograph 3, London

Davies, R.W. 1977a. 'Ateco of Old Carlisle', *Britannia* 8, 271–4

Davies, R.W. 1977b. 'Cohors I Hispanorum and the Garrisons of Maryport', *Transactions of the Cumberland and Westmorland Antiquarian and Archaeological Society* (2nd series) 77, 7–16

de Brisay, K.W. and Evans, K.A. (eds) 1975. *Salt: the study of an ancient industry. Report on the Salt Weekend held at the University of Essex, 20, 21, 22 September 1974*, Colchester

Degrassi, A. (ed.) 1937. *Inscriptiones Italiae XIII: Fasti et Elogia*, Rome

de Kind, R. 2005. 'The Roman portraits from the villa of Lullingstone: Pertinax and his father P. Helvius Successus', in T. Ganschow and M. Steinhart (eds), *Otium: Festschrift für Volker Michael Strocka*, Remshalden, 47–53

de la Bédoyère, G. 1998. 'Carausius and the marks RSR and I.N.P.C.D.A.', *Numismatic Chronicle* 158, 79–88

de Montfaucon, B. 1719. *Antiquitas Explanatione et Schematibus Illustrata*, Paris

Devijver, H. 1976–80. *Prosopographia militiarum equestrium quae fuerunt ab Augusto ad Gallienum* (3 vols), Leuven

de Vries, J. 1956. *Altgermanische Religionsgeschichte* (vol. 1, 2nd edn), Berlin

de Vries, J. 1957. *Altgermanische Religionsgeschichte* (vol. 2, 2nd edn), Berlin

Dittenberger, W. and Purgold, K. 1896. *Olympia V: die Inschriften von Olympia*, Berlin

Dobson, B. and Mann, J.C. 1973. 'The Roman Army in Britain and Britons in the Roman Army', *Britannia* 4, 191–205

Droysen, H. (ed.) 1879/1961. *Eutropi Breviarium ab urbe condita*, Monumenta

Germaniae Historica, Auctorum Antiquissimorum 2, Berlin (repr. 1961, Berlin)

Duncan-Jones, R.P. 1978. 'Pay and numbers in Diocletian's army', *Chiron* 8, 541–60

Duncan-Jones, R.P. 1990. *Structure and Scale in the Roman Economy*, Cambridge

Ensslin, W. 1943/4. 'Arminius – Armenius?', *Das Gymnasium* 54/5, 64–73

Euzennat, M. 1976. 'Une dédicace volubilitaine à l'Apollon de Claros', *Antiquités africaines* 10, 63–8

Fink, R.O. 1958. 'Hunt's *Pridianum*: British Museum Papyrus 2851', *JRS* 48, 102–16

Fink, R.O. 1971. *Roman Military Records on Papyrus*, The American Philological Association Monograph 26, Cleveland

Finley, M.I. 1973. *The Ancient Economy*, London

Fishwick, D. 1972. 'Templum Divo Claudio Constitutum', *Britannia* 3, 164–81

Fitz, J. 1961. 'Legati legionum Pannoniae Superioris', *Acta Antiqua* 9, 159–207

Freis, H. 1965. 'Urbanae Cohortes', *Realencyclopädie der classischen Altertumswissenschaft* Suppl. X, 1125–40

Freis, H. 1967. *Die Cohortes Urbanae*, Epigraphische Studien 2, Beihefte der Bonner Jahrbücher 21, Cologne

Frere, S.S. 1967. *Britannia: a History of Roman Britain*, London

Frere, S.S. 1978. *Britannia: a History of Roman Britain* (2nd edn), London

Frere, S.S. 1987. *Britannia: a History of Roman Britain* (3rd edn), London

Fulford, M. 2006. 'Corvées and *civitates*', in R.J.A. Wilson (ed.), *Romanitas: Essays on Roman Archaeology in Honour of Sheppard Frere on the Occasion of his Ninetieth Birthday*, Oxford, 65–71

Galsterer, H. 1988. 'Municipium Flavium Irnitanum: a Latin Town in Spain', *JRS* 78, 78–90

Garbsch, J. 1970. *Der spätrömische Donau-Iller-Rhein-Limes*, Kleine Schriften zur Kenntnis der römischen Besetzungsgeschichte Südwestdeutschlands 6, Stuttgart

Gillam, J.P. 1970. *Types of Roman Coarse Pottery Vessels in Northern Britain* (3rd edn), Newcastle upon Tyne

González, J. 1986. 'The Lex Irnitana: a New Copy of the Flavian Municipal Law', *JRS* 76, 147–243

Goodburn, R. 1978. 'Roman Britain in 1977: I. Sites Explored', *Britannia* 9, 404–72

Goodchild, R.G. 1946. 'The Origins of the Romano-British Forum', *Antiquity* 20 (78), 70–7

Gordon, A.E. 1952. 'Quintus Veranius, consul AD 49: a study based on his recently identified sepulchral inscription', *University of California Publications in Classical Archaeology* 2 (5), 231–352

Gose, E. 1955. *Der Tempelbezirk des Lenus Mars in Trier*, Trierer Grabungen und Forschungen 2, Berlin

Graham, A.J. 1966. 'The Division of Britain', *JRS* 56, 92–107

Green, M.J. 1976. *A Corpus of religious material from the civilian areas of Roman Britain*, BAR British Series 24, Oxford

Grimes, W.F. 1930. *Holt, Denbighshire: the Works-Depôt of the Twentieth Legion at Castle Lyons*, Y Cymmrodor 41, London

Grimes, W.F. 1968. *The Excavation of Roman and Medieval London*, London

Haarhoff, T. 1920. *Schools of Gaul: a Study of Pagan and Christian Education in the Last Century of the Western Empire*, London

Harper, R.P. 1975. 'Excavations at Dibsi Faraj, Northern Syria, 1972–1974: a preliminary note on the site and its monuments', *Dumbarton Oaks Papers* 29, 319–38

Hartley, B.R. 1966. 'Some problems of the Roman military occupation of the north of England', *Northern History* 1, 7–20

Hassall, M.W.C. 1970. 'Batavians and the Roman Conquest of Britain', *Britannia* 1, 131–6 (= Article 2 in the present collection)

Hassall, M.W.C. 1972. 'Roman Urbanization in Western Europe', in P.J. Ucko, R. Tringham and G.W. Dimbleby (eds), *Man, Settlement and Urbanism: Proceedings of a meeting of the Research Seminar in Archaeology and Related Subjects held at the Institute of Archaeology, London University*, London, 857–61

Hassall, M.W.C. 1973. 'Roman Soldiers in Roman London', in D.E. Strong (ed.), *Archaeological Theory and Practice: Essays Presented to Professor William Francis Grimes*, London, 231–7 (= Article 10 in the present collection)

Hassall, M.W.C. 1976. 'Britain in the Notitia', in R. Goodburn and P. Bartholomew (eds), *Aspects of the Notitia Dignitatum: Papers presented to the conference in Oxford, December 13 to 15, 1974*, BAR Supplementary Series 15, Oxford, 103–17 (= Article 17 in the present collection)

Hassall, M.W.C. 1977a. 'Wingless Victories', in J. Munby and M. Henig (eds), *Roman Life and Art in Britain: a celebration in honour of the eightieth birthday of Jocelyn Toynbee*, BAR British Series 41 (2), Oxford, 327–40 (= Article 5 in the present collection)

Hassall, M.W.C. 1977b. 'The historical background and military units of the Saxon Shore', in D.E. Johnston (ed.), *The Saxon Shore*, CBA Research Report 18, London, 7–10 (= Article 18 in the present collection)

Hassall, M.W.C. 1978. 'Britain and the Rhine provinces: epigraphic evidence for Roman trade', in J. du Plat Taylor and H. Cleere (eds), *Roman shipping and trade: Britain and the Rhine provinces*, CBA Research Report 24, London, 41–8 (= Article 16 in the present collection)

Hassall, M.W.C. 1979a. 'Military Tile-stamps from Britain', in A. McWhirr (ed.), *Roman Brick and Tile: Studies in Manufacture, Distribution and Use in the Western Empire*, BAR International Series 68, Oxford, 261–6 (= Article 8 in the present collection)

Hassall, M.W.C. 1979b. 'The Impact of Mediterranean Urbanism on Indigenous Nucleated Centres', in B.C. Burnham and H.B. Johnson (eds), *Invasion and Response: the Case of Roman Britain*, BAR British Series 73, Oxford, 241–53 (= Article 12 in the present collection)

Hassall, M.W.C. 1982. 'Inscriptions and Graffiti', in G.C. Boon and M.W.C. Hassall, *Report on the Excavations at Usk 1965–1976: the Coins, Inscriptions and Graffiti*, Cardiff, 45–61

Hassall, M.W.C. 1983a. 'The Building of the Antonine Wall', *Britannia* 14, 262–

4 (= Article 4 in the present collection)

Hassall, M.W.C. 1983b. 'The internal planning of Roman auxiliary forts', in B. Hartley and J. Wacher (eds), *Rome and her Northern Provinces: Papers Presented to Sheppard Frere in Honour of his Retirement from the Chair of the Archaeology of the Roman Empire, University of Oxford, 1983*, Gloucester, 96–131

Hassall, M.W.C. 1984. 'The Date of the Rebuilding of Hadrian's Turf Wall in Stone', *Britannia* 15, 242–4 (= Article 6 in the present collection)

Hassall, M.W.C. 1996. 'London as a Provincial Capital', in J. Bird, M.W.C. Hassall and H. Sheldon (eds), *Interpreting Roman London: Papers in Memory of Hugh Chapman*, Oxbow Monograph 58, Oxford, 19–26 (= Article 11 in the present collection)

Hassall, M.W.C. 1999. 'Soldier and Civilian: a debate on the bank of the Severn', in H. Hurst (ed.), *The Coloniae of Roman Britain: New Studies and a Review. Papers of the conference held at Gloucester on 5–6 July, 1997*, Journal of Roman Archaeology Supplementary Series 36, Portsmouth, RI, 181–5

Hassall, M.W.C. 2000a. 'Pre-Hadrianic Legionary Dispositions in Britain', in R. Brewer (ed.), *Roman Fortresses and their Legions: Papers in Honour of George C. Boon*, Occasional Papers of the Research Committee of the Society of Antiquaries of London 20, London/Cardiff, 51–67

Hassall, M.W.C. 2000b. 'The location of legionary fortresses as a response to changes in military strategy: the case of Roman Britain AD 43–84', in Y. Le Bohec and C. Wolff (eds), *Les légions de Rome sous le Haut-Empire: Actes du Congrès de Lyon (17–19 septembre 1998)*, Collection du Centre d'Études Romaines et Gallo-Romaines nouvelle série 20, Lyon, 441–57 (= Article 1 in the present collection)

Hassall, M.W.C. 2004. 'The defence of Britain in the 4th century', in Y. Le Bohec and C. Wolff (eds), *L'armée Romaine de Dioclétien à Valentinien Ier: Actes du Congrès de Lyon (12–14 septembre 2002)*, Collection du Centre d'Études Romaines et Gallo-Romaines nouvelle série 26, Lyon, 179–89 (= Article 19 in the present collection)

Hassall, M.W.C. 2008. 'Footnotes to The Fasti', in H.M. Schellenberg, V.E. Hirschmann and A. Krieckhaus (eds), *A Roman Miscellany: Essays in Honour of Anthony R. Birley on his Seventieth Birthday*, Akanthina Monograph 3, Gdańsk, 31–41 (= Article 9 in the present collection)

Hassall, M.W.C. 2009. 'Inscriptions and Hadrian's Wall', in M.F.A. Symonds and D.J.P. Mason (eds), *Frontiers of Knowledge: a Research Framework for Hadrian's Wall, Part of the Frontiers of the Roman Empire World Heritage Site. Volume I: Resource Assessment*, Durham, 152–4 (= Article 3 in the present collection)

Hassall, M.W.C. 2010. 'The written record and the late Roman frontier', in R. Collins and L. Allason-Jones (eds), *Finds from the Frontier: Material Culture in the 4th–5th Centuries*, CBA Research Report 162, York, 17–19 (= Article 20 in the present collection)

Haverfield, F. 1918. 'Early Northumbrian Christianity and the Altars to the 'Di Veteres'', *Archaeologia Aeliana* (3rd series) 15, 22–43

Hearne, T. (ed.) 1745. *Joannis Rossi Antiquarii Warwicensis, Historia Regum Angliae* (2nd edn), Oxford

Heichelheim, F.M. 1961. 'Vitiris', *Realencyclopädie der classischen Altertumswissenschaft* IX A.1, 408–15

Heighway, C.M. and Parker, A.J. 1982. 'The Roman Tilery at St Oswald's Priory, Gloucester', *Britannia* 13, 25–77

Henig, M. 1980. 'Art and Cult in the Temples of Roman Britain', in W. Rodwell (ed.), *Temples, Churches and Religion: Recent Research in Roman Britain, with a Gazetteer of Romano-Celtic Temples in Continental Europe*, BAR British Series 77 (1), Oxford, 91–113

Henig, M. 1995. *The Art of Roman Britain*, London

Henig, M. 2006. 'Pertinax and his father: imperial portraits in Britain', *SALON* 143, Society of Antiquaries of London Online Newsletter, www.sal.org.uk/salon/archive

Henig, M. 2009. 'Roman Sculpture from the Hadrian's Wall Region', in M.F.A. Symonds and D.J.P. Mason (eds), *Frontiers of Knowledge: a Research Framework for Hadrian's Wall, Part of the Frontiers of the Roman Empire World Heritage Site. Volume I: Resource Assessment*, Durham, 155–8

Heurgon, J. 1951. 'The Amiens Patera', *JRS* 41, 22–4

Hind, J.G.F. 1974. 'Agricola's Fleet and Portus Trucculensis', *Britannia* 5, 285–8

Hind, J.G.F. 2007. 'A. Plautius' Campaign in Britain: an Alternative Reading of the Narrative in Cassius Dio (60.19.5–21.2)', *Britannia* 38, 93–106

Hodgson, N. 2002. 'The Roman place-names *Arbeia* and *Corstopitum*: a rejection of recently suggested meanings', *Archaeologia Aeliana* (5th series) 30, 173–4

Hoffmann, D. 1969. *Das spätrömische Bewegungsheer und die Notitia Dignitatum*, Epigraphische Studien 7 (1), Düsseldorf

Hoffmann, D. 1974. 'Die Neubesetzung des Grenzschutzes am Rhein, an der gallischen Atlantikküste und in Britannien unter Valentinian I. um 369 n. Chr.', in E. Birley, B. Dobson and M.G. Jarrett (eds), *Roman Frontier Studies 1969: Eighth International Congress of Limesforschung*, Cardiff, 168–73

Hölscher, T. 1967. *Victoria Romana: Archäologische Untersuchungen zur Geschichte und Wesensart der römischen Siegesgöttin von den Anfängen bis zum Ende des 3. Jhs. n. Chr.*, Mainz

Hondius-Crone, A. 1955. *The Temple of Nehalennia at Domburg*, Amsterdam

Horn, H.G. 1970. 'Eine Weihung für Hercules Magusanus aus Bonn. Mit einem Nachtrag von Henning Wrede', *Bonner Jahrbücher* 170, 233–51

Hübner, E. 1881. 'Das römische Heer in Britannien', *Hermes* 16, 513–84

Jackson, K. 1970. 'Romano-British Names in the Antonine Itinerary', 68–82, in A.L.F. Rivet, 'The British Section of the Antonine Itinerary', *Britannia* 1, 34–82

Jarrett, M.G. 1964. 'Legio II Augusta in Britain', *Archaeologia Cambrensis* 113, 47–63

Jarrett, M.G. 1966. 'The garrison of Maryport and the Roman army in Britain', in M.G. Jarrett and B. Dobson (eds), *Britain and Rome: Essays Presented to Eric Birley on his Sixtieth Birthday*, Kendal, 27–40

Jarrett, M.G. (ed.) 1969. *The Roman Frontier in Wales* (revised edn), Cardiff

Jarrett, M.G. 1976. *Maryport, Cumbria: a Roman Fort and its Garrison*, Cumberland and Westmorland Antiquarian and Archaeological Society Extra Series 22, Kendal

Jenkins, F. 1956. 'Nameless or Nehalennia', *Archaeologia Cantiana* 70, 192–200

Jobey, G. 1976. 'Traprain Law: a summary', in D.W. Harding (ed.), *Hillforts: Later Prehistoric Earthworks in Britain and Ireland*, London, 192–204

Johnson, J.S. 1970. 'The Date of the Construction of the Saxon Shore Fort at Richborough', *Britannia* 1, 240–8

Johnson, S. 1979. *The Roman Forts of the Saxon Shore* (2nd edn), London

Johnston, J.B. 1934. *Place-names of Scotland* (3rd edn), London

Jones, A.H.M. 1949. 'The Roman Civil Service (Clerical and Sub-clerical Grades)', *JRS* 39, 38–55

Jones, A.H.M. 1960. *Studies in Roman Government and Law*, Oxford

Jones, A.H.M. 1964. *The Later Roman Empire, 284–602: a Social, Economic, and Administrative Survey* (3 vols), Oxford

Jones, C.P. 2005. 'Ten dedications 'To the gods and goddesses' and the Antonine Plague', *Journal of Roman Archaeology* 18, 293–301

Jones, C.P. 2006. 'Cosa and the Antonine Plague?', *Journal of Roman Archaeology* 19, 368–9

Kajanto, I. 1965. *The Latin Cognomina*, Helsinki

Keppie, L.J.F. 1975. 'The building of the Antonine Wall: archaeological and epigraphic evidence', *Proceedings of the Society of Antiquaries of Scotland* 105, 151–65

Keppie, L.J.F. 1979. *Roman Distance Slabs from the Antonine Wall: a Brief Guide*, Glasgow

Keppie, L.J.F. 1982. 'The Antonine Wall 1960–1980', *Britannia* 13, 91–111

Klumbach, H. (ed.) 1973. *Spätrömische Gardehelme*, Münchner Beiträge zur Vor- und Frühgeschichte 15, Munich

Leschi, L. 1948. 'L'album municipal de Timgad et l''Ordo Salutationis' du consulaire Ulpius Mariscianus', *Revue des Études Anciennes* 50, 71–100

Lewis, M.J.T. 1966. *Temples in Roman Britain*, Cambridge

Lewis, N. and Reinhold, M. (eds) 1955. *Roman Civilization: Selected Readings. Volume II: the Empire*, New York

Lewis, N. and Reinhold, M. (eds) 1990. *Roman Civilization: Selected Readings. Volume II: the Empire* (3rd edn), New York

Macdonald, G. 1934. *The Roman Wall in Scotland* (2nd edn), Oxford

MacMullen, R. 1963. *Soldier and Civilian in the Later Roman Empire*, Harvard Historical Monographs 52, Cambridge, Mass.

Magie, D. 1950. *Roman Rule in Asia Minor: to the End of the Third Century after Christ*, Princeton

Mann, J.C. 1961. 'The Administration of Roman Britain', *Antiquity* 35 (140), 316–20

Mann, J.C. (ed.) 1971. *The Northern Frontier in Britain from Hadrian to Honorius: Literary and Epigraphic Sources*, Newcastle upon Tyne

Mann, J.C. and Jarrett, M.G. 1967. 'The Division of Britain', *JRS* 57, 61–4

Manning, W.H. 1966. 'Caistor-by-Norwich and *Notitia Dignitatum*', *Antiquity* 40 (157), 60–2

Mattingly, H. 1967. *Roman Coins: from the Earliest Times to the Fall of the Western Empire* (2nd edn), London

Maxfield, V.A. (ed.) 1989. *The Saxon Shore: a handbook*, Exeter Studies in History 25, Exeter

Maxwell, G.S. 1974. 'The building of the Antonine Wall', in D.M. Pippidi (ed.), *Actes du IXe Congrès International d'Études sur les Frontières Romaines*, Bucharest, 327–32

McWhirr, A. 1979a. 'Tile-kilns in Roman Britain', in A. McWhirr (ed.), *Roman Brick and Tile: Studies in Manufacture, Distribution and Use in the Western Empire*, BAR International Series 68, Oxford, 97–189

McWhirr, A. 1979b. 'Origins of Legionary Tile-stamping in Britain', in A. McWhirr (ed.), *Roman Brick and Tile: Studies in Manufacture, Distribution and Use in the Western Empire*, BAR International Series 68, Oxford, 253–9

Meiggs, R. 1973. *Roman Ostia* (2nd edn), Oxford

Merrifield, R. 1969. *Roman London*, London

Merrifield, R. 1977, 'Art and Religion in Roman London: an Inquest on the Sculptures of Londinium', in J. Munby and M. Henig (eds), *Roman Life and Art in Britain: a celebration in honour of the eightieth birthday of Jocelyn Toynbee*, BAR British Series 41 (2), Oxford, 375–406

Mertens, J. 1974. 'Liberchies-Brunehaut: *castellum* du *Limes Belgicus*', in E. Birley, B. Dobson and M.G. Jarrett (eds), *Roman Frontier Studies 1969: Eighth International Congress of Limesforschung*, Cardiff, 106–11

Milne, G. 1996. 'A Palace Disproved: Reassessing the Provincial Governor's presence in 1st-century London', in J. Bird, M.W.C. Hassall and H. Sheldon (eds), *Interpreting Roman London: Papers in Memory of Hugh Chapman*, Oxbow Monograph 58, Oxford, 49–55

Möbius, H. 1948/9. 'Römischer Kameo in Kassel', *Archäologischer Anzeiger, Beiblatt zum Jahrbuch des Deutschen Archäologischen Instituts* 63/4, 101–18

Momigliano, A. 1950. 'Panegyricus Messallae and 'Panegyricus Vespasiani': Two References to Britain', *JRS* 40, 39–42

Mommsen, T. (ed.) 1894/1961. *Chronica Minora saec. IV, V, VI, VII* (vol. 2), Monumenta Germaniae Historica, Auctorum Antiquissimorum 11, Berlin (repr. 1961, Berlin)

Morris, J. 1978. *Oxford* (revised edn), Oxford

Nash-Williams, V.E. 1954. *The Roman Frontier in Wales*, Cardiff

Nesselhauf, H. and von Petrikovits, H. 1967. 'Ein Weihaltar für Apollo aus Aachen-Burtscheid', *Bonner Jahrbücher* 167, 268–79

Noll, R. 1974. 'Eine goldene 'Kaiserfibel' aus Niederemmel vom Jahre 316', *Bonner Jahrbücher* 174, 221–44

Ogilvie, R.M. and Richmond, I. (eds) 1967. *De Vita Agricolae*, Oxford

Oswald, F. 1936/7. *Index of Figure-types on Terra Sigillata ('Samian Ware')*, Liverpool

Painter, K.S. 1972. 'A late-Roman silver ingot from Kent', *Antiquaries Journal*

52 (1), 84–92

Peacock, D.P.S. 1973. 'Forged brick-stamps from Pevensey', *Antiquity* 47 (186), 138–40

Pearson, A. 2002. *The Roman Shore Forts: Coastal Defences of Southern Britain*, Stroud

Pflaum, H.G. 1948. *Le Marbre de Thorigny*, Paris

Pharr, C. with Davidson, T.S. and Pharr, M.B. (trans.) 1952. *The Theodosian Code and Novels and the Sirmondian Constitutions*, Princeton

Phillip, H. 1930. 'Marsyas', *Realencyclopädie der classischen Altertumswissenschaft* XIV, 1985–2000

Philp, B. 1981. *The Excavation of the Roman Forts of the Classis Britannica at Dover 1970–1977*, Kent Monograph 3, Dover

Piganiol, A. 1962. *Les documents cadastraux de la colonie romaine d'Orange*, Gallia Supplément 16, Paris

Reynolds, P.J. and Langley, J.K. 1979. 'Romano-British Corn-Drying Oven: an Experiment', *Archaeological Journal* 136, 27–42

Richardson, J.S. 1996. *The Romans in Spain*, Oxford

Richmond, I.A. 1935. 'The Rudge Cup: II. The Inscription', 334–42, in J.D. Cowen and I.A. Richmond, 'The Rudge Cup', *Archaeologia Aeliana* (4th series) 12, 310–42

Richmond, I.A. 1936. 'Roman leaden sealings from Brough-under-Stainmore', *Transactions of the Cumberland and Westmorland Antiquarian and Archaeological Society* (2nd series) 36, 104–25

Richmond, I.A. 1943. 'Roman legionaries at Corbridge, their supply-base, temples and religious cults', *Archaeologia Aeliana* (4th series) 21, 127–224

Richmond, I.A. 1955. *Roman Britain*, Harmondsworth

Richmond, I.A. (ed.) 1966. *Handbook to the Roman Wall* (12th edn), Newcastle upon Tyne

Richmond, I.A. 1968. *Hod Hill. Volume II: Excavations Carried Out between 1951 and 1958 for the Trustees of the British Museum*, London

Richmond, I.A. and Gillam, J.P. 1953. 'Milecastle 79 (Solway)', *Transactions of the Cumberland and Westmorland Antiquarian and Archaeological Society* (2nd series) 52, 17–40

Riese, A. 1889. *Forschungen zur Geschichte der Rheinlande*, Frankfurt

Ritterling, E. 1924. 'Legio: Bestand, Verteilung und kriegerische Betätigung der Legionen des stehenden Heeres von Augustus bis Diocletian', *Realencyclopädie der classischen Altertumswissenschaft* XII.1, 1211–328

Ritterling, E. 1925. 'Legio: Bestand, Verteilung und kriegerische Betätigung der Legionen des stehenden Heeres von Augustus bis Diocletian (Fortsetzung)', *Realencyclopädie der classischen Altertumswissenschaft* XII.2, 1329–829

Rivet, A.L.F. 1970. 'The British Section of the Antonine Itinerary', *Britannia* 1, 34–82

Rivet, A.L.F. 1977a. 'Ptolemy's Geography and the Flavian invasion of Scotland', in D. Haupt and H.G. Horn (eds), *Studien zu den Militärgrenzen Roms II: Vorträge des 10. Internationalen Limeskongresses in der Germania Inferior*, Beihefte der Bonner Jahrbücher 38, Cologne/Bonn, 45–64

Rivet, A.L.F. 1977b. 'The Origins of Cities in Roman Britain', in P.-M. Duval and E. Frézouls (eds), *Thèmes de recherches sur les villes antiques d'Occident: Strasbourg, 1er–4 octobre 1971*, Colloques internationaux du Centre national de la recherche scientifique 542, Paris, 161–72

Rivet, A.L.F. and Smith, C. 1979. *The Place-names of Roman Britain*, London

Robertson, A.S. 1969. 'Distance slab of the Twentieth Legion found on the Antonine Wall, at Hutcheson Hill, 1969', *Glasgow Archaeological Journal* 1, 1

Robinson, H.R. 1975. *The Armour of Imperial Rome*, London

Rostovtzeff, M. 1942. '*Vexillum* and Victory', *JRS* 32, 92–106

Roxan, M.M. 1986a. 'Roman military diplomata and topography', in C. Unz (ed.), *Studien zu den Militärgrenzen Roms III: Vorträge des 13. Internationalen Limeskongresses, Aalen 1983*, Stuttgart, 768–78

Roxan, M.M. 1986b. 'Observations on the reasons for changes in formula in diplomas circa AD 140', in W. Eck and H. Wolff (eds), *Heer und Integrationspolitik: die römischen Militärdiplome als historische Quelle*, Cologne/Vienna, 265–92

Rüger, C. 1972. 'Gallisch-germanische Kurien', *Epigraphische Studien* 9, 251–60

Russell, M. 2006a. 'Roman Britain's Lost Governor', *Current Archaeology* 204, 630–5

Russell, M. 2006b. *Roman Sussex*, Stroud

Sadurska, A. 1972. *Corpus des sculptures du monde romain. Pologne 1: Les portraits romains dans les collections polonaises*, Corpus Signorum Imperii Romani, Warsaw

Şahin, S. and Adak, M. 2007. *Stadiasmus Patarensis: Itinera Romana Provinciae Lyciae*, Monographien zu Gephyra 1, Istanbul

Salviat, F. 1977. 'Orientation, extension et chronologie des plans cadastraux d'Orange', *Revue archéologique de Narbonnaise* 10, 107–18

Salway, P. 1965. *The Frontier People of Roman Britain*, Cambridge

Salway, R.W.B. 2007. 'The perception and description of space in Roman itineraries', in M. Rathmann (ed.), *Wahrnehmung und Erfassung geographischer Räume in der Antike*, Mainz, 181–209

Sauer, E.W. 2005. 'Inscriptions from Alchester: Vespasian's Base of the Second Augustan Legion(?)', *Britannia* 36, 101–33

Sauer, E.W. 2007. 'Milestones: Misunderstood Stone Monuments?' Paper delivered to the British Epigraphy Society Spring Colloquium 2007 in Edinburgh, *British Epigraphy Society Newsletter* (new series) 17, 13–14, http://www.csad.ox.ac.uk/bes/newsletter.htm

Saxer, R. 1967. *Untersuchungen zu den Vexillationen des römischen Kaiserheeres von Augustus bis Diokletian*, Epigraphische Studien 1, Beihefte der Bonner Jahrbücher 18, Cologne/Graz

Schallmayer, E., Eibl, K., Ott, J., Preuss, G. and Wittkopf, E. 1990. *Der römische Weihebezirk von Osterburken I. Corpus der griechischen und lateinischen Beneficiarier-Inschriften des Römischen Reiches*, Forschungen und Berichte zur Vor- und Frühgeschichte in Baden-Württemberg 40, Stuttgart

Schulze, W. 1904/66. *Zur Geschichte lateinischer Eigennamen*, Berlin

Seeck, O. (ed.) 1876/1962, *Notitia Dignitatum: accedunt Notitia Urbis*

Constantinopolitanae et latercula provinciarum, Berlin (repr. 1962, Frankfurt)

Sherk, R.K. 1970. *The Municipal Decrees of the Roman West*, Arethusa Monographs 2, Buffalo

Sherlock, D. 1979. 'Plumbatae – a note on the method of manufacture', in M.W.C. Hassall and R.I. Ireland (eds), *De Rebus Bellicis*, BAR International Series 63 (1), Oxford, 101–2

Simpson, F.G. and Richmond, I.A. 1935. 'The Turf Wall of Hadrian, 1895–1935', *JRS* 25, 1–18

Smith, I.G. 1997. 'Some Roman Place-names in Lancashire and Cumbria', *Britannia* 28, 372–83

Speidel, M.P. 1965. *Die Equites Singulares Augusti*, Antiquitas Reihe 1, Bonn

Speidel, M.P. 1974. 'Stablesiani: the Raising of New Cavalry Units during the Crisis of the Roman Empire', *Chiron* 4, 541–6

Steer, K.A. and Cormack, E.A. 1971. 'A new Roman distance-slab from the Antonine Wall', *Proceedings of the Society of Antiquaries of Scotland* 101, 122–6

Stein, E. 1932. *Die kaiserlichen Beamten und Truppenkörper im römischen Deutschland unter dem Prinzipat*, Vienna

Stevens, C.E. 1940. 'The British Sections of the 'Notitia Dignitatum'', *Archaeological Journal* 97, 125–54

Stevens, C.E. 1941. 'Gildas Sapiens', *English Historical Review* 56 (223), 353–73

Stevens, C.E. 1966. *The Building of Hadrian's Wall*, Cumberland and Westmorland Antiquarian and Archaeological Society Extra Series 20, Kendal

Strang, A. 1998. 'Recreating a possible Flavian map of Roman Britain with a detailed map for Scotland', *Proceedings of the Society of Antiquaries of Scotland* 128, 425–40

Stuart, J. and Revett, N. 1794. *The Antiquities of Athens. Volume III*, London

Stuart, P. and Bogaers, J.E. 1971. 'Catalogus van de monumenten', in P. Stuart (ed.), *Deae Nehalenniae: gids bij de tentoonstelling Nehalennia de Zeeuwse godin, Zeeland in de Romeinse tijd, Romeinse monumenten uit de Oosterschelde, Stadhuis Middelburg 17/6–29/8 1971*, Middelburg/Leiden, 60–86

Sutherland, C.H.V. 1967. *The Roman Imperial Coinage. Volume VI: from Diocletian's reform (AD 294) to the death of Maximinus (AD 313)*, London

Syme, R. 1958. *Tacitus*, Oxford

Thomasson, B.E. 1960. *Die Statthalter der römischen Provinzen Nordafrikas von Augustus bis Diocletianus*, Lund

Todd, M. 1966. 'Romano-British mintages of Antoninus Pius', *Numismatic Chronicle* (7th series) 6, 147–53

Tomlin, R.S.O. 1969. 'Numerus Supervenientium Petueriensium', in J.S. Wacher, *Excavations at Brough-on-Humber 1958–1961*, Reports of the Research Committee of the Society of Antiquaries of London 25, London, 74–5

Tomlin, R.S.O. 1972. 'Seniores–Iuniores in the Late-Roman Field Army', *American Journal of Philology* 93 (2), 253–78

Tomlin, R.S.O. 1979. 'Graffiti on Roman bricks and tiles found in Britain', in A. McWhirr (ed.), *Roman Brick and Tile: Studies in Manufacture, Distribution* and Use in the Western Empire, BAR International Series 68, Oxford, 231–51

Tomlin, R.S.O. 1992. 'The Twentieth Legion at Wroxeter and Carlisle in the First Century: the Epigraphic Evidence', Britannia 23, 141–58

Toynbee, J.M.C. 1924. 'Britannia on Roman Coins of the Second Century AD', JRS 14, 142–57

Toynbee, J.M.C. 1962. Art in Roman Britain, London

Toynbee, J.M.C. 1964. Art in Britain under the Romans, Oxford

Toynbee, J.M.C. 1978. 'A Londinium votive leaf or feather and its fellows', in J. Bird, H. Chapman and J. Clark (eds), Collectanea Londiniensia: Studies in London Archaeology and History presented to Ralph Merrifield, London and Middlesex Archaeological Society Special Paper 2, 128–47

Turnbull, P. 1978. 'The Phallus in the Art of Roman Britain', Bulletin of the Institute of Archaeology, University of London 15, 199–206

Turner, E.G. 1963. 'A Curse Tablet from Nottinghamshire', JRS 53, 122–4

Vogel, F. (ed.) 1885/1961. Magni Felicis Ennodi Opera, Monumenta Germaniae Historica, Auctores Antiquissimi 7, Berlin (repr. 1961, Berlin)

von Domaszewski, A. 1967. Die Rangordnung des römischen Heeres. 2: durchgesehene Auflage: Einführung, Berichtigungen und Nachträge von Brian Dobson, Beihefte der Bonner Jahrbücher 14, Cologne

Wacher, J.S. 1969. Excavations at Brough-on-Humber 1958–1961, Reports of the Research Committee of the Society of Antiquaries of London 25, London

Wacher, J.S. 1975. The Towns of Roman Britain, London

Wacher, J.S. 1995. The Towns of Roman Britain (2nd edn), London

Walser, G. 1951. Rom, das Reich und die fremden Völker, Baden-Baden

Ward, J.H. 1973. 'The British Sections of the Notitia Dignitatum: an Alternative Interpretation', Britannia 4, 253–63

Watson, W.J. 1926. The History of the Celtic Place-names of Scotland, Edinburgh

Webb, P.H. 1933. The Roman Imperial Coinage. Volume V, Part II: Probus to Amandus, London

Webster, G. 1966. 'Fort and Town in Early Roman Britain', in J.S. Wacher (ed.), The Civitas Capitals of Roman Britain: Papers Given at a Conference Held at the University of Leicester, 13–15 December 1963, Leicester, 31–45

Webster, G. 1993. The Roman Invasion of Britain (revised edn), London

Webster, J. 2009. 'Religion', in M.F.A. Symonds and D.J.P. Mason (eds), Frontiers of Knowledge: a Research Framework for Hadrian's Wall, Part of the Frontiers of the Roman Empire World Heritage Site. Volume I: Resource Assessment, Durham, 158–60

Wenham, L.P. 1939. 'Notes on the garrisoning of Maryport', Transactions of the Cumberland and Westmorland Antiquarian and Archaeological Society (2nd series) 39, 19–30

Wheeler, R.E.M. 1923. Segontium and the Roman Occupation of Wales, Y Cymmrodor 33, London

Wheeler, R.E.M. 1943. Maiden Castle, Dorset, Reports of the Research Committee of the Society of Antiquaries of London 12, Oxford

Wightman, E.M. 1970. Roman Trier and the Treveri, London

Wild, J.P. 1967. 'The Gynaeceum at Venta and its Context', Latomus 26 (3), 648–

76

Wild, J.P. 1975. 'Review: *Kastell Hesselbach und andere Forschungen am Odenwaldlimes*. By D. Baatz', *Antiquaries Journal* 55 (1), 146–7

Wild, J.P. 1976. 'The Gynaecea', in R. Goodburn and P. Bartholomew (eds), *Aspects of the Notitia Dignitatum: Papers presented to the conference in Oxford, December 13 to 15, 1974*, BAR Supplementary Series 15, Oxford, 51–8

Wilson, P.R. 2002. 'Roman Catterick discussion', in P.R. Wilson, *Cataractonium: Roman Catterick and its hinterland. Excavations and research, 1958–1997. Part II*, CBA Research Report 129, York, 446–75

Wilson, P.R. and Wacher, J.S. 2002. 'Excavations by Professor John Wacher', in P.R. Wilson, *Cataractonium: Roman Catterick and its hinterland. Excavations and research, 1958–1997. Part I*, CBA Research Report 128, York, 46–138

Witts, P. 2005. *Mosaics in Roman Britain: Stories in Stone*, Stroud

Wright, R.P. 1956. 'A Note on the Inscription', 8–10, in S.S. Frere, 'Excavations at Verulamium, 1955: interim report', *Antiquaries Journal* 36 (1–2), 1–10

Wright, R.P. 1970. 'Bronze Rings', 257–9, in J.R. Collis, 'Excavations at Owslebury, Hants: a second interim report', *Antiquaries Journal* 50 (2), 246–61

Wright, R.P. 1974. 'Carpow and Caracalla', *Britannia* 5, 289–92

Wright, R.P. 1976. 'Tile-Stamps of the Sixth Legion found in Britain', *Britannia* 7, 224–35

Wright, R.P. 1978. 'Tile-Stamps of the Ninth Legion found in Britain', *Britannia* 9, 379–82

Zanier, W. 1992. *Das römische Kastell Ellingen*, Limesforschungen 23, Mainz

MARK HASSALL:
A BIBLIOGRAPHY, 1954–2017

Not including published book reviews by the author

1954
'A Pottery Mould from Horsepath, Oxon.', *Oxoniensia* 17/18, 1954, 231–4

1958
'Archaeology of Holton', *Oxoniensia* 23, 1958, 145–6

1970
'Batavians and the Roman Conquest of Britain', *Britannia* 1, 1970, 131–6 (= Article 2 in the present collection)

1971
(With I. Hodder) 'The Non-random Spacing of Romano-British Walled Towns', *Man* (new series) 6 (3), 1971, 391–407

(With R.P. Wright) 'Roman Britain in 1970: II. Inscriptions', *Britannia* 2, 1971, 289–304

The Romans, The Young Archaeologist, 1971, London

1972
'Roman Urbanization in Western Europe', in P.J. Ucko, R. Tringham and G.W. Dimbleby (eds), *Man, Settlement and Urbanism: Proceedings of a meeting of the Research Seminar in Archaeology and Related Subjects held at the Institute of Archaeology, London University*, 1972, London, 857–61

(With R.P. Wright) 'Roman Britain in 1971: II. Inscriptions', *Britannia* 3, 1972, 352–67

1973
'Roman Soldiers in Roman London', in D.E. Strong (ed.), *Archaeological Theory and Practice: Essays Presented to Professor William Francis Grimes*, 1973, London, 231–7 (= Article 10 in the present collection)

'Appendix I: Inscriptions 1969–1973', 211–14, in A. McWhirr, 'Cirencester, 1969–1972: Ninth Interim Report', *Antiquaries Journal* 53 (2), 1973, 191–218

(With R.P. Wright) 'Roman Britain in 1972: II. Inscriptions', *Britannia* 4, 1973, 324–37

1974
(With M. Crawford and J. Reynolds) 'Rome and the Eastern Provinces at the End of the Second Century B.C.', *JRS* 64, 1974, 195–220

(With R.P. Wright) 'Roman Britain in 1973: II. Inscriptions', *Britannia* 5, 1974, 461–80

1975
(With J. Rhodes) 'Excavations at the new Market Hall, Gloucester, 1966–7', *Transactions of the Bristol and Gloucestershire Archaeological Society* 93, 1975, 15–100

(With R.P. Wright and R.S.O. Tomlin) 'Roman Britain in 1974: II. Inscriptions', *Britannia* 6, 1975, 284–94

1976
'Britain in the Notitia', in R. Goodburn and P. Bartholomew (eds), *Aspects of the Notitia Dignitatum: Papers presented to the conference in Oxford, December 13 to 15, 1974*, BAR Supplementary Series 15, 1976, Oxford, 103–17 (= Article 17 in the present collection)

(With R.P. Wright and R.S.O. Tomlin) 'Roman Britain in 1975: II. Inscriptions', *Britannia* 7, 1976, 378–92

1977
'Wingless Victories', in J. Munby and M. Henig (eds), *Roman Life and Art in Britain: a celebration in honour of the eightieth birthday of Jocelyn Toynbee*, BAR British Series 41 (2), 1977, Oxford, 327–40 (= Article 5 in the present collection)

'The historical background and military units of the Saxon Shore', in D.E. Johnston (ed.), *The Saxon Shore*, CBA Research Report 18, 1977, London, 7–10 (= Article 18 in the present collection)

(With R.S.O. Tomlin) 'Roman Britain in 1976: II. Inscriptions', *Britannia* 8, 1977, 416–49

1978
'Britain and the Rhine provinces: epigraphic evidence for Roman trade', in J. du Plat Taylor and H. Cleere (eds), *Roman shipping and trade: Britain and the Rhine provinces*, CBA Research Report 24, 1978, London, 41–8 (= Article 16 in

the present collection)

(With R.S.O. Tomlin) 'Roman Britain in 1977: II. Inscriptions', *Britannia* 9, 1978, 473–85

1979

'Military Tile-stamps from Britain', in A. McWhirr (ed.), *Roman Brick and Tile: Studies in Manufacture, Distribution and Use in the Western Empire*, BAR International Series 68, 1979, Oxford, 261–6 (= Article 8 in the present collection)

'The Impact of Mediterranean Urbanism on Indigenous Nucleated Centres', in B.C. Burnham and H.B. Johnson (eds), *Invasion and Response: the Case of Roman Britain*, BAR British Series 73, 1979, Oxford, 241–53 (= Article 12 in the present collection)

(Ed. with R.I. Ireland) *De Rebus Bellicis*, BAR International Series 63 (1), 1979, Oxford

'The inventions', in M.W.C. Hassall and R.I. Ireland (eds), *De Rebus Bellicis*, BAR International Series 63 (1), 1979, Oxford, 77–95

(With R.S.O. Tomlin) 'Roman Britain in 1978: II. Inscriptions', *Britannia* 10, 1979, 339–56

'Religion in Roman Britain: a topic for projects', *Hesperiam* 2, 1979, 18–33

'The Claudian Conquest 43 AD', in R. Merrifield (ed.), *Roman Britain 55 BC–AD 409*, British History Illustrated 6 (1), 1979, London, 10–16

1980

'Altars, Curses and Other Epigraphic Evidence', in W. Rodwell (ed.), *Temples, Churches and Religion: Recent Research in Roman Britain, with a Gazetteer of Romano-Celtic Temples in Continental Europe*, BAR British Series 77 (1), 1980, Oxford, 79–89 (= Article 14 in the present collection)

'The Inscribed Altars', in T. Dyson (ed.), *The Roman Riverside Wall and Monumental Arch in London*, London and Middlesex Archaeological Society Special Paper 3, 1980, London, 195–8

(With R.S.O. Tomlin) 'Roman Britain in 1979: II. Inscriptions', *Britannia* 11, 1980, 403–17

'Exhibits at Ballots: Roman harness fittings from Canterbury', *Antiquaries Journal* 60 (2), 1980, 342–4

(With L. Webster and D.B. Harden) 'Exhibits at Ballots: the Darenth Park Bowl', *Antiquaries Journal* 60 (2), 1980, 338–40

1981

(With R.S.O. Tomlin) 'Roman Britain in 1980: II. Inscriptions', *Britannia* 12, 1981, 369–96

1982

(With G.C. Boon) *Report on the Excavations at Usk 1965–1976: the Coins, Inscriptions and Graffiti*, 1982, Cardiff

'Inscriptions and Graffiti', in G.C. Boon and M.W.C. Hassall, *Report on the Excavations at Usk 1965–1976: the Coins, Inscriptions and Graffiti*, 1982, Cardiff, 45–61

'Epigraphic evidence for the auxiliary garrison at Cirencester', in J. Wacher and A. McWhirr, *Early Roman Occupation at Cirencester*, Cirencester Excavations 1, 1982, Cirencester, 67–71

'Graffiti', in J. Wacher and A. McWhirr, *Early Roman Occupation at Cirencester*, Cirencester Excavations 1, 1982, Cirencester, 203

'Preface and Bibliography', in I.A. Richmond, *Trajan's Army on Trajan's Column*, 1982, London, v–ix

(With R.S.O. Tomlin) 'Roman Britain in 1981: II. Inscriptions', *Britannia* 13, 1982, 396–422

1983

'The Building of the Antonine Wall', *Britannia* 14, 1983, 262–4 (= Article 4 in the present collection)

'The internal planning of Roman auxiliary forts', in B. Hartley and J. Wacher (eds), *Rome and her Northern Provinces: Papers Presented to Sheppard Frere in Honour of his Retirement from the Chair of the Archaeology of the Roman Empire, University of Oxford, 1983*, 1983, Gloucester, 96–131

'The origins and character of Roman urban defences in the west', in J. Maloney and B. Hobley (eds), *Roman Urban Defences in the West: a review of current research on urban defences in the Roman Empire with special reference to the northern provinces, based on papers presented to the conference on Roman Urban Defences held at the Museum of London on 21–23 March 1980*, CBA Research Report 51, 1983, London, 1–3

(With R.S.O. Tomlin) 'Roman Britain in 1982: II. Inscriptions', *Britannia* 14, 1983, 336–56

'Small Finds: Lead Seal', 63–5, in D. Bramwell, K. Dalton, J.F. Drinkwater, M.W.C. Hassall, K.L. Lorimer and D.F. Mackreth, 'Excavations at Poole's Cavern, Buxton: an Interim Report', *Derbyshire Archaeological Journal* 103, 1983, 47–74

1984

'The Date of the Rebuilding of Hadrian's Turf Wall in Stone', *Britannia* 15, 1984, 242–4 (= Article 6 in the present collection)

'Epigraphy and the Roman Army in Britain', in T.F.C. Blagg and A.C. King (eds), *Military and Civilian in Roman Britain: Cultural Relationships in a Frontier Province*, BAR British Series 136, 1984, Oxford, 265–77 (= Article 7 in the present collection)

(With R.S.O. Tomlin) 'Roman Britain in 1983: II. Inscriptions', *Britannia* 15, 1984, 333–56

1985

(With R.S.O. Tomlin) 'Roman Britain in 1984: II. Inscriptions', *Britannia* 16, 1985, 317–32

(With D.R. Evans) 'An inscription from Roman Gates, Caerleon', *Glamorgan-Gwent Archaeological Trust Annual Report, 1983–4* (pt 2), 1985, 133–4

1986

(With R.S.O. Tomlin) 'Roman Britain in 1985: II. Inscriptions', *Britannia* 17, 1986, 428–54

1987

'Romans and non-Romans', in J. Wacher (ed.), *The Roman World* (vol. 2), 1987, London/New York, 685–700

(With R.S.O. Tomlin) 'Roman Britain in 1986: II. Inscriptions', *Britannia* 18, 1987, 360–77

1988

(With R.S.O. Tomlin) 'Roman Britain in 1987: II. Inscriptions', *Britannia* 19, 1988, 485–508

1989

(With R.S.O. Tomlin) 'Roman Britain in 1988: II. Inscriptions', *Britannia* 20, 1989, 327–45

1990

(With R.S.O. Tomlin) 'Roman Britain in 1989: II. Inscriptions', *Britannia* 21, 1990, 365–78

1992

(With J. du Plat Taylor and A. Small) 'The Fortifications', in A. Small (ed.), *Gravina: an Iron Age and Republican Settlement in Apulia. Volume I: the Site*, Archaeological Monographs of the British School at Rome 5, 1992, London, 59–71

(With R.S.O. Tomlin) 'Roman Britain in 1991: II. Inscriptions', *Britannia* 23, 1992, 309–23

1993

(With R.S.O. Tomlin) 'Roman Britain in 1992: II. Inscriptions', *Britannia* 24, 1993, 310–22

1994

(With R.S.O. Tomlin) 'Roman Britain in 1993: II. Inscriptions', *Britannia* 25, 1994, 293–314

1995

(With R.S.O. Tomlin) 'Roman Britain in 1994: II. Inscriptions', *Britannia* 26, 1995, 371–90

1996

(Ed. with J. Bird and H. Sheldon) *Interpreting Roman London: Papers in Memory of Hugh Chapman*, Oxbow Monograph 58, 1996, Oxford

'London as a Provincial Capital', in J. Bird, M.W.C. Hassall and H. Sheldon (eds), *Interpreting Roman London: Papers in Memory of Hugh Chapman*, Oxbow Monograph 58, 1996, Oxford, 19–26 (= Article 11 in the present collection)

(With B.J. Whipp and S.A. Ward) 'Estimating the metabolic rate of marching Roman Legionaries', *Journal of Physiology* 491 (Suppl.), 1996, 60

(With R.S.O. Tomlin) 'Roman Britain in 1995: II. Inscriptions', *Britannia* 27, 1996, 439–57

1998

'Units doubled and divided and the planning of forts and fortresses', in J. Bird (ed.), *Form and Fabric: Studies in Rome's material past in honour of B.R. Hartley*, Oxbow Monograph 80, 1998, Oxford, 31–9

(With B.J. Whipp and S.A. Ward) 'Paleo-bioenergetics: the metabolic rate of marching Roman legionaries', *British Journal of Sports Medicine* 32 (3), 1998, 261–2

'Perspectives on Greek and Roman catapults', *Archaeology International* 2, 1998, 23–6

(With R.S.O. Tomlin) 'Roman Britain in 1997: II. Inscriptions', *Britannia* 29, 1998, 433–45

1999

'Homes for heroes: married quarters for soldiers and veterans', in A. Goldsworthy and I. Haynes (eds), *The Roman Army as a Community: Including papers of a conference held at Birkbeck College, University of London on 11–12 January, 1997*, Journal of Roman Archaeology Supplementary Series 34, 1999, Portsmouth, RI, 35–40

'Soldier and Civilian: a debate on the bank of the Severn', in H. Hurst (ed.), *The Coloniae of Roman Britain: New Studies and a Review. Papers of the conference held at Gloucester on 5–6 July, 1997*, Journal of Roman Archaeology Supplementary Series 36, 1999, Portsmouth, RI, 181–5

(With R.S.O. Tomlin) 'Roman Britain in 1998: II. Inscriptions', *Britannia* 30, 1999, 375–86

2000

'The location of legionary fortresses as a response to changes in military strategy: the case of Roman Britain AD 43–84', in Y. Le Bohec and C. Wolff (eds), *Les légions de Rome sous le Haut-Empire: Actes du Congrès de Lyon (17–19 septembre 1998)*, Collection du Centre d'Études Romaines et Gallo-Romaines nouvelle série 20, 2000, Lyon, 441–57 (= Article 1 in the present collection)

'Pre-Hadrianic Legionary Dispositions in Britain', in R. Brewer (ed.), *Roman Fortresses and their Legions: Papers in Honour of George C. Boon*, Occasional Papers of the Research Committee of the Society of Antiquaries of London 20, 2000, London/Cardiff, 51–67

'The Army', in A.K. Bowman, P. Garnsey and D. Rathbone (eds), *The Cambridge Ancient History. Volume XI: the High Empire, AD 70–192* (2nd edn), 2000, Cambridge, 320–43

'London: the Roman city', in I. Haynes, H. Sheldon and L. Hannigan (eds), *London Under Ground: the archaeology of a city*, 2000, Oxford, 52–61

(With R.S.O. Tomlin) 'Roman Britain in 1999: II. Inscriptions', *Britannia* 31, 2000, 433–49

2001

(With R.S.O. Tomlin) 'Roman Britain in 2000: II. Inscriptions', *Britannia* 32, 2001, 387–400

2002

(With R.S.O. Tomlin) 'Roman Britain in 2001: II. Inscriptions', *Britannia* 33,

2002, 355–71

2003

'The Tabularium in Provincial Cities', in P. Wilson (ed.), *The Archaeology of Roman Towns: Studies in Honour of John S. Wacher*, 2003, Oxford, 105–10 (= Article 13 in the present collection)

(With R.S.O. Tomlin) 'Roman Britain in 2002: II. Inscriptions', *Britannia* 34, 2003, 361–82

2004

'The defence of Britain in the 4th century', in Y. Le Bohec and C. Wolff (eds), *L'armée Romaine de Dioclétien à Valentinien Ier: Actes du Congrès de Lyon (12–14 septembre 2002)*, Collection du Centre d'Études Romaines et Gallo-Romaines nouvelle série 26, 2004, Lyon, 179–89 (= Article 19 in the present collection)

'Whither Roman Archaeology? Or Wither Roman Archaeology! A London Perspective', *Papers from the Institute of Archaeology* 15, 2004, 1–5

'Whither Roman Archaeology? Or Wither Roman Archaeology! A London Perspective – a Final Response', *Papers from the Institute of Archaeology* 15, 2004, 15–17

(With R.S.O. Tomlin) 'Roman Britain in 2003: III. Inscriptions', *Britannia* 35, 2004, 335–49

2005

(With R.S.O. Tomlin) 'Roman Britain in 2004: III. Inscriptions', *Britannia* 36, 2005, 473–97

2006

'Roman Rochester in its wider context', in T. Ayers and T. Tatton-Brown (eds), *Medieval Art, Architecture and Archaeology at Rochester*, British Archaeological Association Conference Transactions 28, 2006, Leeds, 1–5

(With R.S.O. Tomlin) 'Roman Britain in 2005: III. Inscriptions', *Britannia* 37, 2006, 467–88

'A Modern Pilgrim: Maastricht to Cologne', in M. Meek (ed.), *The Modern Traveller to our Past: Festschrift in honour of Ann Hamlin*, 2006, Belfast, 377–83

2007

(With R.S.O. Tomlin) 'Roman Britain in 2006: III. Inscriptions', *Britannia* 38, 2007, 345–65

2008

'Footnotes to The Fasti', in H.M. Schellenberg, V.E. Hirschmann and A. Krieckhaus (eds), *A Roman Miscellany: Essays in Honour of Anthony R. Birley on his Seventieth Birthday*, Akanthina Monograph 3, 2008, Gdańsk, 31–41 (= Article 9 in the present collection)

'London: Britain's first 'university'? Education in Roman Britain', in J. Clark, J. Cotton, J. Hall, R. Sherris and H. Swain (eds), *Londinium and Beyond: Essays on Roman London and its Hinterland for Harvey Sheldon*, CBA Research Report 156, 2008, York, 117–20 (= Article 15 in the present collection)

'Graffiti on pottery', in N. Bateman, C. Cowan and R. Wroe-Brown, *London's Roman amphitheatre: Guildhall Yard, City of London*, MoLAS Monograph 35, 2008, London, 187–8

2009

'Inscriptions and Hadrian's Wall', in M.F.A. Symonds and D.J.P. Mason (eds), *Frontiers of Knowledge: a Research Framework for Hadrian's Wall, Part of the Frontiers of the Roman Empire World Heritage Site. Volume I: Resource Assessment*, 2009, Durham, 152–4 (= Article 3 in the present collection)

(With R.S.O. Tomlin and R.P. Wright) *The Roman Inscriptions of Britain. Volume III: Inscriptions on Stone, Found or Notified between 1 January 1955 and 31 December 2006*, 2009, Oxford

2010

'The written record and the late Roman frontier', in R. Collins and L. Allason-Jones (eds), *Finds from the Frontier: Material Culture in the 4th–5th Centuries*, CBA Research Report 162, 2010, York, 17–19 (= Article 20 in the present collection)

2012

'The 2nd-century AD garrison of Londinium', in J. Shepherd, *The discovery of the Roman fort at Cripplegate, City of London: Excavations by W F Grimes 1947–68*, 2012, London, 158–63

2017

Roman Britain: the Frontier Province. Collected Papers, 2017, Warminster

INDEX

A page number followed by n. indicates an endnote; for example, 205n.53 indicates endnote 53 on page 205.

INDEX OF REFERENCES TO
THE ROMAN INSCRIPTIONS OF
BRITAIN

Each entry gives the RIB *number, followed by the page number and endnote number where appropriate; for example, 114n.7 indicates endnote 7 on page 114.*

www.ingramcontent.com/pod-product-compliance
Lightning Source LLC
Chambersburg PA
CBHW060816100426
42813CB00004B/1104